Living
Zen

ROBERT LINSSEN

Living Zen

Preface by
CHRISTMAS HUMPHREYS

Foreword by
DR. R. GODEL

Translated from the French by
DIANA ABRAHAMS-CURIEL

GROVE PRESS
New York

Published by Grove Press
a division of Wheatland Corporation
841 Broadway
New York, N.Y. 10003

First Evergreen Edition 1960
New Evergreen Edition 1988
ISBN: 0-8021-3136-0
Library of Congress Catalog Card Number: 60-198

Manufactured in the United States of America

10 9 8 7 6 5 4 3 2 1

PREFACE

Western interest in Zen Buddhism is steadily rising, and the ferment introduced by Dr D. T. Suzuki is beginning to take effect and to appear in visible reaction. For long we have depended on his vast and deeply illumined mind to give us, to the extent that books can ever convey it, that vision of Non-Duality which only the few attain. But if the Zen technique is a true way to Reality it can be and must be adapted to the needs of the Western mind. To what extent the more famous 'devices' used by the Zen Masters of the East can be used by the West in the absence of a Zen Master remains to be seen; much will depend on the speed with which a few minds, albeit in Western bodies, can reach the very high standard required of a Japanese Zen *roshi*, or qualified Zen teacher.

Meanwhile we are producing our own writers, those who, after a long or short intellectual study of Zen, have acquired enough 'experience' to think that they have something useful to say to their fellow students. I understand that the late Eugen Herrigel's *Zen in the Art of Archery* is in the opinion of Zen experts in Japan the best such work so far produced, but new minds are publishing their 'findings' month by month, and between them they may be producing the beginnings of a Western approach to Zen. All of them approach the subject via the intellect; it may be that for the West there is no other way, but in every case the intellect is illumined by a high degree of intuition or 'direct seeing', and the higher that thought can lift us the easier it may be to take the 'leap' which alone will land us beyond the dualism of even the highest thought.

Now Mr Robert Linssen of Brussels enters the field with a work in French in three volumes entitled *Living Zen* of which this book is an excellent English translation. He approaches the field via history, philosophy, psychology and current Western habits of mind. Then, and only then, does he turn to the task of transcending duality. Thus the temple of our understanding slowly rises, as the factors of Western thought are severally analysed, evaluated and built into a whole which transcends all of them. Then comes the jump ... But the abyss into which we fall is found to be the Plenum/Void; the leap is from thought to No-thought; from the ultimate duality of Illusion/Reality to a burst of laughter and a cup of tea. But with what new eyes do we view the saucer, and in what serenity of mind do we clear the table away!

But the reader must climb and jump for himself. He will fall happily.

CHRISTMAS HUMPHREYS

FOREWORD

If the reader will allow himself to fall under the spell exercised by the first few pages of this study on Buddhism, he will soon realize that he is being asked to go beyond the particular forms and doctrines of a philosophy. Of course, he will find in this book all that the title has proclaimed, namely a study and background history of the systems included in Buddhism. The author deals with Mahayana, Hinayana, the Tantras and Zen in particular. But he does not dwell on the immense intellectual edifice which the genius of Eastern thinkers has built round the original flame. It is rather on the flame itself that the author has focused his attention, for it has drawn him directly to the heart of this majestic dialectic superstructure that is Buddhism. Tirelessly he tries to evoke the illumination and the whole truth by the diverse methods of approach of Mahayana, Hinayana and in the flash of Satori.

Therefore one must not expect to find in this book only a study of doctrines and an analysis of systems. This work bears its fruit higher up, towards full sunshine with no shadows; allusion is made everywhere to the inexpressible reality of its radiation.

This preface will be short, in keeping with the spirit of this fine book whose main virtue lies in leading the readers towards silence. To conclude, I shall quote Robert Linssen: 'From the moment when the "thinker" understands, he is silent, and stopping, he looks more serenely within himself and into all things. Tanha, the avidity to "become" is on the point of extinction. The tensions in order to "become" are replaced by the relaxation of that which is. It is the moment of "letting go" of which the Zen masters speak. The death of the entity of the "thinker" is succeeded by the plenitude of life.'

DR. R. GODEL

CONTENTS

PREFACE TO THE SECOND (FRENCH) EDITION

Our friend Mme A. David-Neel, after having read the first edition of these essays, very kindly made various criticisms which have led us to concentrate more on explaining the unorthodox nature of our position.

'Buddhists', wrote Mme David-Neel, 'denounce in particular the theistic tendencies which some people wish to associate with Buddhism.'

Speaking on behalf of the Maha-Bodhi someone declared: 'We cannot admit, as some claim, that all religions are but a manifestation of the Supreme Reality. For the expression "Supreme Reality" has an obviously theist flavour, while Buddhism is well-known to be atheist.'

However our position is a little different.

Basing ourselves on the texts of many specialists in Buddhism in general and Zen in particular, we find that we are unable to share this point of view completely.

We believe that atheism, as we regard it in the West, does not at all correspond with the particular atheism claimed by certain Buddhists.

Nor does Western theism bear any relation to Buddhist thought.

These are the reasons for which we have thought it best to define our position as that of a 'spiritual materialism'.

Nevertheless the expression 'materialism' is somewhat dangerous.

We have here an example of the impossibility of fitting Zen into the framework of current values.

The use of the term 'materialism' might give one the idea that we are attributing a sense of absolute reality to matter as we see it. However, we are aware that the external appearance of the material world is only a concept of the mind. Beyond all these apparent forms there exists nevertheless an energy which is none other than 'Cosmic Mind'.

We have used the expression 'materialism', apparently so inadequate, in order to produce a psychological shock. We are anxious to help the reader to reach a positive approach to the Real. It is not a question of turning our eyes away from matter on the pretext that the ideas that we have of it are subjective.

Understanding of Zen requires a return to the concrete and the giving up of inadequate mental projections which are all too frequent in most of our 'spiritual' doctrines.

The significance that we wish to give to the term 'materialism', therefore, is completely different from that given by the traditional materialistic philosophies.

The Reality of the Universe is a homogeneous Totality-that-is-One both physical and spiritual. This Reality is sufficient unto Itself.

We consider useless and moreover contradictory all recourse to the intervention of a 'Principle' or a 'Person' endowed with any transcendental character.

'Spiritual', because of the profound nature of this Totality-that-is-One, and of its substance which is closer to spirit than to matter.

'Spiritual' again and above all because of the particular character of consciousness and lucidity of 'Satori', or effective discovery of the 'nature of self' and of things, although a new scale of the values we tend to attribute to all these terms might have to be drawn up.

The imperfections of our language often lead us into somewhat paradoxical situations. By identical words we attempt to express values which are radically opposed to each other.

Indeed, if we were to give the term 'God' a transcendental meaning, and wanted to express a person or an entity by this term, we would be moving away completely from the Buddhist concept. Anyway we have insisted repeatedly on this fact later in the book.

But beware! Buddhism is not nihilistic.

Very many texts of Buddhist orthodoxy remind us not to confuse the 'void' with nothingness. The 'void' should be understood as the absence of our usual values, of our distinct perceptions, of our dualistic notions and our familiar references.

Moreover this theme has been developed very clearly by Mme A. David-Neel herself in her notable study on Buddhism.

The texts of Buddhist orthodoxy dwell upon the enlightenment of the Buddha and the incomparable felicity of Nirvâna. Felicity and enlightenment do not grow from nothingness. Their realization, however, depends on a reduction to nothingness of all our false values, as we shall explain in detail later on. When the false values, which are a result of a fundamentally perverted mental optic cease to exist, then in all simplicity, we shall be able to discover our true nature.

In contrast to the climate of suffering inherent in the limitations of the egoistical 'me', which is a prisoner of ignorance and identification with essentially personal and impermament values, the discovery of the 'true nature of self', during which the mask of separativity melts, is a Plenitude.

For the Sage, of course, there no longer exists any dualistic opposition between a petty, egoistical state and a Plenitude, between a banal reality and a Supreme Reality, between ordinary facts and extraordinary facts, between essential things and inessential things. We could say, that all things considered 'ordinary', henceforth, to the integrated being, become extraordinary from moment to moment.

But this book has not been written for Sages or for integrated men.

In order to make ourselves understood, we are using the language of dualism, the halting tongue spoken by all who are prisoners of duality, but begging them all the while to progress beyond it, and furnishing them with the elements which will allow them to bring about this progress within themselves and by themselves.

Nevertheless the letter sent us by Mme A. David-Neel was valuable. Without it we might not have reminded our readers sufficiently to give the terms we use in an attempt to express the Real, a totally different meaning from that generally given them.

And once and for all, let us remember that the terms 'Supreme Reality', 'Totality-that-is-One' and 'Divine', in no way describe an entity which is distinct from ourselves or a person superadded to the existing Universe. Most of the Judeo-Christian concepts are incompatible with the Buddhist standpoint in this domain. We have in fact developed these essential differences in the chapter dealing with the divergencies between Buddhism and Christianity.

Some people will say that though Buddhism is not nihilistic, it is still atheistic. We think that we have dwelt sufficiently on the particular significance we give to the terms 'Divine' or 'Supreme Reality', to be able to affirm the impossibility of categorically classifying Buddhism as atheist or theist, as generally understood. This will become sufficiently evident in reading this book.

Two fundamental notions become apparent from the teachings of the masters of Buddhism in general and Zen in particular.

Firstly, the existence of an essential Reality escaping all our traditional concepts (beyond existence and non-existence as we conceive them), and secondly, the notion of the Zen Unconscious and 'Cosmic Mind' which is closely linked up with the former.

Amongst all the forms of the French language we have had to choose the terms able to evoke the almost intangible climate of the central reality of Buddhism.

Grimm called it the 'basis of the world'. The translators of Lao-Tzu speak of the 'Principle'. The latter term could be applied to orthodox Buddhism, but we have not found it very adequate. Writers on Zen speak of the 'Cosmic Mind' or of the 'nature of the Buddha', or of the 'Body of Buddha'. We have explained in the second volume how these notions are to be understood.

Non-Buddhist writers have tried to find a new term which would have the advantage of being completely disanthropo-morphized.

Carlo Suarès in his *Comédie Psychologique*, prudently speaks of the fundamental 'something' or of the 'plus', the perpetually positive balance sheet of a thousand million apparently negative and positive transformations. Jaspers, too, has proposed a new term: the 'comprehensive' in which all dualities would be integrated and united.

We have ourselves proposed the expression 'Totality-that-is

One', which comprehends and dominates the oppositional aspects which are apparently separated from the cosmos.

From the point of view of orthodoxy, words can be of great importance, but we do not belong to any orthodoxy.

The essence of Zen with which we are dealing in particular, is above all the fact of personal experience.

All work is useful in so far as it is really creative; and this it cannot be if it submits to the requirements of any school of thought. This is why all the great teachers were revolutionaries and creators. This attitude also is in keeping with the spirit of Zen.

Had the Buddha conformed to the average mental outlook of his time, his existence would never have been noticed by the eyes of history.

When Buddhism was introduced into China by two Indians, Matanga and Bhorâna around A.D. 65 at Loyang, it was a long way from the extraordinary impulse to be given it by the revolutionary and least orthodox patriarchs of Zen, such as Bodhi-Dharma, Seng T'san, Hui-Neng and Hsi-Yun.

On behalf of the Maha-Bodhi it has been stated that 'Buddhists could not adhere to the idea expressed in certain Congresses of Religion whose professed aim is to lead mankind towards a central religion consisting of the relations between man and his creator. Such a definition of religion, the writer continues, completely excludes the Buddhists, for what would the Christians and Musulmans say if they were asked to adhere to a discipline whose first rule was: neither God nor soul'.

We have dwelt repeatedly on the fact that in Buddhism there is no 'Creator' and that man has no one to depend on but himself.

Mme A. David-Neel's reminder at this point allows us to explain our position even more fully.

We are deeply convinced of the profound sameness of the experiences of a Buddha, a Lao-Tzu, or a Jesus, but this supposed sameness of the experiences of the Sages, in no way entails similarity in the parodies of their teachings which their successors have tried to codify.

Another comment of Mme A. David-Neel refers to the discredit thrown upon the Hinayana School, also known as the Lesser Vehicle.

Any doctrine which gives a certain importance to the forms, ritual and ceremonies, is considered inferior by us, whether this doctrine belongs to the Mahayana or Hinayana branches of Buddhism, or any other discipline.

On various occasions we have repeated this point of view; Truth is beyond any particular system and must be freed from the tyranny of forms.

Our position is endorsed by the opinion of Mme A. David-Neel when she wrote: 'On the strength of my relations with Zenists, I can say that the opinion of a Zen Buddhist is as follows; all doctrines are equally false because they are doctrines.'

Moreover that is the opinion of one of the most eminent non-conformist and spiritual revolutionaries of the present time: Krishnamurti.

It is in a climate free of any particular conditioning that we have tried to enlighten the reader on the profound Reality of his being and of all things.

INTRODUCTORY NOTE

The greatest truths have always been the most simple, but Aristotle said that 'things divine were all the more obscure in so far as they were more intelligible and luminous in themselves'. Though this may seem paradoxical to the Western reader, the [1] essential notions of Buddhism in general and Zen in particular are extraordinarily simple. So simple are they, that at first we find ourselves unable to grasp their real significance.

We may well recoil slightly on our first contacts with the be- [2] wildering and enigmatic teaching technique of the Zen masters. But however incoherent and even absurd they may appear at a casual glance, unsuspected riches lie hidden therein.

The Zen method of revelation is in violent opposition to the familiar mental routine of our hyper-intellectualized races.

If in spite of everything we insist on cleaving to the 'habitual dream of the ego' we will be greatly upset by the brutal shock of Zen. If we are ripe for the *awakening* and the supreme *simplicity*, we will perceive the pure essence of all that is ineffable in it. That is the vision of 'Satori', the vision of an eternal renaissance in the pure and boundless joy of the Unfathomable.

But the discovery of the *simplicity* inherent in the profound nature of our being and in all things will be difficult in proportion to the over-intellectualization of our minds.

If Zen is approached with the usual mental attitude, it will seem quite incomprehensible. Our average Western intellectuality [3] would consider its paradoxical language simply as a play upon words. Its full significance is revealed only when we approach it in a different manner, making our minds available to the new processes of inner perception which it suggests. A certain flexibility of thought is necessary so that the study of a new subject may be fruitful and revealing.

'To speak of flexibility is to speak of liberty.' An atmosphere of [4] remarkable freedom and independence is to be found in Buddhism in general and Zen in particular.

As an example we may quote here a fundamental rule of conduct taught by the Buddha:

'Therefore, be ye lamps unto yourselves, be a refuge to yourselves. Betake yourselves to no external refuge. Hold fast to Truth as a lamp; hold fast to the Truth as a refuge. Look not for a refuge in anyone beside yourselves. And those, who either now or after I am dead shall be a lamp unto themselves, shall betake themselves to no external refuge, but holding fast to the Truth as their lamp, and holding fast to the Truth as their refuge, shall not look for refuge, shall not look for refuge to anyone beside themselves – it is they who shall reach the topmost Height' (Paranibbâna Sutra).

Out of respect for this liberty, we do not want this work to be considered as yet another doctrinal text whose aim is to condition the mind. We just wanted to present readers with the remarkable elements of simplicity and clarity offered by the superior forms of Buddhism, at the moment when the growing invasion of ideas, theories and 'mental confections' is tending to suffocate the brain. These elements offer the hyper-intellectual tense and anxious people of the present generations, the possibility of a serene, perfectly clear, harmonious and relaxed mental life. By virtue of the fundamental unity of mind and matter, the new inner harmony materializes in action on the concrete plane. In the eyes of the masters of Zen and Mahayanist Buddhism, the 'Nirvâna of the depths and the Samsara of superficial appearances' are one and the same thing. Irresistibly, then, a new sense of values will be expressed by adequate conduct.

Perhaps it is because a growing number of seekers foresee this equilibrium and this source of complete enrichment, that a considerable awakening of interest in the higher forms of Buddhist thought is becoming noticeable.

Very unusual psychological climates will be revealed in this book which differ from those which are familiar to the Westerner who has never made contact with Oriental thinkers.
The words used no longer have exactly the meaning which we

are in the habit of giving them. That which is 'normal' to us, is 'abnormal' in the eyes of the Zen masters. The state of 'Satori' is to them essentially the normal and natural state. At first sight this may seem to us exceptional or inaccessible. Where we see objects or symbols with definite contours, the Sages only see a 'void'. That which appears to them as an inexpressible plenitude, appears [6] a dizzy nothingness to us.

So we will repeat the warning of Dr. Hubert Benoit who in his introduction to the *Zen Doctrine of No-Mind* of Professor Suzuki reminds the reader of the great effort of readaptation that is demanded of him.

Most of the ideas formulated in Zen belong to the class of primordial ideas which explain the ten thousand things, without themselves being explained by anything; these truths explain all things due to a Light which they receive directly from the inexpressible original Truth (*Zen Doctrine of No-Mind*).

Admittedly our commentaries would have great difficulties in reaching the high plane of thought, the clarity and rigour of the Zen masters whose experience and science infinitely surpass ours. Their real significance can only appear in daily practice. Their theoretical rejection or acceptance would have no sense.

This work is not so much destined for the erudite who may wish to complete his intellectual knowledge, as for the practical seeker [7] sincerely wishing to 'see into his own nature'.

Many repetitions will be noticed throughout the different chapters. They are intentional and serve as a guide-point. Without them the uninformed reader might lose sight of the essential background against which our ideas are developed. Without these repetitions the informed reader might think that we have unwittingly allowed ourselves to be led astray by dualistic explanations.

This warning applies above all to the examples we shall use to define certain aspects of Zen thought.

Our task has been rendered the more difficult because we did not wish to separate general Buddhism from Zen in this book, while at the same time devoting more consideration to the latter.

Having now made these reservations for the passages which might present some ambiguity, we hope that the occasions for misunderstanding will be reduced. To this end we have given a brief survey of the general history of Buddhism in order to define the exact position of Zen.

What is Zen? The Japanese philosopher S. Ogata replies:

'It is neither simply a religion nor a philosophy; it is something more: it is *Life itself*. Zen is a special transmission *outside the Canonical Scriptures; it does not depend upon texts*. As Bodhi-Dharma declared *Zen does not waste time with dissertions on abstruse notions such as God, or Truth;* what *Zen requires of its disciples is to look upon their own faces*.'

The essential spirit of Zen is living, dynamic, non-conformist and *non-traditionalist*. We must experience this if we would really enter this domain. Zen is not '*understood*', *it is lived*. This also applies to the higher forms of Tibetan Buddhism.

True to one of the fundamentally revolutionary attitudes of Zen, we have tried to free ourselves from the tyranny of texts so as to seize the inner life in the plenitude of its primal upsurge. For it is in this sense that we have understood the advice of Bodhi-Dharma, founder of Zen, when he said to his disciples: '*Do not let yourself be upset by the Sutra, but rather upset the Sutra yourself*.'

In the light of this freedom, it has become evident that Truth is beyond all systematization of thought. It is this panoramic vision which has guided the choice of the various quotations borrowed not only from Zen, but also from the different forms of Mahayanist Buddhism.

The forms of Buddhism being diverse, an infinite variety of texts exists and to follow them all would be to follow many contradictory tendencies, so a choice becomes necessary.

How to set about choosing them in such a manner that they will not suffer the deformations inherent in personal preferences which may condition us? One way would be to try and find by ourselves in so far as our experiences make it possible, the living sources of Zen inspiration. We have bridged the gaps inherent in the insufficiency of our own experience by direct contacts, sometimes long sometimes short which we were privileged to have with different authorities in this field. We may mention by name Professor D. T. Suzuki (*Zen Buddhism*), Mme A. David-Neel (*General Buddhism and Tibetan Buddhism*), Dayalshanti Ghose (*Samtchen Kham Pa*) (*Buddhism; the direct way*) the Bikkhu Thunananda (*Burma — Southern School*).

We have also undertaken a comparative study of other religious disciplines exposing the essential sameness of the original inspiration.

Truth is dynamic. It is constantly being recreated and renewed. This is the reason for which all the great spiritual teachers have been — and should be — revolutionaries.

Whether it be a Buddha, a Socrates, a Plotinus, a Jesus, or today, a Krishnamurti, it is in the presence of powerful individualities that we find ourselves, men profoundly alive and revolutionary. Their inspiration is a result of a total integration into the process of Life itself.

The anti-traditionalism of the Zen masters or of a Krishnamurti should not astonish us unduly. We lose sight of the nature of the essential Reality of which the Sages are the mouthpieces. Such people are 'dead to themselves'. Their comportment is entirely dictated by the Reality which lives within them. If we wish to understand them it is indispensable for us to learn what this Reality is.

The men who have realized themselves define it as an eternal presence which escapes all our concepts of duration, time and causality. At its approach, this presence reveals itself endowed with an incomparable up-surging and creative intensity. It is truly *from instant to instant* that the Real reveals itself and is lived in the states of 'Satori' or 'Nirvâna'.

This helps us understand why Truth cannot be traditional.

Those who might say that it is traditionally revolutionary and non-traditional would not be wrong.

Let us realize, however, that though the authentic teachers are revolutionary, it is not in order to make revolution a system, but because the Reality in which they are integrated is a state of constant renaissance and revolution. In it there is no past, no memory, no points of reference or succour.

Men who are liberated are in a state of intense awakening in comparison with which the supposedly positive and practical world appears fast asleep. Superstitions, beliefs and false mental values act as so many spiritual narcotics which transform the collective dream of humanity into a nightmare. Zen, however, tells us that 'the earth is a paradise', but only 'correct vision' will allow us to discover its hidden riches.

It was in this state of mind awakened to the Present that the Buddha opposed the ritual *habits* and diverse forms of magic practised by the Brahmins. The essential element of buddhist teaching consists in throwing off the spell which the '*force of habit*' cast on our minds.

Ignorance is the result of the action of force of habit on our thoughts and on our inner states. Thus we are plunged in a lethargy both individual and collective which is responsible for all our unhappiness.

It was in such a state of mind that Socrates constantly sought to 'undermine' the mental *habits* and established values of the Athenians whom he was addressing. In his remarkable study on *Socrate et le Sage Indien*, Dr. R. Godel writes:

'*In order to rouse his audience out of their sleep, and to draw them away from the routines of thought* and behaviour in which they delighted, Socrates applied to each one the technique best suited to his temperament. Some people will awake only when disconcerted; to these, by his arguments, mimicry and gestures he would administer a *brutal shock, similar to the discharges of an "electric-ray"*.'

For his part Jesus drove the merchants from the Temple and never ceased challenging the doctors of the Law. He, more than anyone else intentionally trod underfoot the strict conformism of the Jews and rose against the ritual practices of his time.

While Buddhism was declining owing to vain metaphysical quarrels which were essentially alien to the wisdom of the Buddha,

Bodhi-Dharma, the founder of Zen, vehemently denounced the [12]
vanity and absurdity of intellectual preoccupations in this field.
Hui-Neng and most of the patriarchs of Zen were great revolutionaries. In Tibet, Padma Sambhava and Marpa the Translator
gave a considerable impulse to Tibetan Buddhism by their non-
conformist attitude and living experience.

Today independent thinkers and non-Buddhists such as Krishnamurti are laying the new bases of the most complete spiritual
revolution known up till now.

The teaching of accomplished men of all times has respected
Liberty, Infinitude and the perpetual renewal of Reality, and has
condemned the negative role of egoism, attachment and habit.

This leads us to think that a single spiritual sap feeds the inner
life of those, who triumphing over the limitations of their egoism,
effect the full discovery of themselves.

They all realize a vision of indescribable infinitude, in which [13]
dualities, the habitual distinction of opposites have no place. Only
Unity remains in its ineffable character.

Neither rites nor efforts of thought can realize or conceive this
fundamental unity.

The Mundokopanishad says that this essence

'cannot be seized either by the eye or by the senses, either by
austerity or *by religious rites*. It is by serene wisdom, *by the pure
essence*, that the Unique indivisible can be seen in meditation'
(*Mundokopanishad*, III 8-9).

The sense of unity and homogeneity of the Real has also been [14]
defined by Plotinus:
'*they see all things as the same* . . . and they perceive themselves in
others. For all things are diaphanous in this place; nothing is obscure or resistant. In this place, for the same reason, movement is
pure, because it is not troubled by a motive-force differing from
itself' (Plotinus, *Aeneiad*, X4, 8).

There is no space here to develop the idea of a common inspiration at the root of the early teachings of the great masters. Without

number are the texts of the Ancient Egyptians, Musulmans, Zoro-
astrians, Hindus, Greeks, Buddhists and Christians which evoke
the supreme Unity of the Real, the luminous and trans-luminous
aspects of the pure essence, and the obstacles raised by mental
activity and egoism. These considerations would lead us towards
an intellectuality we particularly wish to avoid. Besides such
developments have been the subject of specialized studies on comparative mysticism. They have been carried out by eminent
writers and scholars in most countries.

If emphasis is laid here on the identity of inspiration at the origin
of the early teachings of the Sages, it is so as to throw into relief
the *eternally living character of the Unique Reality* of which they were
the interpreters.

We will try to grasp, apart from the Scriptures, *the eternally active presence* which they seek to express. We must go beyond letters
and symbols *actually to find at first hand in ourselves the Flame Itself.*

According to Bergson our logic is founded on solids . . . it bears
the stamp of solids and is only at ease amongst them. For this
reason we demand concrete, palpable and static facts. But Reality
makes game of our limitations and our attempts at imprisonment.
It cannot be codified. No framework can hold it. It is for us to
rise to its level.

That is why the Zen Masters tell us that after having read a text
we should, however paradoxical this may seem, free ourselves
from the particular conditioning it may have imposed on our
minds. If this is not done scrupulously, we cannot directly experience its living unforseeable reality.

As has been said 'that which is well conceived is expressed
clearly'.

These words are correct when definite objects are to be described or concrete notions to be expressed.

The essential Reality of Buddhism in general and Zen in particular escapes any mental representation. Therefore it is indescribable, unthinkable and inexpressible.

Were some clever person regretably to give us an approxima-
tive symbolic representation of it, this would be the final and
greatest obstacle which would remain for us to vanquish.

That is the reason why these symbols which are so sought after, studied, cultivated and adored by a whole class of 'spiritual or religious' minds, are in fact the worst conditioning factors of the mind.

The absence of images and symbols which is characteristic of the higher forms of Buddhism and Zen, is extremely useful. Often it irritates us, and at first we criticize it.

Nothing could be more natural. But a deeper study of the question will finally reveal to us that this absence of precise sign-posting is really a blessing.

The role of transcendental wisdom consists not in conditioning the human mind, but in liberating it. All doctrines using symbols and mental clichés enslave it by leading it imperceptibly into a process of imitation, which is all the more serious in that it is subtle.

Part One

Dates	Hinayana School	Mahayana School
560 B.C. birth of the Buddha		The original Prajnâpâramita Sutras of the Mahayana Saddharma-Pundarika Lotus of the Good Law Prajnâ-
200 B.C.	writing of the Pali scriptures	
80 B.C.		pâramita (Great) Sandhinir-
A.D. I		mocana Sûtra (Yogacarin School) Lankâvatâra Sûtra
A.D. 100		Vajracchedikâ Sûtra.
A.D. 160		
A.D. 200		Nagâr-Juna
A.D. 333	final codification of the Buddhaghosa	
A.D. 420		Wall Contemplation in
A.D. 498-563	the oldest catalogue of the Chinese Tripitaka	Mahayana (Bodhidharma, founder of Zen)
A.D. 518		'On believing in Mind' poem
A.D. 600		by Seng Ts'an (Zen) 'Sermons of the Sixth Pat-
A.D. 638-713		riarch' by Hui-Neng (Zen)
A.D. 870		'Huang-Po Doctrine' by Hsi-Yun (Zen)
A.D. 960		Kalasakra-Tantra (Tantrism)
1267		Foundation of the Rinzai (Zen)
	manual of Yogavacara	
1620		Awakening of Buddhism in
1890		Japan Taisho-Issaikyo (publication
1924-29		of the Chinese Tripitaka in Japan)
1926-34		Essays in Zen Buddhism, by D. T. Suzuki
1941		First important translations of Zen into French (D. T. Suzuki, trans. by P. Sauvageot, René Daumal)

CHAPTER I

Summary History of Buddhism

BUDDHA was born in Kapilavastu, capital of the kingdom of the Sakyas, about 560 B.C. Numerous archaeological discoveries testify to his historical character, but the detailed circumstances of his life are less well known. We know that the Buddha was a prince called Gautama Siddharta, son of the Queen [17] Maya Devi and of Suddhodana, king of the Sakyas.

The kingdom of the Saykas was a little state situated at the foot of the Himalayas in a region which now forms part of the state of Nepal.

Tradition has it that round the age of twenty-nine, and although married and father of a son, Siddharta Gautama left his palace and led the life of the wandering monks or 'Sannyasins'. Every precaution had been taken to spare the young prince the sight of anything connected with pain, poverty, disease and death. The moment came, nevertheless, when after having led a life of pleasure, he had an unexpected meeting. By a strange coincidence, in one day, he saw an old man, a sick person, a corpse and a man of religion.

These meetings released in him an intense inner turmoil. The sight of suffering hereto carefully hidden from him, moved him to profound reflection. The discovery of the fundamental impermanence of all things, the spectacle of poverty and death directed him to the study of spiritual problems. He went to study with the [18] Brahmins, and frequented various well-known schools of philosophy, but he was disappointed.

He then started on a series of ascetic practices and progressively severe mortifications, but he gained nothing from the latter despite the prolonged and cruel experiences he underwent.

History tells us that enlightenment or 'waking from the dream' came to him whilst he was meditating seated at the foot of the 'Bodhi-Tree'. At first he had to forget all he had learnt in order

better to follow the course of his own thoughts. As a result of
[19] correct attention, he discovered the fundamental development of
all beings that exist, and afterwards reached the unfathomable
experience of Nirvâna.

The 'Lalita-vistara' relates the vow made by the Buddha before
reaching enlightenment:

> Let my body be dried up on this seat,
> Let my skin and bones and flesh be destroyed:
> So long as Bodhi is not attained . . .
> My body and thought will not be removed from
> this seat.

Buddhist tradition tells us in the Majjhima-Nikaya (XXVI,
p. 167), the first words of the Buddha after his enlightenment.

'Then, disciples, myself subject to birth, but perceiving the
wretchedness of things subject to birth and seeking the incomparable security of Nirvâna which is birthless, to that incomparable
security I attained, even to Nirvâna which is birthless.

Myself subject to birth and decay, but perceiving the wretchedness of things subject to growth and decay and seeking the incomparable security of Nirvâna which is free from growth and
decay, to that incomparable security I attained, even to Nirvâna
which is free from growth and decay.

Myself subject to disease, but perceiving the wretchedness of
things subject to disease and seeking the incomparable security
of Nirvâna which is free from disease, to that incomparable
security I attained, even to Nirvâna which is free from disease.

Then, I saw and knew: "Assured am I of deliverance; this is my
final birth; never more shall I return to this life!"' (Suzuki, *Essays
in Zen Buddhism*, vol. I, p. 158).

The rigorously individual character of the Enlightenment of
Buddha is made apparent in a declaration made by the Master on
meeting the ascetic Upâka on the road to Benares. The original
version figures in the Dîgha-Nikâya (XXVI):

All-conqueror I, knower of all,
From every soil and stain released,
Renouncing all, from craving ceased,
Self-taught; whom should I Master call?
That which I know I learned of none;
. . . .
I truly have attained release,
Alone, enlightened perfectly,
I dwell in everlasting peace.
                    (Suzuki, *Essays in Zen Buddhism*)

We draw the attention of the reader particularly to the lines underlined by us in this declaration, the others clearly bearing the stamp of an exclusive deification superimposed by the commentators.

The Buddha devoted himself to preaching during close on fifty years.

His influence was considerable, and among his disciples were all the intellectual élite of India and several kings.

He died of dysentery round the age of eighty-one. He was expected to preach in a neighbouring town and refused to listen [20] to advice of his disciples who begged him to rest and be attended to.

Before dying, the Buddha said to his cousin Ananda:

'It may be, Ananda, that in some of you the thought may arise "The word of the master is ended, we have no teacher now!" But it is not thus that you should think. The Truths and the Rules of the Order, which I have set forth and laid down for you all, let them, after I am gone, be the Teacher to you.

Behold now brethren, I exhort you to remember, "All things that are born must die. Work hard for your own freedom from sorrow."'

When the Buddha died about 480 B.C., a great number of monastic communities were formed in north-east India. As no suc-

cessor had been explicitly designated, the monks took as sole guide
the elements of the doctrine left by the Master. These were not
written down, but memorized by the monks and transmitted
orally for nearly four centuries.

There was one supremely important thing in the eyes of the
Buddhists: *to live the Dharma*. The importance of the texts was
secondary and derivative. This state of things soon gave rise to
tendencies, diverging only slightly at first but more widely as the
centuries passed.

Amongst the most considerable were those generally known
under the name of 'Ancient School of Wisdom'.

As we have already mentioned elsewhere, the great masters such
as a Buddha, or a Jesus, never had the intention of founding a
definite religious system. It is also remarkable that they never
wrote a treatise, in the sense understood by our writers and philosophers. It was their successors or their disciples who spontaneously rebuilt the structure of their discourses, dwelling on this or
that aspect which to them appeared to need emphasis.

In Buddhism this role was filled by Sâriputra. Tradition tells us
that he entered very early into the religious life under the guidance
of Sanjaya, a complete sceptic. He came into contact with the
Buddha's teaching shortly after and obtained full Enlightenment
within a fortnight of having joined the Order. Sâriputra was a
learned man but Buddhist writers credit him with too great a
reserve and a dryness inherent in the very analytical tendencies of
his mind. Though he died six months before the Buddha, his way
of understanding the doctrine inspired Buddhist communities
during fifteen to twenty generations. But the *Abhidharma* of which
he was the founder, did not receive the unanimous adhesion of
the monks.

Amongst the opponents of the interpretations of Sâriputra, we
may mention the group of Sautrântika which had the greatest
influence, as well as Ananda, one of the earliest disciples of the
Buddha.

The Mahayana and Sautrântika thought arose as a reaction
against the Abhidharma tendencies of the Sarvâstivâdin founded
by Sâriputra.

Four hundred years had to pass after the death of the Buddha before the Mahayana literature began to develop. The Prajnâpâramita Sûtra, the Lotus of the Good Law and the Avatamsaka Sûtra were the first elements of it.

That which is known generally as *Hinayanist* Buddhism, is believed to have been founded by Sâriputra.

The *Hinayana* or '*Little Vehicle*', split into two branches. One known under the name of *Theravadin* developed in the East of India, and today dominates in Ceylon, Burma and Siam. The second branch known as *Sarvâstivâdin*, arose in the west of India and during fifteen centuries developed in the regions of Gandhara, Mathura and Cashmere.

As a reaction to the teaching of the Ancient School of Wisdom or *Hinayana*, the New School of Wisdom or *Mahayana* was established between the second and first centuries before our era.

The Mahayana sprang from a branch known by the name of *Mahâ-Sanghika* (the great assemblies). This latter comes down in direct line from the original doctrine. During the reign of Asoka, about 240 B.C., the *Mâha-sanghika* became separated from an old conservative tendency, the *Shtaviravâda*, and its subsequent development became very important. Four centuries later, the *Mahayana* gave birth to the tendency of the *Mâdhyamikas* founded around A.D. 150 by Nâgarjuna. Two hundred and fifty years later towards A.D. 400, the influence of the Sankhya-Yoga philosophy resulted in the founding of the *Yogacâra School* by Asanga. Finally around A.D. 500 the developments of the Tantric magic in India favoured the growth of *Tantra* or *Magical Buddhism*. The *Tantra* underwent considerable development in Nepal, Tibet, China, Japan, Java and Sumatra.

Specialists generally agree that the creative impulse of the Buddhist doctrines arising from developments in India, ceased some 1500 years after the Enlightenment of the Buddha.

It is only in the non-Indian developments which followed that Mahayanist Buddhism, fusing with the indigenous elements, realized its most remarkable developments.

Amongst these are the elements of fusion or synthesis such as the *Rnyin-ma-pa* in Tibet which absorbed most of the ideas of the indigenous Shamanism. Other elements, in contact with the less imaginative temperaments of the Chinese and Japanese, unexpectedly recovered the purity of the original inspiration. Such was the case of *Zen*, founded by Bodhi-Dharma towards A.D. 500.

We have not sufficient space to enable us to present the various philosophical differences of the divers schools of Buddhist thought. We only wish to draw the reader's attention to the difference existing between the two fundamental tendencies of Buddhism: the *Hinayana* or Little Vehicle, and the *Mahayana* or Great Vehicle. Both schools teach the impermanence of beings and of things.

They demonstrate the fundamental vacuity of the ultimate nature of the Universe.

However, the conceptions of the Mahayana were far more abstract than those of the Hinayana, the essential difference being the following:

To the Hinayanists, Nirvâna, or the essence of the depths, is distinct from Samsâra, or 'surface manifestations'. In Mahayanist Buddhism, Nirvâna and Samsâra are one and the same thing. 'Samsâra is Nirvâna, and Nirvâna is Samsâra.' In other words, mind and matter are the opposing but complementary facets of a single reality, in a sense that we will develop on various occasions later in this book. This is the essential basis of Mahayanist Buddhism which serves as a point of departure for the developments of Zen.

LITERARY DOCUMENTATION

During nearly four centuries after the death of the Buddha, the Buddhist Scriptures were not written down. The doctrine was transmitted orally.

The Scriptures were divided into 'Vinaya' which dealt with monastic discipline, and 'Dharma' or 'Sûtra' which expounded the doctrine.

There is an important division between the 'Sûtras' and the 'Sastras'.

A 'Sûtra' is a text which Buddhist tradition considers as having been uttered by the Buddha himself. It always begins with the words: 'Thus have I heard ... The Master was living at ...' The 'I' designates Ananda, the leading disciple of Buddha who reported all the Master's words.

A 'Sastra' is a treatise written by someone whose name is known, and it can be considered as an apparently more systematized commentary than the 'Sûtras'.

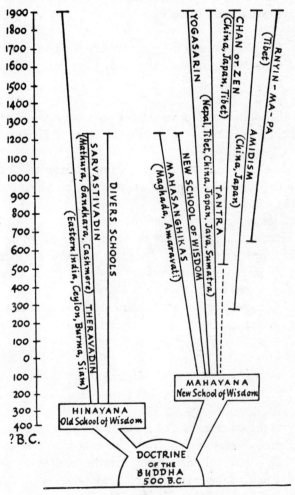

Fig. I.

Amongst the first works of Mahayanist literature one should mention the Prajnâpâramita Sûtras, the Lotus of the Good Law, and the Avatamsâkara Sûtra.

The Sanscrit word 'pra-jnâ-pâramita' means literally 'the act of going-beyond-wisdom'.

Translations of the 'Prajnâpâramita Sûtras' spread as far afield as China where they exercised considerable influence after A.D. 180.

Present-day Zen, may be considered an adaptation of these doctrines in China and Japan.

Of the Scriptures which have survived to the present day, the authorities on Buddhism generally study three main collections.

(1) *The Pâli Tripitaka*

The Pâli Tripitaka comprises the Scriptures of a school of Hinayana (Lesser Vehicle) known under the name of Theravadin.

(2) *The Chinese Tripitaka*

According to an ancient catalogue, dating from around A.D. 518 the Chinese Tripitaka comprised 2113 works, of which 276 survive to the present day.

(3) *The Tibetan Kanjur and Tanjur*

The Tibetan Kanjur consists of some hundred volumes of Sûtras, of which 13 deal with Vinaya or monastic discipline, 21 with the Prajnâpâramita or 'Perfect Wisdom', 45 are mixtures, and 21 are devoted to Tantrism.

The Tanjur, consisting of 225 volumes is made up of commentaries and 'Sastras'.

TEXTS WHICH HAVE SERVED AS BASES OF INSPIRATION
TO THE MASTERS OF ZEN

Contrary to the other schools of Buddhism, Zen does not possess any particular Sûtras which could be called a 'fundamental Canon'. Nevertheless, Bodhi-Dharma recommended the *Lankâvatâra Sûtra* to his disciple Houei-k'o. The *Vajrasamâdhi Sûtra*, the *Nirvâna Sûtra*, and the *Vajracchedikâ Sûtra* (Diamond Sûtra), are generally considered to be the fundamental elements of Zen inspiration.

However, certain reservations should be made when speaking of the 'texts which have inspired the Zen masters'. Professor D. T. Suzuki says the following about this:

'I wish to make some remarks against certain scholars who consider the philosophy of Sunyata to be really the foundation of Zen. Such scholars fail utterly to grasp the true purport of Zen, *which is first of all an experience and not at all a philosophy or dogma.* Zen can never be built upon any set of metaphysical or psychological views; *the latter may be advanced after the Zen experience has taken place, but never before*' (D. T. Suzuki, *Essays in Zen Buddhism*, vol. I, p. 186).

The main work of Bodhi-Dharma is entitled 'Mahayanist Wall-Contemplation' (Tai-tcheng-pi-kouan). Amongst his successors was Seng Ts'an who left a poem which is a remarkable contribution to the interpretation of Zen. Some fragments of this poem are reproduced in this book. It is entitled 'On believing in Mind' (Hsin-hsin-ming).

We shall end this very brief survey by pointing out a fundamental work of Zen, that of Hui-Neng, father of Chinese Zen. The title is '*Sermons of the Sixth Patriarch*' (Lu-tso T'an-ching).

We must also mention the work of Hsi Yun, the third descendant in direct line of the Sixth Patriarch Hui-Neng. This work is known as 'The Huang-Po Doctrine'. It has been translated into English under the title of 'The Huang-Po Doctrine of Universal Mind'.

Most of the teaching in these above-mentioned documents have been commented on in the books of Professor D. T. Suzuki who is universally recognized as the greatest authority on Zen Buddhism. Amongst his works we may mention: *Essays in Zen Buddhism, Studies in Zen, Living by Zen* (translated into French under the title of *Essais sur le Bouddhisme Zen*) and *Manual of Zen Buddhism*. The doctrine of Hui-Neng has been studied by D. T. Suzuki in a work entitled *The Zen Doctrine of No-Mind*.

CHAPTER II

Short Historical Sketch of Zen

THE history of Zen has two aspects; a somewhat obscure, legendary one, and an historical one. The legendary aspect developed alongside the great historical events already described. Professor D. T. Suzuki relates it in the following words:

'Sakyamuni was once engaged at the Mount of the Holy Vulture in preaching to a congregation of his disciples. He did not resort to any lengthy verbal discourse to explain his point, but simply lifted a bouquet of flowers before the assemblage, which was presented to him by one of his lay disciples. Not a word came out of his mouth. Nobody understood the meaning of this except the old venerable *Mahakasyapa*, who quietly smiled at the Master, as if he fully comprehended the purport of this silent but eloquent teaching on the part of the Enlightened One. The latter perceiving this opened his golden-tongued mouth and proclaimed solemnly, "I have the most precious treasure, spiritual and transcendental, which this moment I hand over to you, O venerable Mahakasyapa!"' (*Essays in Zen Buddhism*, vol. I, p. 165).

From the point of view of the Zen masters, it is of no importance whether this happened or not. The historical reality of the succession of the Buddha by Mahakasyapa, as head of the Faith, is generally admitted. The first allusions to this event are to be found in a Chinese history of Zen entitled 'Transmission of the Lamp', written by Li-Tsun-hsiu in 1029.

However the faithful of certain branches of Buddhism consider that there is a line of twenty-eight patriarchs from the Buddha till Bodhi-Dharma, founder of Zen.

They are generally called as follows:

(1) Sakyamuni (The Buddha)   (3) Ananda
(2) Mahakasyapa   (4) Savanasa

(5) Upagupta
(6) Dhritaka
(7) Micchaka
(8) Buddanandi
(9) Bodhamitra
(10) Bhiskhu Parsva
(11) Punyayashas
(12) Asvaghosha
(13) Bhikshu Kapimala
(14) Nagârjuna
(15) Kanadeva
(16) Arya Rahulata

(17) Samghanandi
(18) Samghayashas
(19) Kumarata
(20) Jayata
(21) Vasubandhu
(22) Manura
(23) Haklenayasas
(24) Bhikshu Simha
(25) Vasasita
(26) Punyamitra
(27) Prajnatara
(28) Bodhi-Dharma

In fact the history of Zen begins about A.D. 520 when Bodhi-Dharma went to China. There he taught the essential elements of the Lankâvatâra Sûtra and the Vajrasamadhi Sûtra. After Bodhi-Dharma (480-528), his Chinese disciple Houei-k'o (486-593) became the principle interpreter of Zen. He was succeeded in his turn by Seng-Ts'an who died in 606. The details of his life are mainly unknown, but he left a remarkable poem 'Hsing-hsin-ming' which we print here, from the excellent translation published in Professor D. T. Suzuki's *Manual of Zen Buddhism* (pp. 76-82).

ON BELIEVING IN MIND

The Perfect Way knows no difficulties
Except that it refuses to make preferences.
Only when freed from hate and love,
It reveals itself fully and without disguise.
A tenth of an inch's difference,
And heaven and earth are set apart:
If you wish to see it before your eyes,
Have no fixed thoughts either for or against it.
To set up what you like against what you dislike —
This is the disease of the mind:
When the deep meaning (of the Way) is not understood

Peace of mind is disturbed to no purpose.
(The Way is) perfect like unto vast space,
With nothing wanting, nothing superfluous:
It is indeed due to making choice
That its suchness is lost sight of.
Pursue not the outer entanglements,
Dwell not in the inner void;
Be serene in the oneness of things,
And (dualism) vanishes by itself.
And when oneness is not thoroughly understood,
In two ways loss is sustained . . .

Wordiness and intellection —
The more with them the further astray we go;
Away therefore with wordiness and intellection,
And there is no place where we cannot pass freely.

The moment we are enlightened within,
We go beyond the voidness of a world confronting us.

Try not to seek after the true,
Only cease to cherish opinions.
Abide not with dualism. . . .

Quit it, and things follow their own courses,
Obey the nature of things, and you are in concord with the Way.

If an eye never falls asleep,
All dreams will by themselves cease;
If the mind retains its absoluteness,
The ten thousand things are of one Suchness.
When the deep mystery of one Suchness is fathomed,
All of a sudden we forget the external entanglements:
When the ten thousand things are viewed in their oneness,
We return to the origin and remain what we ever have been.
Forget the wherefore of things,
And attain to a state beyond analogy. . . .

The ultimate end of things where they cannot go any further,
Is not bound by rules and measures:
In the Mind harmonious (with the Way) we have the principle of
    identity.
In which we find all strivings quieted.

There is nothing left behind,
There is nothing retained,
All is void, lucid, and self-illuminating. . . .

In the higher realms of True Suchness
There is neither 'other' nor 'self'. . . .

Tao-hsin (580-651) known as the *fourth patriarch*, succeeded
Seng Ts'an. Since the coming of Bodhi-Dharma a veritable spiritual renaissance had become apparent in Zen Buddhism. Seng
Ts'an's admirable poem, parts of which we have given, are an
eloquent testimony to this. This unexpected renaissance developed
during the centuries immediately succeeding Bodhi-Dharma. The
patriarchs after him were mostly exceptional.

Houng-jen (601-675), the *fifth patriarch*, can be considered as the
spiritual father of *Hui-Neng* whose work is almost as important as
that of Bodhi-Dharma.

Historians generally believe that without Hui-Neng – the
sixth patriarch – (also known under the name of Wei-Lang) Zen
would never have reached the developments it did at the beginning of the T'ang period of Chinese history.

Most of his sermons comment the profoundest texts of the
Mahayana and in particular the Nirvâna, Vajracchedika, Lan-
kâravatâra, Vimalakîrti Sûtras. They are striking by reason of
their vigour and inner dynamism. During the VIIIth century
A.D., the work of Hui-Neng (The Sermons of the Sixth Patriarch) occupied a foremost place in Zen.

Hui-Neng died at the age of 76, in the year 712. When he
received the robe of Bodhi-Dharma from the hands of Houng-
jen, the latter told him that he need no longer hand it down to a
successor as Zen had been fully recognized by the outside world.
It is for this reason that there was no seventh patriarch.

After the death of Hui-Neng, Zen split up into several schools many of which still exist in China as well as in Japan.

One is known as the Soto school, and another descends from the line of Houiai-Jang, successor to Hui-Neng, and is represented by the Rinzai school (Lin-Tsi). Among the successors of Hui-Neng we may mention the masters Hsi-Yun of Huang Po and Hui Hai.

Some opponents of Zen try to discredit it by insisting that it is only a tardy and secondary branch of Buddhism developed in regions far off from the original birthplace.

But they are losing sight of the eternally living character of Truth or Dharma to which we have frequently referred.

It is indeed fortunate that Buddhism should not have been entirely submerged by the too fertile imagination of the Hindus amongst whom it was born. Zen, which most of the pre-eminent authorities look upon as the pinnacle of Buddhism, has re-found, thanks to the less romantic and imaginative temperaments of the Chinese and the Japanese, the primitive purity of the Wisdom of the Buddha.

The fact that Zen should be considered as a non-Indian development of Buddhist thought, must give it all the more value to positive minds. The absence or lack of Scriptures in Buddhism, which some treat as a weakness, gives it, on the contrary, an element of strength.

In proportion as the teachings of a master are codified, his successors imperceptibly sink into an attitude of imitation. It is most probable that if Buddhism had had more Scriptures, we would never have known such remarkable masters as Bodhi-Dharma, Seng Ts'an and Hui-Neng. *The lack of precise and rigid ideas which is criticized by some, forces sincere seekers to find experiences of a far more individual and profound character than those suggested by the too perfect and systematized codification of a text.* It is for this reason that the superior forms of Buddhism in general and Zen in particular have led thousands of men and women to Enlightenment.

The first purity of the experience of the Sages cannot be transmitted by the prestige of a tradition or supposed revelation. It must be wholly created by living experience.

This is precisely the attitude adopted by Zen masters.

Another important fact is being lost sight of: though Zen is a non-Indian development of Buddhism, the texts which were its inspiration all come from the Mahayana and the Prajnaparamita, amongst which the Lankâvatâra Sûtra and the Vajracchedika Sûtra should be mentioned.

But apart from the prestige which these texts should have, the Zen masters have exceeded verbal expression in order to live the wisdom they seek to express. Therefore we should rejoice in the fact that strong non-traditionalist individualities have existed, who, rejecting the form and the letter, have re-discovered the LIFE behind these texts and realized the miracle of a renaissance of their pure spirit, beyond and in spite of their dead letters.

CHAPTER III

Is Buddhism a Philosophy?

THE term 'philosophy' generally does not exist in Buddhist texts, and in Zen it is even harder to find.

Both disdain metaphysical speculations on first causes, God, the absolute, etc.

Contrary to what is generally thought in the West, Buddhism in general and Zen in particular are essentially practical. They require us to free our minds from the general preoccupations which usually form the basis of all our philosophies: notions of good, of evil, etc.

Hui-Neng, one of the founders of Zen has left us this well-known injunction:

'Do not think of good, do not think of evil, but look at this very moment upon your original physiognomy, the one which you had even before you were born . . .' (*Sermons of the Sixth Patriarch*).

Tilopa, a master of Tibetan Buddhism, has left us this further advice:

'Do not think, do not imagine, do not analyse.'

Buddhism in general and Zen in particular are essentially 'non-mental'. *Man only attains 'correct vision' from the moment when no idea, no 'fabrication' of the mind any longer comes between him and the fact.* But were we to take what has just been said as a 'philosophical' position, we would be beside the question. That was simply the declaration of an essentially practical attitude to life, to be effectively realized from one instant to another.

This is why we would define Buddhism as a dialectic pragmatism of a psychological and non-mental nature.

This pragmatical attitude is the result of the actual process of the inner Enlightenment of the Buddha.

After having consulted the best-known Brahmins of his time, Siddharta Gautama was disappointed. Rejecting all the knowledge he had acquired, he restricted himself to observing attentively all the *actual facts* before him. Amongst these facts he picked out suffering, the impermanence of all things, and the continual flux of his thoughts. A penetrating view of the fundamental process of his inner life revealed to him the illusion of the 'I-process'. The mirage of his personal consciousness was replaced by the vision of his profound nature.

Buddhism does not dwell on metaphysical speculations developing the origin of suffering. It merely notes the fact and gives us a practical means for its elimination.

One must also add that this elimination is not the result of fleeing from the problem, but on the contrary, of a direct approach to it.

Buddhism confines itself to declaring that suffering originates in ignorance; the latter corresponding more exactly to a sleeping [24] state, a state of individual and collective lethargy. Nirvâna is the waking state outside this dream.

Buddhist thought avoids losing itself in speculations on the origins of the dream of ignorance; as a living process, it tends to turn us back irresistibly on ourselves. It requires us to be more attentive. Inattention is the greatest of sins in the eyes of the Zen masters. Perfect attention consists of an attitude of *non-mental observation* of concrete facts arising during daily life. It is a living method of approach whose practical character is attached to mind as much as to the matter.

For this reason Buddhism is pragmatic. It aims at the radical transformation of all our values by denouncing their contradictions. If it finds it necessary to use thought, it does so only in order to go beyond it. Therefore it is dialectic. However the importance which it gives to our mental processes, and the accent it places on the knowledge of ourselves, has constituted an extraordinarily [25] penetrating psychology from which most of the eminent psychologists have drawn inspiration.

The superior forms of Buddhism in general and Zen in particular are 'maieutic' rather like that of Socrates. 'Maieutic', or 'science of spiritual delivery' tries to unite the psychological elements favourable to the delivery of the mind. The latter being enslaved by mental 'habits', it will be necessary to eliminate the energy which feeds them. Socrates and the Zen masters tend to exhaust the possibilities of thought by obliging it to demonstrate to itself by its own means, its powerlessness to discover the Real. When thought realizes its impotence to 'give birth' to the essence of things, it is silent; and in this very silence the 'giving birth' is [26] realized. These are the essential lines of Socratic maieutics, and they correspond wholly with those of Zen and of Krishnamurti.

Independently of the aspects just defined, popular Buddhism is generally presented in the form of the 'Four great truths' and the 'Eightfold Path'.

Buddhist Tradition tells us that the 'Four essential Truths' were preached at Benares by the Buddha shortly after his illumination. They are generally simply listed as follows:

(1) Evidence of suffering.
(2) Designation of ignorance as the cause of suffering.
(3) Possibility of being delivered from suffering.
(4) Course to follow.

The fourth one is known by the name of the 'Eightfold Path' and consists of :

(1) correct vision
(2) correct intentions
(3) correct speech
(4) correct conduct
(5) correct way of living
(6) correct effort
(7) correct attention
(8) correct concentration.

In the higher forms of Buddhism, the last two branches are often considered as the most fundamental. Without 'correct attention' there can be neither 'correct vision' nor 'correct action'.

Here we shall try to define in more familiar language the general philosophical position of Mahayanist Buddhism.   [27]

The study of the elements of 'correct vision' as taught by the masters of the 'Secret Oral Tradition' and Zen, is far more involved than supposed at first.

The idea of 'seeing correctly' implies that at first we are capable of *seeing all*, and *seeing it correctly*. 'Seeing all' means to see beyond the body and the familiar peripheral layers of consciousness. 'Seeing all' when we look at the Universe, is to see as clearly beyond its merely superficial appearances. It means to penetrate into its profound essence by means of what is most intimate and inexpressible. But we can only do so by fully revealing ourselves to ourselves, in the totality of that which we are both on the 'surface' and 'in depths'. Only the essence can see the essence.

Today any man of average learning knows that the material Universe originates from a fundamental energy.

This energy is ONE, in spite of an appearance of multiplicity of forms, colours and properties. This energy is the *basis* of the world. The material aspects of the Universe and of our own persons are only secondary and derivative as regards this energy. In other words the old values of reality which we attribute to the outside world must be entirely recast. Recent progress in modern physics constitutes a striking confirmation of the soundness of the doctrine of 'Correct Vision'. The multiplicity of the aspects of the surface world familiar to us is based upon the Unity of a common essence before which the mask of separativity disappears. Everything is bound to all.

Only an indefinable Reality which physicists call energy remains; metaphysicists call it: Pure Being; mystics: God; and Buddhists: 'the basis of the world' or 'the Body of Buddha'. This Reality is prodigiously moving, fluid and creative. But the mental [28] representations given us by men of science still need far-reaching transformation. In physics as in biology, we are forced to admit the existence of 'non-physical' forms of energy. The psycho-physical aspects of the human being are closely linked. It is difficult for a scientist to find out exactly where one begins and the other ends. Considerable progress in psycho-somatics prove their constant interdependence most strikingly. As knowledge of physics and biology advance we see that a certain priority should be given to the non-physical forms of energy. We shall speak further of this later on.

For the moment it is important to remember that in man and in the Universe a close interdependence lies between two apparently opposed but complementary forms of the Real: the 'psychical' form, and the 'physical'. As Spinoza taught: 'The substance is ONE, but the modes are innumerable.'

In the light of recent discoveries in physics as well as in the Buddhist teachings, eventually we shall see that our ideas of 'substance' are very far from the facts.

If we examine minutely our states of consciousness, we notice their constant fluctuations, their inherent discontinuity. The study of the ultimate depths of matter reveals identical fluctuations and a fundamental discontinuity. Everything moves, is transformed, both materially and psychologically. This is the fundamental declaration of Buddhism: the impermanence of the aggregates of elements. 'Correct attention' should lead the seeker to the discovery of his impermanence. There is not really any continuous entity always identical with itself but a perpetually changing succession of 'cause and effect'. There is no static 'I-process', but a continuously moving and fluid succession of moments of consciousness stripped of all permanent individuality.

The belief in the reality of the 'I-process' comes from the rapidity with which our moments of consciousness follow each other. We shall examine their elements in more detail later on.

After having unmasked the illusion of his 'pseudo permanent individuality', the attentive seeker discovers the profound nature of his being. He experiences this common essence in which things and beings are bathed. From that moment he sees that *he is himself the Reality in such a homogeneity that all distinctions have vanished*.

That which distinguishes Buddhism from other religions is total respect for the homogeneity of the Real, the consequences of which are the absolute disappearance of all the dualities of observer and observed, spectator and spectacle, adorer and object adored, [11] and above all, the subject of the experience and his experience.

Thus, as we shall show more fully later on, we have always been the Real, but a mental optique, falsified by identification, had stopped us having a clear and direct vision. The Satori of Zen, or the Nirvâna of the higher forms of Buddhism are nothing other than this simple, clear and direct vision.

CHAPTER IV

Is Buddhism a Religion?

IF religion means an ensemble of imposed or proposed dogmas, and rites served by priests presented as 'ministers of God', then Buddhism is not a religion in the sense commonly given by the West to this term. At most we could call it such in its popular and Tantric forms.

If religion means an organization of spiritual aspirations whose aim is to understand and pass beyond the tangible world by freeing ourselves from the impulses attaching us to it, then the various forms of Buddhism could be qualified as religious.

Buddhist Scriptures recommend rules of correct conduct grouped under three main headings: *morality, contemplation and wisdom.* Their fundamental aim is to dissolve the illusion of individuality, this being the result of a process of linking up the 'aggregates' known as 'skandhas'.

They are:

(1) the body
(2) sense reaction
(3) the perceptions
(4) the impulses and emotions
(5) the acts of consciousness.

There, where only exists an impersonal network of causes and effects between the five elements, we see an entity. Buddhism considers belief in an individuality as an invention of the 'ego' which automatically is superimposed on the five aggregates.

We should point out however that most of the lower forms of Buddhism adopt what has been said above somewhat automatically.

In the higher forms and in Zen especially, we find an atmosphere of *vigilance* imposing on the seekers an effective experimental realization of this process.

The more a religion consists of a strict conformism to certain precepts, models or principles established as a system, the further is its outlook from that of Zen. The latter does not worry about [33] Scriptures, nor precepts, and even less with any rules of codified morality.

That is why if the different forms of Buddhism can be considered as forming a religion, as much can no longer be said for Zen. However, we will state that the latter is *basically religious*. 'Religion', in the eyes of someone who has awakened to an authentic inner life, is a term related to oppression or death. This is a consequence of the abuses and superficiality of certain aspects of Christianity in the course of history. Terms such as 'God' and 'religion' have been so betrayed and misrepresented that most writers have felt the need to replace them by new and more adequate expressions which have the merit of dissipating undesirable ambiguity.

There are religions, apparently alive, but which spiritually are dead. On the other hand there are religions apparently dying but which are very much alive. This is the case of Zen and the higher forms of Buddhism.

If we take the term 'religion' in its purest etymological sense, that is *re-ligare*, to reunite, bind again, then Zen and the higher forms of Buddhism may be considered as a religion. In this sense, the 'religious' man tries to discover the secret link which binds him to the divine presence which dwells in him as in all things. In this particular perspective we can consider religion as the science of the possible relationships between the human finite and the divine infinite. But here we have fallen into the trap laid by [31] words. We find ourselves distinguishing between the 'human finite and the divine infinite', when, in the eyes of the Zen masters, these distinctions, from certain points of view, are devoid of meaning. This shows us how great is the difficulty of making a correct definition of the religious position of Buddhism.

In consulting the *Dictionnaire Larousse*, we find that religion is defined as a series of *obligations* which men have towards God.

In this case, the higher forms of Buddhism and Zen are certainly not religions. In fact the notion of any *obligation* whatsoever is completely alien to the spirit of Zen particularly. Moreover, in Buddhism there is no allusion to a 'God' as distinct from us or outside our profound being. The fact of considering religion and its ensuing laws as *obligations*, is absurd.

All obligations imply shades of coercion, imposition and even violence which are contrary to any veritable religion, which can only be realized in the spontaneity of love and freedom of the mind.

THE ROLE OF MONKS IN BUDDHISM

The monks either live in communities or as lone hermits.

The whole fraternity is called the *Sangha*.

In most of the higher forms of Buddhism and in Zen, the monks refuse to consider themselves as *intermediaries* between the divine, the universe and man.

They devote themselves to the exercise of correct attention in order to discover their true nature, and respect the injunction of the Buddha to 'be each a lamp unto himself'.

When we say they devote themselves to the 'exercise of correct attention', we refer to most of them, for in fact the greatest Zen masters say that one does not 'practise' correct attention.

To consider it from that point of view, would confer on it an artificial character.

This would be further aggravated by a notion of compartition between the hours of exercise and 'normal' hours.

In the spirit of Zen, lucidity and vigilance should be continuous, and are inseparably united to the totality of the processes of Life, and better still, are Life itself.

In the Zen monasteries, the monks devote themselves to practical work, and try to realize it to perfection. This depends on pure, non-mental attention, allowing the realization of what certain Buddhist writers call 'perfect adequacy'.

'The infinite is in the finite of every instant', said one of the greatest masters of Zen.

The higher forms of Buddhism are totally bereft of the sense of spiritual authority which so strongly permeates present-day Christianity. Here is one of the most characteristic counsels of Zen [36] which tells the Disciple: 'Do not put another head above your own.'

Nevertheless, correct attention realized in such an atmosphere of independence and spiritual liberty, leads to an effective transcendence of the illusory 'I-process'. Though the Zen monks refuse spiritual authority, as generally understood in the West, they are working towards the discovery of an *identical nature*. This community of essence, or 'Body of Buddha', is the determining factor [37] of harmony, fraternity, compassion and true communion.

ABSENCE OF DOGMA

The attitude of Buddhism is very independent. The ideas of Zen are comparable with the modern currents of free thought. 'Cease to cherish opinions', Seng Ts'an, one of the great patriarchs of Zen tells us.

The essence is freedom. Attachment to any ideas is contrary to freedom. Zen teaches us not only that attachment to an idea is a factor that conditions the mind, but also that the simple preference for one idea rather than another, for one value rather than another [38] equally enslaves the mind'. The central reality of our being and of all things is 'Cosmic Mind. All mental preferences imply an addition of psychic energy to a privileged point in the infinitude of cosmic mind. From the moment when we create privileged points, distinctions and preferences, we are exiling ourselves from the infinite Freedom of the Real. Any particularization gives a hold to the innumerable processes of relativity. This spirit of freedom has been clearly defined in a Zen counsel: [39]

'The perfect way knows no difficulties *except that it refuses to make preferences . . . A tenth of an inch's difference and Heaven and Earth are set apart.*'

The psychological atmosphere of the higher forms of Buddhism and of Zen bears the marks of extraordinary sensitivity and delicacy in relation to the problem of spiritual freedom. As it is, we could define Zen as spiritual free thinking. In contrast to this, we cannot help feeling the oppression and violence implied in certain forms of Christian dogmatism, which not only proposes but also imposes a series of systematized ideas in the name of a supernatural revelation.

THE APPARENT DOGMATISM OF NON-DOGMATISM

The independent and non-dogmatic position of Zen runs counter to minds conditioned by an attachment to particular beliefs.

While lecturing in various countries, the author of this book met with certain dogmatic listeners who could not admit the possibility of a fundamental freedom and a non-conditionment of the mind.

We would draw the reader's attention to the fact that in spite of appearances we are not engaging upon any polemic. This warning applies also to the non-ritualist position to be developed later on.

Some people lose sight of the fact that the real polemist defends particular ideas and beliefs with which he has identified himself. He is fighting in order that the point of view of his own personal ideological preferences may triumph.

We have no personal idea. We are not defending any special belief with which we have identified ourselves. *We are not fighting anything.*

The Zen masters have nothing to 'defend', for the simple reason that they possess nothing.

They teach us that wisdom consists in '*no longer cherishing opinions*'.

Pure freedom is the essential law of the spirit. Such an affirmation is not a concept, for veritable Freedom cannot 'be conceived'. It is lived, but it cannot be lived till concepts cease. The cessation itself is Liberty. It is in itself the most imperious spiritual reality there could be. However, its importance seems to escape the average man.

To the eyes of a Sage, freedom and non-conditioning of the mind appear as urgent on the spiritual plane as is air to the drowning person nearing final suffocation.

To pretend that the non-dogmatism of the Sages and the Zen masters is in itself a dogmatism, is just to play upon words. That is a trap laid by the intellect as a means of self-defence for those who are prisoners of dogmas to which they cling desperately.

The non-dogmatism of the Sage is not due to his personal adhesion to any particular system of anti-dogmatic ideas. It is simply an impersonal consequence of the essential law of total liberty of cosmic mind to which his is submitted.

It is not *he* who decides to rise up against dogmas and beliefs; but it is the divine and essential Reality which quite naturally itself imposes on the Sage its fundamental nature of Freedom, Spontaneity and eternal resurgence.

Let us beware then of easy answers and snares laid by the intellect.

They can lead us to mechanical and unintelligent arguments similar to that put forward by the listener who solemnly affirmed that an attitude of non-conditioning of the mind as recommended by Zen or Krishnamurti was really a conditioning. . . .

At first the position of the authentic sages as regards the problems of Freedom and non-conditioning of the mind, always appears to be intransigent. When we try to explain this point of view, some people accuse us of intolerance.

We would emphasize particularly that to the Sages (or integrated men) the world seems plunged in a veritable lethargy, at once individual and collective. And this is not merely a manner of speaking.

Zen wants awakeners . . . Like Diogenes, it seeks true men who realize the plenitude of their profound nature in whatever it may have that is creative, dynamic and intensely awake. The Zen Unconscious is not a form of sleep, but a state of supreme lucidity so perfect that it is unconscious of itself.

Most seekers forget that between *being awake and dreaming, the Light and Darkness, Freedom and servitude, there is no half way. The passage from one to the other constitutes a veritable psychological mutation.* These are the essential reasons for the sudden character of 'Satori' and the Krishnamurtian liberation.

And now we find ourselves obliged to declare one of these terrible thoughts which are always liable to be misunderstood: he who is in the plenitude of the Light cannot be 'tolerant' towards the darkness. He who is in the plenitude of Freedom cannot be tolerant towards the servitudes and conditionings of the Mind.

Tolerance as we see it would appear to him in this field as the most unpardonable duplicity, because he knows that the slightest trace of shadow which remains and resists the light, irreparably prevents the psychological mutation of 'Satori'.

Nevertheless we must insist on the fact that this intolerance is not of the type we generally condemn. The apparent intolerance of the integrated man or of the Sage, is not comparable with that known to dogmatic and intolerant men.

For these men are intolerant by reason of the attachment of their minds to particular systems of thought with which they have identified themselves.

The integrated men no longer identify themselves with any system of thought and are free from all personal attachment to a particular belief.

They are 'dead to themselves', and *only LIFE commands in them*.

The intolerance of a man who is prisoner of a particular political or religious ideology, leads to the violence and fanaticism inherent in the desire to impose this ideology. In fact by these means the man is trying to affirm himself and is using his ideas as instruments of expansion and domination.

The apparent intolerance of the integrated man does not lead to any violence.

It does not try to impose itself. It is basically non-violent, because the Sage does not try to impose himself nor dominate. All that matters to him is the rhythm of Life, universal and impersonal.

That is exactly why one does not bargain with Life.

One compromises with men. One does not compromise with God. And we are all used to easy bargains, half-measures and compromises. It is through the latter that the 'I-process' preserves itself and will on no account disappear.

The half-hearted, the timid and the tepid do not enter the 'Kingdom of God'. The proportion of error we tolerate in others is the proportion we tolerate in ourselves.

When on the psychological plane we are totally dead to ourselves, we are no longer able to be the accomplices of the half-measures and compromises which enslave others. However, we do not impose on anyone the vision of Freedom, which the supreme Reality has suggested to us.

If the Sages speak to us of it, it is because being animated by compassion and infinite love, they have understood, felt and realized the painful character of the ignorant and lethargic state of the world. The Sage proposes, he does not impose anything. However the truth for which he is the mouth-piece is unconditional, and the secret of his power is that it is no longer his truth but Life Itself.

RITES

In most of the Indian developments of Buddhism, magic is of considerable importance. Tantric and magic rites have also developed in Tibet. However, they do not exist in Zen. **41**

In the spirit of Zen all ritual, every magical or tantric practice, hinders deliverance of mankind. They show that the mind is a prisoner of false values through establishing distinctions and preferences in the domain in which they are specifically forbidden.

'Satori' or experience of the Real is realized from one instant to the other.

The Southern school of Zen insists on its *sudden, unexpected* and **42** *spontaneous* character.

A too elaborate preparation of the mind creates an inner tension hampering the spontaneity of the experience. A subtle and secret anticipation of the unconscious paralyses all possibility of its uprising.

That is why the Zen Masters insist on the fact that Satori may be realized on any occasion. Salvation is found in the ordinary things of everyday life. Moreover life in general ceases to be divided be- **43** tween 'ordinary' things and others which could be called 'extra-ordinary'.

The ultimate experience may be released by a common occurrence such as the fall of a stone, or as readily by the sight of a lovely flower or the contemplation of a sunset. The inner attitude of approach to an event is far more important than outer circumstances.

'Every perception is an occasion for Satori', say the Zen Masters. But the occasion cannot be fully grasped if the mind is conditioned by any kind of ritual.

This highly purified attitude of Zen towards dogmas, rites and Scriptures, is defined in the 'Four Maxims':

'A special transmission outside the Scriptures;
No dependence upon words and letters;
Direct pointing to the soul of man;
Seeing into one's nature and the attainment of Buddhahood.'

It is obvious that all ritual implies a preparation, an examination, a training and a waiting period which engenders a subtle state of spiritual tension.

The spontaneity and upsurging character of 'Satori' are totally incompatible with such inner attitudes in which the resistances of the 'I-process', far from disappearing, are strengthened on the unconscious plane.

The attitude of devotion which accompanies religious ceremonies and rites, depends on certain definite forms inherent in the symbols chosen by the faithful.

In the spirit of the Zen Masters the cult of no matter what symbol will never allow us to attain the Supreme Reality, of which we wrongly suppose the symbol to be a perfect representation.

No symbol is capable of representing that which the Zen Masters call the 'Cosmic Mind'. To wish to conceive the latter in the form of a mental cliché or of an image, is in practice equivalent to denying it.

Most of those who profess to adore or pray to God, in fact only adore a mental projection of the divine which has been fabricated by their mind. The materials for this artificial edifice are taken as much from the individual consciousness and unconscious as from the collective unconscious.

They all belong to a dead past without any relationship with the Divinity Himself.

That is why most of the religious experiences realized within the framework of symbolic religions, lead the mystics to the contemplation of their own mental creations.

These states of auto-hypnosis have no common measure with [45] the Supreme Reality itself.

There is a distinction which we must realize, and to which the veritable teachers attach great value: our mental representations of the divine must not be confused with the divine itself.

Here the defenders of Roman Catholicism will say that the experience of the saints has proved that the cult of symbols can bear fruit.

We will answer this in three different ways which will enable us to define our point of view more accurately.

Firstly, if there have been 'saints' in the Catholic church or any other symbolic and ritualistic and religious organization, we have serious reasons to think that they reached realization *in spite* of the environment in which they lived. This environment being radically opposed to the natural laws of the spirit, we should admire all the more what they have accomplished despite psychological surroundings so contrary to genuine spiritual development.

A study of the incidents of the lives of most of them, shows how they had to fight against the pettiness of the organization under whose auspices they realized their experiences.

The experiences of certain Christian mystics such as was Catherine of Sienna, show us that they had first reached the 'Formless', only to fall later within the limitations of symbols. After the great joy of the informal vision, the mind of the saint intervened and created tragic anxiety: where were the symbols of the adored?

She had, we might say, and unknown to herself, transcended them, by means of her personal quality and despite the limitations inherent to Christian symbolism.

It was only afterwards that the symbols achieved their work of degradation and corruption. By an easily understood process of compensation, the saint finally 'saw' the images and symbols whose absence had worried her.

Secondly, it would be absurd for us to suppose that saints have flourished only in the Christian faith. The fact that for centuries various other religions have not taken the trouble to codify and register the number of their ascetics and saints for purposes of propaganda is not reason enough for supposing that they did not exist. 'Saintliness' is not the privilege of religious organizations. It can and should belong to the laity.

Thirdly, it is definitely important not to confuse saintliness with wisdom. The saint is one whose 'I-process', by asceticism, mortifications, traditional religious practices and rites, comes to realize a state of purity.

His needs are reduced to a minimum, he is chaste, eats little, and lives in contemplation and prayer. *But fundamentally the saint remains an 'I-process'.* Only from being impure, his 'I-process' has become 'pure'. The attractions of exterior life have given way to those of the inner life. But beyond these changes and transformations, the centre of personal consciousness remains intact and intends so to remain. *The 'saint' does not transcend the illusion of the 'I-process'. The Sage on the other hand has transcended the 'I-process'.*

The mystic experience of the 'saint' is that of a *dualistic communion* during which the entity of the 'I-process' remains aware of the distinction between itself and the object of its veneration. The experience of the Sage on the contrary is a *Monist integration*, during which identification with the personal consciousness is definitely extinguished.

Certain saints have described the states of their mystical experiences as veritable fusions with the divine. They speak of total non-dualistic identification with God. They have not, however, definitely reached the state of the Sage, and from the moment their experiences are over, they return to the ordinary, personal state of consciousness.

Between the state of saintliness and wisdom there is a veritable mutation of an essentially psychological and spiritual nature volatilizing henceforth the usual limits of the 'I-process'.

To the saint chastity and simplicity of needs are the means; to the Sage they are the consequences.

The saint may have lofty thoughts but they cannot penetrate the limits of the mental plane. He does not yet succeed in grasping the key to the process which dominates his thoughts and gives to his 'I-process' the illusory appearance of a continuous and real entity.

The Sage has transcended beyond the mind and has definitely freed himself from identification with the body, the emotions and thoughts.

The mystic emotion of the saint is often the result of a simple transposition of the sexual energies to the affective plane. A physical sensualism is only succeeded by a psychic sensualism. A detailed study of the ecstatic processes of most mystics and the very nature of the words used in their descriptions of their experiences prove this point of view beyond doubt.

The state of the Sage is not of an emotional or mental nature.

The mystical state of the saint is the result of prayers and gross or subtle mortifications that never break out of the 'I-process'.

The mystical state of the Sage is not the consequence of 'personal manipulations', but on the contrary, of their complete cessation.

The saint submits himself to discipline. The Sage has passed beyond all disciplines.

The emotional intensity and religious exaltation felt by the officiants and active or passive participants in certain rites, are the consequence of the manipulation of particular idea-forces and archtypes of the collective unconscious.

These idea-forces and archtypes are bearers of a considerable potential of psychic energy. During thousands of years they have been fed by the thoughts of millions of human beings.

And yet each day they are thought and re-thought.

Therefore they continually gain power.

But this power, considered by some as a help, is a hindrance.

These idea-forces are the supreme crystallization of the 'Cosmic force of Habit' on the mental plane.

Adversaries of this point of view reply that idea-forces and mental archtypes do not only arise from the human mind. The neo-platonists for example spoke of paradigms. These designated idea-forces or cosmic archtypes previous to human evolution.

This point of view does not change the problem in any way.

Essentially the aim of Wisdom is to free us from the tyranny of forms. Whether they be physical or mental, whether they be the result of a non-human cosmic process, the problem is the same. The identification of forms, whether they are natural or manufactured by the mind or the human body, always remains a process of enslavement to the past.

The fact that certain archtypes could be considered as emanating from the divine Great Work, is not an argument likely to prove that *for us* there exists a seizable link between these archtypes and the Supreme Reality of the divine.

We are losing sight of the irreversible character of the divine processus.

That which we — in our dualistic image of the world — conceive as emanations of the divine, cannot help us to find the divine itself. To try and cover in the opposite direction the supposed succession of stages between Him and ourselves does not make sense.

It is because most religions and philosophies have lost sight of the irreversible and asymmetrical nature of the processes of Life, that they lead us into these impasses.

To Zen, and the Sages in general, the Supreme Reality is *LIFE*. These are the basic reasons for the sudden and instantaneous character of Satori.

[48] We cannot realize Eternity by means of time which is a false emanation of Eternity. Therefore we are forced to free ourselves from mental identification with time.

We cannot discover light by means of darkness which is a false emanation of light. Therefore, we are forced to deliver our mind from the false values which engendered the notion of 'darkness'.

It is impossible to realize the Real by means of the 'individual I-process' or pseudo-entity which is a false emanation, a mirage, of the Real. Therefore we are forced to outline the errors of the mental optique which have given rise to the illusion of the pretended reality of the 'I-process'.

In the degree in which we are willing to submit to the influences of idea-forces or archtypes, human or so-called divine, we shut ourselves from all possibilities of Satori.

The veneration of forms and energies contained in the forms of the past, is incompatible with the eternally renewed presence of the divine.

The Zen Masters teach us, besides, that the Supreme Reality is not outside us. It is not only in us, but we are IT.

From this particular point of view all ritual takes on a doubly contradictory character.

Firstly it is artificial because it is specially prepared and isolated from the total processes of Being. We separate it from the natural realities of life which should include everything and exclude nothing. We also have a tendency to seek outside ourselves that which in a certain respect we are already.

Secondly, it is directed at mental representations, vestiges of a far-off past whose very nature is a total negation of the Real.

The religious emotion felt by the faithful and certain mystics during ritual, derives in order of importance from five funda- mental factors.

(1) A sincere but unfortunately ill-directed research because ill-informed, as well as an element of unconscious erotism of thought and sublimation of the sensualism of the 'I-process'.

(2) The 'occult' or psychic efficacity of the ceremonial magic itself, based on esthetic considerations of form and simple relationships (the golden Numbers), and colours.

(3) The psychic environment exerts an influence which draws its power from the psychic forces of accumulated devotion. These psychic forces called 'agregor' by some writers, work on the mind of the faithful.

The forms inherent in ceremonial magic should be added to these just mentioned.

(Manipulations of the idea-forces attached to certain symbols.)

(4) There is a phenomenon of auto-hypnosis, at once individual and collective. The faithful, unconsciously influenced by the psychic currents which surround them, tend to imagine that the

particular states experienced by them confirm the accuracy of their thoughts and prayers. The detection of these errors can be helped if we know that an authentic inner state does not depend on any specially chosen outer circumstance.

(5) Confusion arises between the esthetic emotion caused by the obviously moving edifice of chants and particularly beauti-
⁵⁰ ful musical arrangements on the one hand, and religious emotion on the other.

The idea that a place has been specially consecrated also provokes in the faithful a state of mind favourable to the emergence of a whole series of false values.

⁵¹ The Masters denounce as follows the dangers inherent in ritual practices.

(a) A tendency to depend on the practice of rites to find a pseudo-religious atmosphere.

(b) Inner laziness.

(c) A tendency to inertia and spiritual death through the fact that the 'religious' state is gradually sought after through the medium of elements borrowed from 'without' by the ritual, whereas they should be sought 'within' by a strictly individual process of auto-enlightenment, independent of all ritual.

(d) A tendency continually to seek simple sensations. The putting to sleep of the transcendental spiritual process of the waking state.

Being incapable of perceiving the inner riches of the divine State itself, the faithful try to 'saturate themselves in the favourable psychic atmosphere' and seek the easy way through an 'exterior' psychic bath, instead of recovering in themselves and by themselves the existential and in-formal felicity of their own veritable nature.

(e) An inevitable tendency on the part of the faithful to identification with and attachment to the places in which the ritual takes place and to decorum.

(f) In the end the faithful tend to become uprooted psychically and spiritually.

They can no longer do without ritual.

This last acts as a spiritual drug. Inevitably a separation is established between 'ordinary' life, and the time given to ritual.

(g) The practice of rites becomes an escape.

It tends to render the man insensible to the circumstances which he considers as ordinary and inessential in contrast to those of rites which he looks upon as extraordinary and essential.

So Man sinks into the habit of routine practices which paralyse all possibility of a really living spiritual or religious experience. Ritual never goes beyond the sphere of the lower mind.

True spirituality lies beyond forms and symbols, and can only be realized in absence of premeditation, in spontaneity and immediacy of the mind.

CHAPTER V

The Notion of God in Buddhism

MANY writers consider Buddhism atheistic and in order to support their theory they point out that the term 'God' is never mentioned in Buddhist texts. Clearly this is not a sufficient reason to qualify it as an atheist philosophy.

Teachers of Buddhism in general and Zen in particular, have too clear a vision of the infinitude of the Real to give it a name. Reality is inconceivable, and nothing can be said about it. Not only are our usual distinctions unable to give us an idea of the Supreme Reality, but they are in themselves the most serious obstacles which separate us from it.

Though the term 'God' never appears in the texts of Buddhism in general and Zen in particular, the terms 'pure essence' or 'the basis of the world', or 'cosmic mind' or even 'The Body of Buddha' are used frequently.

Indeed the teachers of Zen consider the God of whom the Christians speak merely as a mental projection of their own psyche, bearing moreover all the marks of the limitations of that.

Our anthropomorphisms seem to them rather naive. The idea of an external God who rewards some while punishing others, is completely alien to them.

As Professor D. T. Suzuki says:

'In Christianity we seem to be too conscious of God, though we say that in him we live and move and have our being. Zen wants to have even this last trace of God-consciousness, if possible, obliterated' (*Essays in Zen Buddhism*, vol. I, p. 350).

In Zen to think of God is to deny God. To base oneself on such attitudes in order to affirm the atheism of Zen or of Buddhism, only proves that their deeper significance has not yet been understood. The essential preoccupation of Buddhism in general and Zen in particular is waking out of the dream of ignorance and illusion. The moment this dream is dissipated, the Supreme Reality is revealed in all the infinitude of its splendour.

Though the Buddhists do not indicate it by the term God, nevertheless it is the central object which they try to realize and towards which they direct their efforts and 'non-efforts'.

None the less, certain similarities exist between Christianity and the popular forms of Buddhism. In the latter detailed descriptions are to be found of attributes applying to the 'nature of Buddha'.

In Zen, however, the divine is not a thing which is discussed. [53]

That which we name 'God', cannot be 'known' as we generally know things. 'God' is lived. But He can only be lived when attachment to our usual knowledge has ceased; then from that moment we discover His nature in us, and this nature mingles with all things.

'If the mind retains its absoluteness, the ten thousand things are of one suchness' said Seng Ts'an, a Zen Master.

In this new perspective, the Divine is not distinct from us.

We are it, but we do not know it . . . Eyes have we, but we see not. . . .

Here we shall develop the same subject in a different and unfortunately still more intellectual language. That to which we so imperfectly refer as the 'concept of the divine', requires in Buddhism various ways of approach, whose interconnection and varied shades of meaning might enlighten us.

When before we said 'we are Divine', this affirmation had no exclusive or restrictive character. We are It, just as are the paving-stones over which we walk and the dead branch at the side of [54] the road. We are It in 'depth' and 'on the surface', for nothing is outside the Body of Buddha. Its complete homogeneity includes all that is actual and virtual in the domain of mind and of matter.

Our shock on hearing that a mere stone or a piece of dead wood *is the Divine*, is due to the fact that we *know nothing about their real nature*. All that we have in mind are mental representations of their exterior contours and superficial appearances as perceived by our senses. But their essential physical reality is quite different. The little we have learned from recent research in physics has given us much to think about.

Lack of information as to the exact structure of matter, was responsible for the pessimism which marked certain forms of materialism during the past centuries. We can say that the materialists of the past worshipped a God whom they did not know. The 'God of Matter' has just taken off his mask of glacial immobility, and, behold, is transformed into a prodigiously moving, fluid, impalpable energy. His countenance, which once appeared sombre and dull, is now lit up with ever more dazzling clarity. The silent fairyland of light, perpetually unfolding in the heart of the smallest grain of sand, far exceeds in splendour the most brilliant display of fireworks that we could ever hope to see.

The physicists give us a glimpse of the essence of matter taking on such a spiritual character that it looks as though modern physics is irresistibly leading us to the creation of a *spiritual materialism*.

This offers a striking similarity with the higher forms of Buddhism.

In view of what has just been said, we shall be able to understand better the hidden sense of the following anecdote which is familiar to the students of Zen. A disciple asked the instructor by what means he might obtain 'Satori' or vision of his true nature. The master answered by simply raising his staff and saying: 'If you understand this, you will have understood the whole Universe.'

From the point of view of Zen, no difference exists between the profound nature of our being and that of any object, that of all things. There is only a difference of 'surface' which is the result of diversity in the degrees of complexity and flexibility of their organization. *In our eyes*, these differences are very important. We have identified ourselves with them to such an extent that they represent all that we are. This is the origin of the spiritual drama inherent in our inner poverty.

To Zen, the aspects of the world which are familiar to us, are a consequence of an inadequacy of perception, but when this gains in depth, the differences of surface are integrated in a whole which is infinitely more vast and of which they are but an insignificant reflection.

If the Divine as seen by the Zen Masters had to be defined in simple language, we would describe it as the Totality-that-is-One of the visible and invisible aspects of the Universe.

This Totality-that-is-One is absolutely homogeneous. We will develop this more fully later on. It knows no duality and includes all that which in the dualistic manner we call the physical and psychical aspects of the Universe.

By virtue of the analytical tendency of our thoughts which divide, sub-divide and classify arbitrary divisions are set up in the midst of this Totality-that-is-One: the material division, the psychic and the spiritual. The watertight compartments which separate these different modes of the Real are the work of our thoughts.

In fact there are no 'modes' in the Real. There are no separate planes, no watertight compartments, nor mind in opposition to matter.

This language has become so familiar to us, because it is inseparable from our partial way of seeing things, that we are obliged to use it repeatedly while at the same time recognizing its weaknesses. Without recourse to a concession made to our funda- [56] mentally perverted vision, we would find ourselves most of the time incapable of explaining anything at all.

The notion of the Totality-that-is-One of the divine which to us is composed of two opposed, but complementary aspects such as mind and matter, can be illustrated by an example well known to physicists.

In certain experiments the electron behaves like a solid corpuscle. The physicists who first caught a glimpse of it under this aspect, hastily concluded that the nature of the electron was essentially corpuscular. In the course of other experiments, however, a different group of physicists observed an undulatory behaviour of the same electrons. These physicists concluded that the ultimate constituents of matter were of an essentially undulatory nature. But as Prince Louis de Broglie proved, there was nevertheless but *one and the same type of electron which according to the angle under which it was examined, revealed itself either as a corpuscle or as pure radiation.*

In other words the undulatory and corpuscular aspects of the electron *are opposed but complementary*; opposition does not appear as such, except to observers who each examine only one aspect of the same reality with the aid of different and particular scales of observation.

This is the fragmented approach of the mind which perverts the clear vision which we should have of all things, and ourselves.

The Nirvâna of Buddhism in general and the Satori of Zen are [57] nothing other than the experience of this clear non-mental, non-fragmented vision of the Totality-that-is-One in its indivisible homogeneity. In the light of this new clarity, the limitations of egoism and consciousness of self vanish for ever and, instead of the [58] nothingness which many expect, such an experience permits the realization of the highest peaks of love and pure intelligence.

However let us not lose sight of the fact that the terms 'Love', 'intelligence', or 'Supreme Reality' take on a meaning in the minds of the Masters of Buddhism different from that with which we are familiar.

CHAPTER VI

The Illusory Character of Aid, of Salvation, of all Systems

WHEN the personality of him who is imperfectly called the 'founder' of a religion becomes more important than his teaching, then all kinds of deviation become possible. [59]

The progressive deification of the teacher slowly confers on him the character of sole saviour, and his followers believe that no salvation is possible outside the only way laid down by him. [60]

The Zen Masters have a very different standpoint on the notions of 'salvation', exterior help, the redemption of sin, and the familiar 'dogmas' of Christianity.

Here is a passage from Professor D. T. Suzuki on the subject: (*Essays in Zen Buddhism*, vol. I): [61]

'To comprehend fully the constitution of any existent religion that has a long history, it is advisable to separate its founder from his teaching, as a most powerful determinant in the development of the latter', p. 40.

'By this I mean that the *founder so called had in the beginning no idea of being the founder of any religious system which would later grow up in his name; . . .*', p. 40. [62]

'The Christian edifice is built around the person of Jesus. Buddhists may accept some of his teachings and sympathize with the content of his religious experience, but so long as they do not cherish any faith in Jesus as "Christ" or Lord, they are not Christians', p. 44.

'In other words, *Christ did not found the religious system known by his name, but he was made its founder by his followers . . .*', p. 44. [63]

'*Buddhism did not come out of the Buddha's mind fully armed*, as did Minerva from Jupiter', p. 45.

'Inasmuch as Buddhism is a living religion and not an historical mummy stuffed with dead and functionless materials, it must be able to absorb and assimilate all that is helpful to its growth. This is the most natural thing for any organism endowed with life', p. 46.

The further it may be from the spirit of Freedom and Independence with which it was imbued by the Buddha, the more Buddhism resembles present-day aspects of Christianity. In fact in popular Buddhist texts we often see expressions such as 'to take refuge in the Dharma'.

These notions however are completely alien to Zen.

In Zen there are no miracles, supernatural interventions, ways nor refuges. We bear the whole responsibility for our actions and no Sage whomsoever he be has the right to encroach on our free will.

We are at the same time responsible for our slavery and our freedom; the chains of our enslavement have been forged by ourselves, and only we can break them.

The task of the Sages is to show us the obstacles to our liberation, for that can only be realized in the living fire of our experience, our joys and suffering.

Only ignorance, laziness and cowardice can lead us to seek outside aid for no authentic wisdom could assume the responsibility of inducing man to take up an attitude of evasion which is so harmful to his development.

Nor have we anything to acquire, say the Zen Masters. We have nothing either to receive from the outside, nor anything to build up or 'make' in the usual sense of the word. Rather have we to 'undo' the complex accumulations of our false values.

Everything is present. We are the Real but we do not know it, as Zen tells us repeatedly. From the depths of our spirit to the material structures of our physiology, *nothing is lacking*. It suffices merely to establish a co-ordination, a functional harmony between the different components of which we are made up. The lack of harmony between the different levels of our beings, and the very sense of division into different compartments which our spirit loves to create, come from an essential error of our mental vision. The mirages engendered by it, however, disappear as soon as it is adjusted by 'correct attention'.

Therefore one thing seems fundamentally necessary: *to know ourselves*. In this alone lies that which we could very imperfectly call 'our salvation'.

It is useless to seek anything outside ourselves, because all outside search is undertaken in a direction radically opposed to that which the mind should naturally take. We could compare the process of development of our inner life with the growth of a plant which must direct its roots down into the fertile soil that nature has prepared for it. The depths of the unconscious and of the conscious are to us the fertile soil into which the roots of our being must spread, in order to obtain the vivifying contact of its essence. It is a strictly individual process. All expectation from outside, all cult of authority, all hope of a miracle, are just so many elements which paralyse the development of our psychic roots towards the buried centre which is the source of Life in us.

If we attain the perfectly clear vision of what we are we no longer need 'to go elsewhere'. The exterior 'ways' become to us ways of perdition.

Most men, however, choose these very ways, for they are more comfortable and require no effort. Ludovic Rehault expressed this perfectly when he said that we would really like to be 'carried to Nirvâna in a sedan-chair'.

But Truth mocks our weaknesses, pettiness and false values. We must raise ourselves to its level, and not require it to descend to the level of our limitations.

It is only on this condition that we are able to realize the plenitude of that which we were and are to all eternity. Then from that moment there is no saviour, nor way, nor outside salvation.

Just as all men and women of all the people of the Earth have said and will say at the moment of their Awakening, so do we say *simply*: 'I am the Way'.

Christians say that such an affirmation is a proof of pride. Pride is the result of an excessive sense of consciousness of self. To say that the affirmation 'I am the Way' is arrogant, is not to understand that this could not properly be said by anyone except by a being who is totally 'dead' to himself and delivered from all the pitfalls of personal identification.

CHAPTER VII

The Nature of Things

AFTER having examined in what way Buddhism in general and Zen in particular may or may not be a religion, we shall now consider it as a *science*. The doctrine of 'Correct Vision', which forms the essential element of the higher forms of Buddhism, can be defined as the science of the Real whose invariable aim is to discover the profound nature of things. We have already pointed out that the approach to the problem does not conform with the familiar processes of philosophical speculation. Buddhism confines itself to declaring the impermanence of beings and things. This declaration is made with the minuteness of a penetrating analysis which extends to the uttermost confines of the material and psychical structure of human nature. The same process of observation is applicable to the material environment of everyday life. The history of a Universe is one of thousands of millions of transformations, thousands of millions of births, developments and deaths. The essential law of the infinitely great and the infinitely small is that of *change*.

Here is what Carlo Suarès says in his *Comédie Psychologique*:

'Nothing in the Universe is ever stable. *Everything is movement*; not only does matter, of which things are made, hide from our analysis, but of the most banal object which we come across, we are unable to say which are the elements it needs in order to be that object. This table has four legs. A table with a broken leg still remains a table. But a table from which the four legs have been removed becomes only a flat piece of wood. At what moment did it cease to be a table? . . .

That which is commonly called an object is a provisional state of movement, a state whose limits we can only rarely define either in time or space.

Everything, from ourselves to this planet, to the sun, to the thousand of millions of solar systems which surround us is only *perpetual transformation*' (pp. 97-100).

If we examine the intimate structure of matter in the light of recent revelations in physics, we notice the prodigious rapidity of the revolutions of electrons round atomic nuclei.

This notion of fundamental impermanence and perpetual change taught by the doctrine of 'Correct Vision', has been [72] demonstrated by the best Western thinkers. Here is a remarkable citation from a work by Professor Edouard Le Roy:

'Wherever our gaze alights, does it ever find motionless bodies? Repose is always only relative and apparent. To what point does a being mobilise itself before us?

The answer to the experience is significant: as it grows in precision and refinement, it no longer finds immobility, nor constancy, but perpetual trepidation. There are no longer definite terms: *a ceaseless becoming appears. Only change has reality in itself, and it alone is found everywhere as a fundamental basis.*

It is impossible to challenge this fact. All observable objects move, and the elements composing each object are revealed when analysis is applied to them ... as a prodigious inter-weaving of flux and wave, an incalculable structure of vibratory levels, so that in the strict meaning of the word all that we *grasp in the Universe is movement superimposed on movement....*' (*L'Exigence Idéaliste*, pp. 5 and 7).

Buddhism teaches us that when we carry out careful research in the domain of our inner life, we reach conclusions which are absolutely identical to those which apply to the domain of matter. Our states of consciousness vary unceasingly.

We are never identical with ourselves. There where we believe we see a permanent entity, there is really a succession of 'I-processes' which are transformed and recreated from one moment to another.

Carlo Suarès expresses it as follows:

'The objects expressed by the states of movement are not only tables, cars, our planet, stars, but also *emotions, ideas and the "I"*, *the subjective world itself*. Therefore in the last analysis we find in both the subjective world as in the objective world, the irreducible something which is expressed by movement' (*La Comédie Psychologique*, p. 101).

This undefinable 'something' is what Buddhists call the 'basis of the world'. As this is beyond all mental representation, Buddhism calls it the Void.

Is this 'void' really 'void' or nothingness as we conceive it?

Indeed, a literal translation of most of the texts might lead us to think so.

Nothing however would be more contrary to the truth than to admit the nihilism of Buddhist thought. Such a belief could only arise in very imperfectly informed minds. Most of the canonical texts say that Nirvâna or Satori have nothing in common with the annihilation of human nature in the heart of a total vacuity.

'*Do not think of the void as an emptiness*', is written in the Tchag Tchen Gyi Zindi.

We will see later on that the '*Void*' or '*Sunyata*' *is really only the negation of our usual values, of our separate conceptions*. We forget that [73] it is counterbalanced by the *Plenitude of 'total perception'*. The term 'perception', however, as much as any other term, is inadequate for the correct translation of the experience of the nature of things.

We can see immediately the insurmountable difficulties we have to encounter in our efforts to define the profound nature of things. One might as well try to solve the problem of squaring a circle.

The Orientals who are more prudent, generally are more inclined to tell us that which Reality is not.

They proceed by negation. As the very nature of the Real forbids all mental representation, all definition, it could not be otherwise.

That is why the purest teachings are in an exceptionally difficult position, difficult in proportion to their purity. They can affirm

nothing. Their role is limited to denouncing the obstacles which
hinder our awakening to our real nature.   74

But nothing can be said of the latter. It is, however, and above
all, the positive reality, whose inexhaustible riches can be lived by
each of us. This eminently positive reality is not 'known' as we
'generally know things'. Let us bear in mind the words of
Socrates uttered after his Awakening: 'I know that I know
nothing'.

These are the reasons for the apparent negativity of the higher
forms of Buddhism, of Zen and of Krishnamurtian thought.

'Our logic, born of solids is a logic of solids', said Bergson. Our
mind feels at ease in the contemplation of objects and images
with definite contours. We like to hear that a table is square,
Louis XVI style, measures one yard square and costs twenty
pounds.

Things are intelligible to us in so far as they can be analysed in
relation to our familiar standards of value, weights and measures.

But nothing like this can be said about the profound nature of
the Universe; we can only say that which it is not. Therefore we
will say that it is not an object, has no size, weight, form, price,
no substance, beginning, duration, no colour, odour, temperature,
and so forth.

The nature of the Real forbids all mental representation or
attribution. The eloquence of our learned theologians who at this
point become inexhaustible chatter-boxes, is just a spiritual
swindle, the seriousness of which cannot escape the inquiring
mind. Nevertheless it is this kind of eloquence and the prestige of
exterior decorum which exercises such a marked influence on the
masses of today. It is one of the distinctive signs of the decadence
of the modern world.

The teachers of Buddhism are more laconic and above all, more
modest. For is it not written in the Tao Te Ching that:

> 'He who knows does not speak
> He who speaks does not know.'

If the profound nature of things escapes our mental representa-   75 tion, a kind of synchronism exists nevertheless between what it is in us and what it is in the heart of the outside world.

In other words, only the Reality in ourselves can reveal the Reality of that which surrounds us.

This full revelation of ourselves is obtained by the practice of 'Correct Vision'. This leads the seeker to a direct view of the *'essence of Reality which is movement'*, as the Buddhist philosopher Santarakita expresses it.

The essential bases of our experimental approach to 'the profound nature of things', are defined in a commentary on the Tchag Tchen Gyi Zindi by Madame A. David-Neel (*Le Bouddhisme*, p. 66).

'A tree, a stone, an animal cease to be seen as solid and durable bodies for a relatively long period of time and, in their place, the practised disciple discerns a continual succession of sudden manifestations only lasting as long as a flash of lightning, *the apparent continuity of the objects he is contemplating, and his own person, being caused by the rapidity with which these flashes of lightning succeed one another.*

Having reached this point, the disciple has attained what, for Buddhists constitutes *"Correct Vision"*.

He has *seen* that the phenomena are due to the perpetual play of energy *without having as support any substance from which to emerge,* he has *seen* that impermanence is the universal law and *that the "ego" is a pure illusion caused by the lack of penetration and power of perception.*'

The identical nature of the processes at work in mind and in matter, is continually expounded in Mahayanist Buddhism and in Zen. A brief study of the essential ideas arising from recent progress in modern physics will allow us to see its striking similarities to the doctrine of 'Correct Vision'. If these observations cannot help us to define exactly the nature of things, they can nevertheless bring us nearer to certain aspects of it.

REALITY TRANSCENDS THE DUALITY OF 'MOBILE AND IMMOBILE'

A clarification of our views on the problem of movement is desirable. Without this there might seem to be a number of contradictions.

It may be said with good reason, that movement is a function of time. As Kant expressed it: 'We create time ourselves as a function of our receptive apparatus.'

This is obvious.

Therefore we must make it clear that in the preceeding lines we have considered movement as the essence of phenomenal reality.

The complete Reality of the universe includes the phenomenon and the noumenon. It is neither movement, as we know it in the manifested universe, nor immobility, as suggested by the mind (that is to say the notion of immobility in opposition to our idea of movement).

It is obvious that Reality Itself, in its entirety, is beyond the traditional oppositions of mobility and immobility.

Moreover these divisions are arbitrary. The experience of Satori is a result of emancipation from the arbitrary practice of partitioning our mind.

It is absolutely useless and vain to try and imagine or think of a reality that includes and dominates at the same time the two aspects of mobile and immobile. All discussion in this field leads us astray.

The mystery is solved only by the realization of Satori. As we have said elsewhere, though the real cannot be thought, it can be lived.

The non-mental integration of the complete Real shows us that:

(1) Total Reality is not movement as created by our mind in function of its subjective values of time and space. It is not a question of a movement of *transfer* (which would be absurd) but of *re-creation*. The term 'movement' no longer applies correctly to re-creation.

(2) Total Reality is not absolute immobility as most metaphy-

sicists, philosophers or theologians have imagined. It is closer to what Krishnamurti calls the 'creative void' or also 'creative immobility'.

Everything is the Zen Unconscious. All, absolutely all, is Cosmic Mind.

Everything is in good total Reality. Nothing, absolutely nothing, is outside this 'Totality-that-is-One'.

Absolute immobility cannot contain any mobility, not only of transfer, but also of creation.

THE ILLUSION OF IMMOBILITY IN PHYSICS

Generally we have no idea of the extent to which recent discoveries in both physics and biology have led man into a strange and prodigiously living world.

There is perpetual movement in the objects we consider the most inert. The apparent outer immobility of a stone, really hides a silent life within so intense that the human imagination is unable to visualize it.

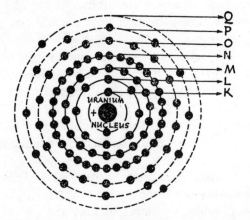

Fig. 2

The uranium atom, the most complex body, with a set of 92 electrons.
The nucleus contains 146 neutrons and 92 protons.

The molecules of a diamond, symbol of hardness, oscillate 19,000 billion times per second. On looking at an old rusty screw, we do not think for one moment that for every second that passes, the iron molecules will have made 10,000 billion oscillations.

Each molecule of air in a hermetically sealed room makes a fantastic series of circuits in all directions at the speed of 500 metres per second. This speed is that of a missile discharged at 1.125 miles per hour.

Having examined the domain of molecules let us glance at the world of atoms.

It is well known that molecules are the result of a combination of atoms.

The molecule of sodium chloride – cooking salt – is the result of the combination of one atom of sodium and one of chloride.

(The reader may refer to Figures 3, 4 and 5.)

Atoms are like minute solar systems having at their heart a positive nucleus around which circle minute planets known as 'planetary electrons'. Ten million atoms would have to be laid side by side in order to cover one millimetre.

While in our solar system the planet Neptune takes 164 years and Jupiter 11 years to complete their revolution round the sun, the planetary electrons of the microcosm make 5,760,000 thousand million *revolutions per second* around the minute sun serving as central nucleus. If one penetrates further into the mystery of the atomic world, even greater frequencies are discovered in the intra-atom.

THE ILLUSION OF CONTINUITY

We learn in physics that considerable empty spaces exist between the constitutive elements of matter. As an example let us take a block of platinum measuring one cubic decimetre and weighing 21 kilos. In this very solid block, in appearance so perfectly homogeneous and compact, the atoms are separated from each other by spaces which, proportionately, are as considerable as those existing between stars in the macrocosm.

If the nuclei of atoms in one square metre of copper were packed together without spaces between them, their total volume

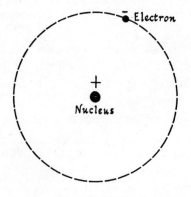

Fig. 3

The hydrogen atom is the most simple of the elements. It is composed of one negative electron revolving round a central positive nucleus, which, in turn, is made up of one positive electron and one neutron.
The negative or planetary electron makes 6,570,000 thousand million revolutions per second round the nucleus.

would be about one cubic millimetre. Joliot-Curie tells us that if the nuclei of atoms making up the mass of a man weighing 70 kilos were packed like grain in a bushel, their volume would be that of one of those minute specks of dust floating in the air and which are only visible in the light of sunbeams streaming into a dark room.

These few examples show us the extent to which the material world is really 'empty' of the elements which constitute our notion of matter.

THE NATURE OF ATOMIC CORPUSCLES

We have a natural tendency to imagine the final constituents of matter in the form of minute spherical grains endowed with solidity. The atomic corpuscles are far from being like minute

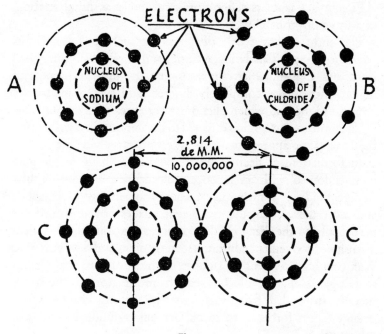

Fig. 4

Schematic drawing of a molecule. The molecule of sodium chloride (cooking-salt) is the outcome of the combination of two atoms: one atom of sodium with one of chloride.

solid beads with definite contours. Their real nature is very different from the drawings in the text-books.

They are simply 'centres of force', 'zones of influence' and 'series of waves'.

What is meant exactly by an atomic corpuscle? Let us see what one of the most eminent physicists has to tell us about it.

'*By corpuscle*', Louis de Broglie tells us, '*one means a manifestation of energy or a quantity of movement, localised in a very small volume and susceptible of transporting itself to some distance at a finite speed*' (*Matiere et Lumière*, p. 62).

It must be remembered once and for all that matter is no longer a simple assemblage of elementary particles whose permanence and individuality are based on the image of perfect solids.

Present-day scholars define atomic corpuscles as singularizations of a wave of probability.

The most recent work of physicists such as Joliot-Curie, Lawrence, Fermi, Chadwick, Maurice and Louis de Broglie, Niels Bohr and Oppenheimer, show us that the ultimate depths of matter offer aspects completely different and even diametrically opposed to those in which phenomena are presented on our scale.

The more our research is directed to the inmost secrets of matter, [78] the less matter appears material. We find ourselves face to face with formations of fleeting waves, veritable phantoms of pure light endowed with an inconceivable density in spite of their strange fluidity. Whirlpools of energy apparently more subtle and more unreal than the evanescent images of a dream, dance perpetually to the dizzy rhythm of unceasing rounds. This silent intensity of movement continues secretly night and day, year after year, century after century right in the heart of apparently inanimate objects. The whole Universe from the atom to the star is literally suspended from this intensely moving reality whose strange aspect forces us to reconsider our traditional notions of substance.

Here is how Pierre Rousseau expresses it:

'In the last analysis the material world fades away and yields to a round of unreal phantoms. We rejoice in almost touching with our finger the final substance of nature, but we perceive with confusion that what we are touching, *far from being substance, is only a complicated disguise*' (*De l' Atome à l' Etoile*, p. 78).

James Jeans eminent mathematician and astronomer uses similar language when he says:

'The tendency of modern physics is to *reduce the whole universe to waves, and nothing but waves.*

These waves are of two kinds: captive waves which we call matter, and free waves which we call rays of light.

These concepts reduce the whole Universe to a world of potential or real light' (*The Mysterious Universe*).

One reality arises, however, from beyond the ruins of our old values; this Reality is energy that is fundamentally ONE, but whose modes of expression are innumerable.

When we ask ourselves what this energy is, exactly, we find [78(a)] that no definition can present it precisely to our mind.

We become aware of it because of the *interferences* established between its different modes. Physicists teach us that energy possesses inertia, that radiation has weight. In 1905 Einstein established a relationship of equivalence between mass and energy according to a well-known formula. E (the total energy of an object) $= mc^2$ (is equivalent to its mass m multiplied by the square of the speed of light c^2).

The mass M of the Universe, well-known to specialists of physico-mathematics, is considered one of the great and fundamental constants.

Let us not forget, however, that most of the current theories are still only mental representations of phenomena and should therefore be considered in the light of their provisional and relative characters.

TOWARDS THE DISAPPEARANCE OF THE NOTIONS OF SUBSTANCE

Whatever the future corrections of present-day conceptions in physics may be, the current ones unquestionably force us to revise the ideas we may have concerning substance.

The evidence of this becomes striking when we examine closely the nature of the electron. Louis de Broglie, writing of this says:

'*the electron is a* (material) *particle only in so far as it is susceptible on occasion of manifesting itself locally with all its energy. The wave associated with the electron is not the physical vibration of some thing . . . it is only the field of probability*' (*Continu et Discontinu*, p. 56).

Professor Edouard Le Roy says more or less the same thing when he recommends us to revise our notions of substance. From this, however, we should not proceed to sort of nihilism. Though our notions of substance may have to be completely recast, this does not imply a definite disappearance of apparent reality itself. Substance is not *entirely* eliminated; its nature is changed and from being static in our eyes, it becomes dynamic. All that has happened is that it represents a *function and not a thing in itself.*

Professor Edouard Le Roy defines this point of view remarkably well.

'When one asks oneself what materiality can be in itself, a metaphysical thesis dominates the whole question: that which affirms • the necessity of conceiving *change as fundamental and primitive reality, as substantial reality, subsisting by itself without requiring support*; the "thing" on the other hand, only appears by itself in a secondary and derivative role, symbol or sediment, figure of interference formed by the meeting of an adverse flux, or aspects of a slower rhythm seen in contrast with a more rapid rhythm.

In short: *intrinsic substantiality of change: no need of a something that changes* and which invariably in its depths, has the mobility of a "being" opposed to a "becoming" and which serves as its support.

Change is sufficient unto itself and basically, is the only thing that really exists' (*Exigence Idéaliste et le Fait de l'Evolution*, p. 44).

Few Western thinkers, without realizing it, have described with such perfection one of the essential bases of Buddhism in general and of Zen in particular. Already at this point in our research we see that most of our familiar notions are incapable of resisting the assault of a profound and penetrating insight. Our mental representations of continuity, immobility, solidity and substance are revealed in their impressive fragility. The 'Correct Vision' is a devouring fire which volatilizes the last vestiges of our notions of things, objects and entities. All that remains is the ever present reality of a Flame about which nothing can be said.

The summit of intellectual renunciation of the non-essential towards which the present men of science and particularly physicists should strive, is described in a work of Dr. Roger Godel.

'The vision of the man of science who has reached the farthest point in his research, melts into a strange world: *it is a pure system* [19] *of energy from which has disappeared – lost, evaporated – the common notion of substance.*

For this dynamic universe, whose *effects only* (and not essence – the last Reality) can be seized by the intellect, the scholar tries to account by creating a code of figures, a 'grid' of numbers in the framework of which lies his conception of the cosmos. But is this grid of numbers, this Universe of mathematical symbols, Tensors and Invariants, anything but a projection of our mind in need of creating? Here our thought has reached the limits of its activities: *it cannot go beyond them.* A gigantic effort of liberation, with regard to the naive play of the senses, has brought it to the position where the cosmos appears to it entirely *stripped of its fictitious attributes.*

All the qualities – substance, hardness, colours, volume – which sensory experience conferred on "things", have lost their pre-eminence.'

We are now in a position more easily to grasp the notion of 'void' spoken of in Zen and the higher forms of Buddhism in their commentaries on the 'profound nature of things'. It has become clear that the latter escapes our familiar mental representations and is therefore 'voided' of our usual distinctions.

TRANSCENDING THE DUALITIES AND THE LIMITS OF ANALYSIS

In order that the reader may more readily follow the general trend of our thought, we think it desirable to give here a brief survey of [20] the following chapters, their inter-relation and the themes to be developed in them.

We shall examine briefly the limits inherent in all processes of analysis and as a consequence, the necessity of transcending the duality of observer and observed. This is an approach to the non-dualistic concept which is one of the essential bases of Buddhism.

On the other hand we can summarize the previous chapters as a progression towards the uttermost confines of the physical world.

We have tried several times to penetrate the strange sphere of pure energy which has gradually brought us nearer to the psychic world. Where is the dividing line between these two worlds?

In our opinion, it does not exist. The traditional problem of the 'demarcation', is a pseudo-problem. Understanding this, we feel ourselves better prepared to study the relationship between physics and psychology. We propose to glance very briefly at certain identities in the processes of physics and psychology, such as the similar processes responsible for the apparent continuity of matter and consciousness, inertia and the habits of mind and matter.

We shall finally reach the apparently disappointing conclusion of the absolute impossibility of an *exact definition of the nature of things*.

This can only be defined negatively as the '*Void*' of our usual values.

We can but point out the obstacles to the perception of this paradoxical 'void' which is a plenitude. We therefore propose to study attentively the main obstacles which both for Buddhism and certain modern psychologists are 'the force of habit', attachment or avidity for 'becoming'. These various observations will help us better to devote ourselves to the most thankless of all tasks: that of commenting the states of Nirvâna or Satori; states which are essentially supra-intellectual and defy all possibility of verbal expression.

The Swiss physicist Eugene Guye has stated one of the most [81] important laws both for the domains of material and psychological phenomenology: *the scale of observation creates the phenomenon*.

A very simple example may enable us to perceive its truth. If we were to place an equal number of black and white marbles at some two or three yards distance, we would see both colours distinctly. If we were to increase the distance thereafter to some hundred yards, we would have the impression of seeing a grey homogenous mass. The new scale of observation has given rise to a new phenomenon.

Thus the Universe seems to us material or spiritual according to the scale of observation used.

This example shows clearly the nature of the limitations inherent in all possible methods of analysis.

This limitation is the basis of Heisemberg's 'relation of uncertainty' familiar to physicists. It expresses the importance of the interaction and the interferences existing between any process of observation and the things observed. At our usual scale of observation these interferences are negligible. *In the world of the infinitely small they become considerable, but it is only in the world of thought that their action takes on full scope.*

A simple example may help us to understand this. We know that the position of an aeroplane in the night sky can be ascertained by training powerful searchlights on it. The projection of this intense flux of 'photons' does not in any way affect the course of the aircraft. But in the atomic world things happen very differently. As the means of research available, pencil of photons stream of electrons, etc., in order to observe an electron are almost of the same size as the electron itself, considerable pertubations will follow. Therefore it is impossible to locate an electron accurately. All that can be obtained is an image resulting from *interference* with the stream of 'photons' used for its observation.

We never see a 'free' electron. It can only be perceived *after* the **"** inevitable perturbation of our analysis.

Therefore our methods of analyses come up against an unsurmountable barrier.

If we wish to go beyond it, we find ourselves obliged to abandon the dualities of observer and observed.

The interferences inherent in the duality of observer and observed can only give relative, partial and contradictory images.

The method of approach suggested by Zen and the superior forms of Buddhism render possible the suppression of the interferences arising between 'observer' and 'observed'. Then there is no longer question of a particular scale of observation, nor of an observer. All that remains is the state of integration which abolishes all dualities and consequently all personal perceptions of distinct phenomena.

Movement is the profound essence of the Universe. Pure movement cannot be perceived in the flash of its first spontaneity by an ordinary observer, who from certain points of view is a degradation of it. 'Things' and 'entities' are but states of movement which have been provisionally slowed down, petrified by the rhythm of habit. Never can a state of movement which is set in the sterile rhythm of habit and repetition reach or recognize pure movement.

The movements of 'entities', whether operating on the spiritual or material planes, are never other than movements of 'things'.

Pure movement is not the movement of any thing. For in pure movement all dualities and distinctions have died out. Only pure movement 'in the observer' can recognize pure movement 'in the object observed'. In this paradoxical perspective observer, observed and observation are integrated in the ever-present reality of pure movement which from moment to moment is the Unthinkable.

Dr. Roger Godel writes:

'He who desires to know the potential of energy, dissimulated in the fields of psychic interiorization, should follow the rule of all science: *use the adequate instrument.* As an appropriate instrument there is none other — and this has proved an excellent one — than the detector of resonances that is the human mind. *Only the mind which has been placed in accord of resonance can measure the mind.* The physicist can resort to an analogous procedure when, amongst the vibrations of light, he chooses a specific length of wave and uses it to explore, by a phenomena of resonance, the properties of a material molecule' (*L'Experience Liberatrice*, p. 314).

The 'mind which is in tune' with the profound essence of things transcends the familiar dualistic methods of analysis. This tuning-in is established on the plane of Unity, which can never be reached by the lower strata of concrete intellectuality. Dualistic intellectual analysis cannot solve the problem of the Totality-that-is-One, because the part cannot contain the whole.

CHAPTER VIII

Complementarity of Physics and Psychology

D R. ROGER GODEL'S example which has just been quoted, illustrates how profoundly contemporary scholars have penetrated the identity of the processes of mind and matter; and [83] it is gratifying to see how much ground has been covered in this direction by scientific philosophy.

In fact, until recently, physics and psychology were considered as separate sciences with no relationship between them.

Recent progress, however, has shown that these two branches of science far from excluding each other, are in fact complementary and mutually fecund.

The comparison of physics and psychology are deemed essential not only by great physicists such as Louis de Broglie, Jordan, C. A. Meier, Oppenheimer, Niels Bohr, but also by most of the great contemporary psychologists such as C. G. Yung, C. Baudouin and others.

This opinion is also fully shared by eminent doctors and biologists, amongst whom are Dr. Roger Godel (Ismailia – Egypt), Professor T. H. Morgan, biologist (University of California), Professor H. S. Burr (Yale School of Medicine – U.S.A.), Professor Arnold Gessel (U.S.A.), Professor Northrop (U.S.A.) and others. This list is far from being complete.

Today we see learned cyberneticists in frequent consultation with specialists in the anatomy of the brain and with psychologists.

In the course of these interesting encounters, the experiments of each of these scientists are illuminated mutually by a number of unexpected discoveries.

Recent progress in psycho-somatics proves the importance of interaction between the physical and psychic sectors.

Recent experiments have shown the extent to which the physico-chemical balance in the human body can be upset by [84] purely affective states such as anger, fear, grief and suppression.

Quoted here is the striking example commented on by Dr. Roger Godel:

'While experimenting on anxious subjects we were able, in the course of examination, to note a rise in the level of acetone bodies in the blood, important oscillations in the glycemic content, an increase in blood viscosity and coagulation, while hormones (pituitary, supra-renal and pancreatic) and adrenal and biliary neuro-secretive products flowed into the organism.

These phenomena — and many others which are associated with them — prove therefore that *an energizing effect has intervened in correlation with the subjective experience and the emotion felt; they measure* — rather crudely it is true — their extent.

One cannot reject the evidence of experimental facts; the intensity of an emotional shock corresponds with an energetic tension which is likely to bring about a change of state.'

We could indefinitely continue quoting the most eminent scholars and thinkers who deal with the psycho-physical unity of man and the world. We will conclude this brief review by quoting a phrase from Bertrand Russell, the English philosopher:

'*Matter is less material and the mind less spiritual than is generally supposed. The habitual separation of physics and psychology, mind and matter is metaphysically indefensible.*'

Recent progress in the physical sciences compels us to strip ourselves inwardly and change all our old values. *The very fact that this process of renouncing the old view-points, which have been so laboriously acquired by the mind, is a result of minute observation of matter, reveals once again the close psycho-physical interdependence of a man and the world.*

Earlier we have said that only the Real in ourselves could by a kind of secret resonance recognize the Real in apparently distinct beings and things. Is it not interesting to note that as man tries to discover the profound nature of matter, the search itself irresistibly obliges him to alter his points of view, channel his thoughts in a new direction, and improvise something new.

Without man realizing it, the sacrifices of the old values which he has had to make lead him on to such decantation of thought that it approaches the pure essence of his deeper nature. In other words: *The Study of the profound nature of things in the physical world, causes such transformations in the mind of the attentive observer that he draws near to the discovery of his true nature.*

It could not be otherwise because of the *identity of essence of the observer and observed on the one hand, and the unity of mind and matter* [85] *on the other.*

APPARENT CONTINUITY OF CONSCIOUSNESS

Buddhism, in the doctrine of 'Correct Vision', teaches us that the processes responsible for the apparent continuity of matter are identical with those which engender the apparent continuity of consciousness.

Physics has shown that all distribution of apparently continuous energy on our usual scale of observation is, in fact, basically discontinuous. All energy is manifested by successive leaps and bounds like the second hand of a chronometer. Living organisms conquer space by 'quantic' jumps. Everything that exists is prolonged in duration by quanta.

Popularizers of science have given us numerous examples to illustrate this process.

The simplest amongst them is that of the staircase.

At a certain distance from this, all that can be seen is the acclivity. But, on approaching it, successive levels formed by the steps can be seen, giving the slope a sense of discontinuity. The flight of stairs represents the apparently continuous movement of all phenomena, of all distribution of energy. The steps represent the process of the discontinuous climbing which is carried out by successive leaps.

As Robert Tournaire, the French chemist, expresses it:

'Everything that lives conquers space by quantic jumps and

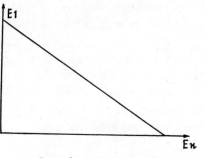

Our scale: apparent continuity.

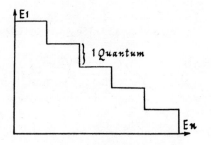

Fig. 5

Atomic scale: quantic discontinuity.

Distribution of energy, apparently continuous
on our scale, is discontinuous on the atomic
scale and is effected by 'leaps' or 'quanta'.

realizes duration through quanta. A molecule polymerizes itself
and becomes a living micella by the quantic process. . . .

On the one hand life is an electronic organization which is the
cause of the instability and complexity of the living molecule; on
the other hand it is a harmonized quantified process. There, where
the quantum no longer has a negligible value, in the heart of the
microcosm, physical life begins; there where the quantum
assumes a relatively negligible value, the physical world reigns.
Life is a conflict between two worlds. Death is the flight of the
quantum. In its turn, is not this basic dualism just the expression of
a radiation of which our Universe and ourselves form an essential
part? This seems probable to me.

But it is worth while asking oneself *whether we impose this fine and quantic granulation on substance, or whether it is real. It is possible that it may be ourselves and our photons that impose this fine granulation* . . . and thus is explained how the boundary between the physical and spiritual world could be conceived' (*La Naissance de la Vie*).

That which present-day scientists state about the apparent continuity of matter has been taught by Buddhism for thousands of years. Applying this process to the domain of the mind, it compares it to a flame.

If one looks absent-mindedly at a candle the flame appears immobile. We know, however, that nothing is immobile within its apparently definite contours. The flame is recreated every instant; and, during its continual flux, the flame feeds on thousands of millions of stearine molecules which melt and are consumed in combination with the oxygen in the air. In this way the heat of the flame is continually recreated and maintained.

The higher forms of Buddhism and Zen teach that the process of the consciousness of self is identical with this.

On observing ourselves we have an impression of continuity of consciousness. We seem to glide uniformly in time from yesterday through today towards tomorrow.

We do not doubt, and in no case do we wish to doubt this apparent continuity. Nevertheless, on the plane of consciousness, we are *burning* in the same way as all flames on the material plane.

The fuel for the flame of the 'I-process' are the 'skandas' which we have already mentioned elsewhere under another form. There are five of them:

(1) The material body or form
(2) Sensations experienced by the body.
(3) Tactile or visual perceptions
(4) Impulses and reactions of the will in contact with the aforementioned
(5) Consciousness of the whole of this process.

These are all linked up in a closed cycle in both the comparison of the candle-flame, and in that of the 'I-process'.

The stearine is melted by the heat of the flame and, by this melting, combines with the oxygen of the air; this combustion in turn, radiates the heat which allows the process to continue.

Buddhists compare the heat of the flame with the 'consciousness of self'.

As the flame is maintained by the combustion of the stearine so is the 'consciousness of self' in its turn by the extremely complex and rapid superimposition of perceptions and sensations, of emotions, thoughts and memories.

Into this chain of cause and effect, stripped of all individuality, an identification has slipped in. The mirage of the 'I-process' is only an arbitrary superimposition born of ignorance.

Canonical texts of the different schools of Buddhism in general and Zen in particular abound in citations similar to the one repeated here:

'Nobody accomplishes the action, nobody enjoys its fruit, only the succession of actions and their fruit turns in an unceasing round like the cycle of tree and seed, without anyone being able to say where it started.

Those who do not perceive this succession believe in the existence of an ego; some think it is eternal, while others declare that it is perishable' (*Visudhi Magga*).

86   Being in the habit of considering ourselves as 'entities', not on any account will we recognize our fundamental contradiction. But as the deeper layers of our unconscious are closer to where our misapprehension develops, a fear, a fundamental anguish lies at the very depth of our being. Literally we are 'suspended over the abyss' of the Real. Something within us KNOWS, or is on the point of knowing that all our affirmations, our greed, violences and agitations are so many desperate reflexes aimed at hiding from ourselves the fundamentally illusory and phantasmal character of the individuality we imagine ourselves to be.

The flame of the 'I-process' is in the *habit of burning* and does not wish to be extinguished. An immensely powerful *instinct of preservation* dwells therein, and expresses itself indirectly through the desire to enjoy, to feel as a distinct entity, and to be objectified in a thousand ways. Buddhist teachings call this fundamental avidity 'Tanha'. This subject we hope to examine in detail later on.

'Tanha' is the 'craving to become'. Because we no longer know how to BE in all simplicity according to the nature of things, we [87] seek to BECOME.

Being incapable of conjugating the verb TO BE, we conjugate instead the verb TO HAVE. But as the verb TO HAVE can lead us nowhere for nothing lasting can be acquired, we seek indefinitely to HAVE MORE. Such is the source of our enslavement.

The tensions inherent in the processes of 'becoming' have a certain heaviness in contrast to the relaxation and spontaneity of Being. The verbs 'to have' and 'to appear' are stamped with a grossness and vehemence far removed from the delicacy and lightness of 'to Be'.

These nuances have been felt by Rilke in his admirable poem called 'A God can do it'.

> For song as taught by you is not desire,
> not wooing of something finally attained;
> SONG IS EXISTENCE. For the God not strained.
> But when shall we exist? And he require
> the sun and the stars to enter our existence?
> Youth, you may feel that love will conquer death,
> but that's not it, — learn with untired persistence
> to forget your celebrations. They flow past.
> Singing in earnest is another breath.
> A breath for nothing. A blowing in the God. A blast.

Buddhism, in its study of the processes of consciousness, draws our attention to the importance of mental activity, which is the essential fuel of the flame of the 'I-process'.

If we try to immobilize it by an act of will we immediately notice the appearance of resistance. It would seem as if our mental activity were bent on keeping its disordered rhythm with all its habitual and contradictory characteristics. If we succeed in overcoming this rapid and instinctive self-defence by fixing our thought on one point to the exclusion of all else, we notice after some time that a more marked agitation apparently tries to compensate our attempt at provisional immobilization.

Mental activity is the expression of an extremely powerful force which seems to escape our control. This force is none other than 'Tanha', the craving to 'Become', the permanent reaction to the obscure *fear* of being nothing.

Generally we have no idea of the importance of the experimental study of this problem within ourselves and by ourselves.

As long as the operational processes of our mental activities have not been grasped by us, all our actions will bear the mark of irresponsibility.

In fact we are not in possession of our faculties; we are possessed by them. We do not really think; we are thought.

At every moment, either vague or definite, though more often vague, images, words and forms appear and disappear in us.

In the degree in which we do not succeed in discovering the fundamental motives which rule our mental activities, our emotions and our actions, indeed our whole life will be but a nebulous dream whatever may be the realism that we claim to possess.

Why do we think? How do we think? What do we think? Who thinks?

By not answering these four questions correctly we remain the slaves of our irresponsibility.

The first question to which we should devote all our attention is precisely the one which no one has thought of except the Masters of lucidity and awakening, a Buddha, a Krishnamurti. Who thinks? We have just seen that there is no 'thinker-entity', but a succession of thoughts.

From then on all our attention is focussed on the operational process of this thought: 'How does one think? Why does one think?'

If we are much more acted upon than acting ourselves, as Bergson said, what is this mysterious force which 'acts us'? What is this strange power which from moment to moment during all our life causes an unceasing sequence of images to rise up, whose continual coming and going obsesses us at certain moments?

We said above that certain strata of our unconscious dimly know that the 'I-process' is merely a mirage, a result of disordered mental activity. A certain part of ourselves knows or foresees that we could not exist without the rapid succession of thoughts which are born and die. Buddhists state that *interstitial voids* known as Turya, exist between thoughts. *The apparent continuity of consciousness stands out against the background of a basic discontinuity.*

Two and a half thousand million human beings live without ever perceiving this. The same process of consciousness rules over all human lives. The same magical force seems to plunge them [89] irresistibly into the dream of static continuity and confers on them the illusory characteristics of permanent individualities. What is this force?

It is 'Tanha', the craving to 'become', the fear of being nothing.

A dim foreboding lurks in the depths of every human being: something in him knows that if for a single moment, he should find himself face to face with the interstitial void between two thoughts, the reign of its illusory continuity would be over instantly.

The 'I-process's' instinct of preservation will do everything possible to hide from our eyes the ever-latent fissures through which the liberating light might pass.

Correct vision consists in delivering us from this comedy which we are playing to ourselves, and in seeing ourselves as we are. This is the essential of Nirvâna or Satori: clear vision of THAT WHICH IS.

That which most Occidentals consider as nothingness, is really a plenitude. *Such is the nature of things*; an eternal incandescence, flaming and silent, which is neither existence nor non-existence.

The discovery of the profound nature of things allows us to grasp the inner, anonymous and eternal greatness hidden in them. It transfigures the imperfect image we have made of the world and allows us to see in each fragment of lowly matter an indissociable element of the Eternal Living God.

The feeling of re-discovery of this true grandeur is expressed by Rilke in his poem:

All will be great and powerful again,
the lands simple and the waters folded,
the trees gigantic and the walls very small;
and in the valleys, strong and multiform,
a people of shepherds and tillers of soil.

And no churches that embrace
God like a fugitive and then commiserate him
like a captured and wounded animal.
The houses, hospitable to all knockers for admission
and a feeling of unbounded sacrifice
in all business and in you and me.

No waiting for a beyond,
and no gazing up above, only longing
not to deconsecrate even death, but to
practise oneself submissively on the earthly
so as to be no longer new to his hands.

CHAPTER IX

The Force of Habit

THE Lankâvatâra Sûtra says:

'What is meant by the Void, in the highest sense of final Reality, is that in the acquisition of an inner understanding through Wisdom, *there no longer is any trace of the force of habit* engendered by erroneous conceptions arisen from a past without beginning.'

The effects of '*force of habit*' are considered as being the major obstacles to the awakening of Satori.

'We do not perceive the world as it is in reality. Our *productive imagination, fed by the energy engendered by habit,* superimposes on this (the world) an illusory construction, a mirage, images similar to those seen in dreams' (*Vajracchedika Sûtra*).

These two citations show the importance attached to the force of habit by the Masters of Buddhism in general and Zen in particular.

Consequently all their technique of action will be aimed at shattering the sterile dreams of our mental routines.

True Sages of all times have suggested a sudden reversal of all the values with which we have become identified through *force of habit*.

This requirement of renewal is to be found in Buddhism and in the pure teachings of Christ; but it is more particularly in Krishnamurtian thought that it seems to be most urgent.

This overthrowing of values is the highest form of conversion in the etymological sense of the word. In Sanscrit the term is 'paravritti', 'para' meaning transcendence, and 'vritti' the whole of the mental habits.

To most Occidentals the term 'conversion' is interpreted as

meaning adherence to a new or different system of thought or a particular religion. For instance, to say that someone has been converted to Catholicism is common parlance. To the Sage, however, such an affirmation is meaningless. True conversion *is a final release from the hold which the forces of habit exercise over us.*

The mere fact of a change of habits does not free us from the fundamental routine-process of the mind. Face-to-face with the Real it is as false to remain the slave of one's own mental habits as it is to take over those of another person or of a body of persons.

The processes of individual and collective memories, their reciprocal interferences with the individual and group conscious and unconscious, which the great modern psychologists have insisted upon, have indeed been known to the masters of Buddhism for thousands of years.

The Lankâvatâra Sûtra states:

'The consciousness of ideas supporting the consciousness attached to the senses (to the eye, vision of forms etc.) distinguishes an objective world, and is thus kept in movement (product of new ideas regarding what it perceives). It *attaches itself to the objective world and, by the effect of multiple forces of habit, it feeds the Alaya Vijnana* (store-house of consciousness).'

THE FORCE OF HABIT IN MATTER

To us who are contemplating it, the Universe has two aspects.

One we shall call the 'surface aspect'. In this everything is ruled by mechanical laws. Everything is *habit* therein. The strict determinism of phenomena is possible where habit prevails. An astronomer can predict, as Leverrier did in the last century, that at such and such an hour, and at such and such a minute, the planet Neptune would be at a certain place in the sky.

The other aspect we shall call the 'aspect of depth'.

This is the aspect revealed to us by modern physics. In this domain mechanical laws, determinism and causality are inadequate. The deeper we go *the further away we are from the rhythms of habit* and nearer the wake of a perpetually unseizable Reality, a kind of eternal rocket of which we see but the extinguished debris. In depth we have only creations, up-surging and ceaseless renewal.

Looking awhile into the intimacy of the atomic world without losing ourselves in the ultimate confines where all notions of things and substance disappear, we again observe a certain influence of the force of habit.

A hydrogen atom can be considered the expression of the habit acquired by materialized energy in the form of a negative electron of turning indefinitely round another form of the same energy known as the positive nucleus.

From this particular point of view, *we could, as we see it, define matter as a constellation of dead habits.*

Amongst these habits we will point out those of chloride and uranium, which consist of the repetition of thousands of millions of identical revolutions of electrons chasing one another every second round an atomic centre during thousands of millions of years.

If so-called 'inanimate' matter seems to us a constellation of dead habits, so-called 'living' matter allows us a glimpse of the work of an intensely creative energy whose rhythms seem far from being repetitive and habitual. Though it is true that the seeds of a particular flower are in the 'habit' of always developing into the same flowers, there is nevertheless in this living structure processes which differ greatly from those that we see in inanimate matter.

We know that the latter is ruled by a principle of degradation of energy expressing the *habit* of the lowering of its successive qualities in the course of its various transformations.

In opposition to this descending movement, living matter offers us many examples of 'ascent' in the qualities of its energy.

In so far as Life — this indefinable reality — enters into matter, it introduces a regeneration of energy. Life tends to oppose the rhythms of habit.

The essential law of Life is a law of renewal, of pure creativeness and change.

Nothing is more opposed to the process of Life than repetition and routine.

The higher forms of Buddhism and Zen can be defined as declarations of the laws of Life in the province of the mind.

The aim of the Zen masters is to free man from the yoke of mental servitude in which he is held through the *force of habit*.

Habit to them is synonymous with death. The symbolism of Satan has no other meaning. To our dualistic mind, *Satan symbolizes the force of habit whose static aspects are opposed to the dynamic fluidity of Life.*

Satan represents the sum of the forces which resist the renewal of LIFE.

CHAPTER X

The Action of the Force of Habit on the Mind according to Psychological Types

THE history of a Universe can be regarded as a *perpetual development towards more freedom and mobility*. We are indeed aware that from the Sages' point of view these dualist considerations are secondary and only apply to our conception of the world.

But we are forced to use the relative language with which we are more familiar.

Looking at so-called inanimate matter we see that it is completely incapable of expressing 'on the surface' the intensity of movement that is taking place within itself.

A block of stone is entirely subject to modifications of temperature, pressure and environment. Nothing within resists the coercion of its surroundings.

The first rudiments of organization only appear in minerals. These show a budding sensitivity the extent of which is not generally suspected. Damaged crystals heal themselves as do more highly organized beings. When dissolved they always re-crystallize into the same forms according to their electronic composition relative to the atomic system of which they are constituted. They are sensitive to anaesthetics. The growth of minerals sometimes occurs independently of the laws of gravity. We are confronted here with the birth of two tendencies; firstly, an initial expression of the inner forces of the atomic field in the external behaviour, in the forms of the crystals dependent on this field. In completely unorganized matter there is no visible link between the inner structure of the atoms, their movements and the total expression presented by the object.

Secondly, a tendency to suffer environmental conditions to a lesser degree, certain crystals forming as a result of a process of horizontal or vertical growth.

In the vegetable kingdom the difference is even more apparent. Plants are far more sensitive by reason of their adaptability and their more complex organization, but the position of their roots binds them to the ground and prevents every other kind of mobility. In the animal kingdom we find immediately a greater degree of independence.

Animals possess infinitely greater freedom of movement than plants. In order to observe the growth of mobility in man, we ought first to study another domain. Evolution being much more psychic than physical, it is in the domain of the mind that a progressive tendency towards autonomy and liberty must be sought.

Are not the complexity and delicacy of human cellular architecture, so flexible, active and adaptable, such that the dynamism, creativeness, freedom and mobility of Life can be seized in the freshness of their perpetual flux.

Such are the possibilities suggested by the Zen masters.

If the dominion of the force of habit seems to extend its all-embracing power as far over the realm of matter as over that of mind, it is nevertheless possible to escape its influence.

Zen masters consider that the possibility of deliverance from our chains is all the more evident as these are part of the individual and group mirage under whose spell we live.

Nevertheless though Zen insists particularly on the sudden nature of deliverance from the 'force of habit' it is certain that mankind approaches the moment of realization by stages.

From this dualistic point of view the psychological evolution of man can be divided into three phases.

These phases will be considered here in particular as the story of a struggle in which (to us) two tendencies are opposed: the *inertia of the 'force of habit', and the dynamism of the force of Life.*

First phase: the birth of the 'I-process'
Second phase: the maturityof the 'I-process'
Third phase: the transcendance of the 'I-process'.

We must add that the force of habit and the dynamism of Life are expressed identically in mind and matter and therefore we shall take some examples from the system of the latter in order to explain the former.

To illustrate this idea, here is an experiment carried out by the English biologist A. Baker (University of London), which by analogy will help us define our ideas. This scientist had noticed that the cells of some living tissue when dipped into colouring matter, resisted the attempt of the stain to penetrate its inner structures. But on the death of the cells by violent electric action, the invasion of colouring-matter into the cellular structure was instantaneous.

Hence, if we wish Life to express itself in the spiritual realm, we should free it from environmental psychological constraints. A truly living mind does not allow itself to be invaded by mental dyes surrounding it. *Mental habits* such as dogmas, systematized thought, beliefs and fixed ideas play the part of mental dyes of which our mind must rid itself if it wishes to be ready for the state of pure perception.

In view of the foregoing, the characteristics of the three phases of the psychological evolution of man can be summarized as follows.

First phase: *Birth of the 'I-process'*.

The personality is barely discernible. During this 'pre-individual' phase *the grip of the force of habit is all-powerful*. Man imitates and copies, and does not yet think for himself; as yet he is not an individual. His mind suffers the invasion of the mental dyes of his environment: prejudices, beliefs and systematization of thought. His mentality is that of the sheep of Panurge; no liberty, no initiative, only blind obedience to the predominating opinions of the moment. This, ultimately is the psychosis of mass movements whose strength obliterates individual judgment and annihilates all sensibility, to end up finally in the disasters of totalitarian experiments.

In this first phase, the mental energy seems to conform to the process of energy-degradation by its tendency to inertia and its lack of creativeness.

Second phase: *Maturity of the 'I-process'*.

From the beginning of this phase the attitude of automatic and mechanical imitation tends to disappear. Servile obedience to the mental imperatives of slogans and catch-words appears in all its puerility. Rhythms of routine and repetition gradually begin to show their negative and superficial side. The bastions of the 'citadel of the force of habit' are beginning to show their first cracks, and from being imitative, man becomes creative. He no longer bows blindly to the accomplished facts of proposed or imposed values, he dares to doubt, and begins to reconsider problems of all kinds for himself. *He is already making attempts to withdraw himself from the influence of the values established by the force of mental habit.* A psychological virility appears in him which demands more autonomy, initiative, creativeness and liberty. The mind, whose essential law is liberty, will at first try to seek it in the free affirmation of its new autonomous powers. However, the day will dawn when, having exhausted all its possibilities of expression, it will understand that it is a prisoner of its own creation.

From the moment when the 'I-process' perceives the narrowness of its own limits it starts evolving towards the third phase.

Third phase: *Transcendence of the 'I-process'.*

This phase is one which nearly all men at present consider unrealizable, but which, however, is the norm of cosmic nature. It is not super-human, but is simply the accomplishment of the possibilities inherent in human nature.

Man has become aware of the dream-state into which he has fallen as a result of the force of habit; the moment he frees himself from its hold he realizes the sum of his humanity. The highest mission of man is to manifest the fullness of his being.

95　From the Zen Masters' point of view only a man like this can be considered normal. The 'part' of him no longer thinks it is the 'Whole'. Correct attention and vigilance have at last unmasked the comedy he was playing to himself, and because he is dead as an entity, he is alive to the fullness of Life Itself.

This process of liberation cannot be realized by those who accept easy solutions and the consolation of dreams.

The transcendance of the 'I-process' requires an acuteness of consciousness as well as exceptional qualities of awakedness. These can only be obtained by an intense life during which we grapple with experiences with the whole of our beings. A certain maturity is required before this transcendance may be realized.

The soil of the soul must be ploughed with the sharp shares of joy and suffering which follow each other like the continual tempering and retempering of the best steels in order to render them more malleable; for it is by these inner alternations that the soul acquires malleability.

But this suppleness cannot be acquired by fleeing from life, and avoiding obstacles.

Too many idealists have a tendency to oppose a flat refusal to the demands of the concrete.

What has been said above has been admirably expressed in *Citadelle* (*The Wisdom of the Saints*) by Saint-Exupery:

'And this one here, who is lying in the sand near a dried-up well which is already evaporating in the sun, how well he walks in his dream; and how easy for him become the great strides towards deliverance. . . .

But he who really walks, bruises his ankles on the stones, struggles with brambles and tears his nails on the scree . . . As for the water, he creates it slowly with his flesh, with his muscles, with the blisters of his palms, with the cuts on his feet. To stir up the contradictory realities he draws the water from his stony desert with the strength of his wrists.

You know your vocation from its weight within you. And if you betray it, it is yourself that you are disfiguring, but learn that your *truth is not the discovery of a formula . . . because the new being, which is unity disengaged from the disparity of things, does not impose on you at all as the final solution of a conundrum, but as an appeasement of the disputes. . . .*

Likewise there is no progress without the acceptance of that which is.

If something is opposed to you and tears you, let it grow, it is that you are taking root and that you are stirring. . . .

Blessed is this tearing which causes you to be delivered of yourself: because no truth shows itself and is reached conspicuously. And those which are proposed to you are but comfortable arrangements and are like drugs taken in order to sleep.

Know, that each contradiction without solution, each irreparable dispute obliges you to grow in order to absorb it. . . .

And you yourself, if you want to grow, employ yourself against your disputes, they lead towards God. It is the only way in the world.'

CHAPTER XI

Memory-Habits and the Birth of the 'I-process'

THE automatisms of memory constitute the most subtle and overwhelming conditioning factor of the human being. This chain-reaction is so subtle and so delicate that at present nearly all men are totally unaware of it.

The shadow cast by old mental habits darkens the light of each present instant. Still the Zen Masters say that Satori or Nirvâna require from us a total presence to the Present. We realize this when no longer a trace of the memory-habits of the past corrupts the freshness and transparence of each present moment as it comes to us.

The plenitude of non-mental consciousness (or Zen Unconscious) can only be in the Present. Whenever in the present moment our mind projects a memory-image from the past, thereby betraying an attachment thereto, our consciousness is torn and divided between the present and the past. It is this division which is the fundamental element of the tension which engenders the 'I-process'.

The function of the mind is not to store up memories but to understand the process of its own functioning in the Present.

Experience of Satori, or deliverance from conceptions engendered by the forces of memory-habit can only be realized in the acuteness of a consciousness which is dying to its own past.

This sense of adherence to the Present and the intense awareness it needs, is admirably conjured up by Saint-Exupery in *Citadelle* (*The Wisdom of the Saints*).

'The sense of things does not at all reside in the ready-made provisions that the sedentary people consume, but in the heat of transformation, of walking, or of desire.

Then you will say to me, towards what shall I aspire, since goals have no significance?

And I would answer you . . . that to prepare the future is only to found the *present*. And let those others wear themselves out in Utopia and in dream-conduct which follows distant images, fruit of their invention. For the sole true invention is to decipher the present under its incoherent aspects and its contradictory language . . . You do not have to foresee the future but to allow it. . . .

Know, therefore, that all true creation is not at all presumption as to the future, pursuit of chimeras and utopia, but a new face, read in the present which is a reserve of material in bulk, and it is not up to you to complain or rejoice, because simply like yourself, they are, having been born. . . .

Therefore let the future unfold its branches one by one. . . .

But do not believe that to think the present is simple . . . for then the very material which you should use resists you, whereas your inventions about the future never will. . . .'

A simple example can illustrate the process of degeneration inherent in memory-habits. To a certain extent it can help us to understand by analogy the way in which the 'I-process' is built up and can show us clearly the necessity of freeing ourselves from the grip of our own past.

Nowadays people know the mechanism of sound recording. Vibrations in the air caused by the spoken word or by music, cause electrical variations in the microphone. This is then amplified and applied to an electro-magnetic head. This head creates a current known as the 'conductor current' which creates an 'induced current'.

The steel wire or tape on which the recordings will be made, unrolls continually throughout the session passing the gap of the electro-magnetic head. In this manner it receives a residual magnetization which produces a faithful image of the variations of acoustic pressure picked up by the microphone.

In other words the steel wire or tape will be magnetized to a greater or lesser degree according to the strength or weakness of the sound.

In a certain sense these wires or tapes have a memory of the words spoken or music played into the microphone. Human memory is the result of a somewhat similar though infinitely more complex process in the formation of cerebral engrams, but in the general outline the two processes show certain similarities.

The images which we see cause continual transformations amongst the cones and rods of the retina. These transformations engender a nervous influx which determines the electro-magnetic perturbations of a memorial character known as engrams, in the cerebral neurons.

All that we see and do not wish to see, all that we hear and do not wish to hear is inscribed in the neurons by cerebral electricity. Thus innumerable engrams are born and accumulated, possessed of persistent 'remanence' in spite of cellular renovation.

Progress realized in the realm of radioactive isotopes have indeed permitted the discovery that the constitutive elements of neurones in particular and the brain in general are not exempt from the process of cellular renovation of the whole organism. Therefore the engrams are more closely related to the undulatory aspects of energy than to its corpuscular aspects.

By continual accumulation they form the 'I-process' which fed by them, increases in bulk and is transformed from moment to moment.

In this process one particularly important fact should attract our attention: *There is a unity of direction in the fundamentally degenerating work of the memory-habits.* Each new memory is instantaneously conditioned by the whole of the older memories. This unity of direction forms one of the essential elements which gives the 'I-process' its character of apparent continuity.

As Krishnamurti said, the new facts of each present instant are corrupted by the old habits of which the 'I-process' is the sum-total and the living incarnation.

All the activities of the human mind are inscribed in a strictly limited cycle of mutually conditioned states which react on one another. Man's urgent task therefore is to break through this sterile cycle of the force of habit.

'*Without his thoughts, the thinker does not exist,*' says Krishnamurti.

This truth which we find expressed in most Buddhist texts, can be illustrated by an example.

Let us not forget however that all our examples amount to concessions made to our dualistic mode of mental operation and therefore contain all its weaknesses.

Schematically the brain could be drawn as a point or centre of pure perception endowed with extraordinary sensibility.

Everything happening around this point is continually registered as electro-magnetic perturbations. And though at the beginning they were impersonal and without any individuality, they have become mechanical memories comparable with those of sound recorders. They accumulate endlessly round our centre or point of hypothetical perception.

Finally this accumulation of memory becomes so complex and dense that secondary phenomena begin to appear. The memories become so loaded that suddenly by the natural effect of a certain 'law of mass', reciprocal action takes place between the different layers of superimposed engrams. Secondary currents spring up and set off a whole process of 'parasitic' phenomena. The Sages believe that consciousness of self is nothing other than a 'secondary current', a 'parasitical phenomenon'.

Thus an entity has been built up on what was a simple impersonal non-individualized process of pure perception. It has been erected as a result of the *impression of psychological solidity given by the complexity of the memory accumulations.*

So where there was just one anonymous process amongst the thousands of millions of anonymous processes in the unfathomable Cosmic Play, a 'thinker' is born. And since then we have acquired the habit of considering ourselves as entities.

However an attentive examination of the image we make of the 'I-process' gives rise to several troubling conclusions. Let us turn our attention for a few moments to the brain. It is the place where the image of the 'I-process' rises as well as all our mental representations.

Looking with the eye of a scientist we see first of all that the nerve-tissue of the brain is formed by a complex network of neurons. These are continually and tremendously active. Viewed close up, their action is transformed into a flux of electrical phenomena, and continual depolarization and re-polarization alternating with the speed of lightning. Finally only a pure field of energy remains where the intangible interferences of the waves of probability seem to operate. In short, instead of a static 'I-process' and the petrified images which it fabricates, a sole dynamic reality appears: that of Pure Movement.

This is what Dr. Roger Godel says:

'In the light of this vision *what becomes of the ego?*

Nothing other than the unseizable product of this mobility that no observation, however keen, could ever stabilize in a formula. Nothing other than the shadow and the flickering of a distant light.

The visible and tangible body, like other sensory elaborations, is a product of nervous activity; it depends for its very existence on a certain state of the neurons, it depends on the reciprocal relations uniting these centres; such conditions are eminently precarious, impermanent and of relative character. *This unstable and strange phenomenon that is the "me" or ego, escapes all definition.* Let us admit that it dwells implanted diffusely between the cortico-parietal, thalamic, diencephalic, mesocephalic and paraventricular centres of the brain, exploring from there the divers associated territories in order to integrate them in a certain representation. *Can one reasonably confer the characteristics of the Real* – for example the mathematic Invariable – *to this play of forces without identity and without duration, to this electronic flux in perpetual mutation?*

Consequently the concrete notion of a corporeal or psychic ego evaporates or, rather, rejoins in the inner world of images other subjective experiences. Let us look closely at its claims to existence; they are those which are possessed by every object perceived by our senses. *The me, (ego) is nothing other than an object from the point of view of discriminating thought, established on the most profound level of the intellectual sphere; and this object – like every psycho-sensorial representation – situated on the relative plane, vanishes on analysis. . . .'*

We wished to show these various methods of studying the 'I-process' in order to prove the similarity of their conclusions: the *notion of a permanent ego is illusory*. Nevertheless the pseudo-entities that we are, use for their defence, the very process of their enslavement.

Here mental automatisms express all the power of the 'force of habit'. How escape from their clutches? Only a *new* approach can help.

For most of us, 'word' has become 'thing'. Words have an immense influence which extends not only into the domain of the mind, but also into those of the emotions and nerves. There are appliances capable of measuring the extent of emotional reaction that results from hearing a familiar word spoken. In certain cases words, such as God, give rise to considerable nervous and psychic vibration. It is a question of noting the automatic and mechanical character of the reactions aroused in us by these words, for then we would realize that the memory content is for the most part formed by words closely linked with emotional states and visual perceptions.

Our supreme enemy is *the word*. Each new experience loses its character of revelation in the degree in which the force of memory-habits of the past place this enemy between the present action and ourselves. Many sincere seekers consider that the terms 'universal love', 'cosmic consciousness', 'divine ecstasy', and Nirvâna or Satori, only have as a true counterpart a simple combination of memory-automatisms enveloped in the agreeable aroma of a sweet quietude unfortunately corrupted by the rhythm of habit.

It is of the utmost importance to free ourselves from the influence exercised by words and from attachment to our memories.

We will refer here again to the example of the sound-recording machine.

Let us assume that one of our conversations was recorded on magnetic wire.

After having played it back several times, we might wish to record some music. Before undertaking a new recording, the magnetized wire must be *'neutralized' or made receptive. To this end a special device will demagnetize it and 'wash' it of its recorded memory*.

We are in exactly the same position. We must make ourselves receptive to the creative impulses of a reality which is renewed from moment to moment.

Therefore it is during each present moment that the living steel wire that we are must be 'washed', so that it may be made *receptive to the perception of THAT WHICH IS.*

This means that we must rid ourselves of what remains of the 'force of habit' on all planes of existence. This is the main reason for the constant vigilance which all the authentic teachers advise us to adopt.

Is it not written in the Dhammapada:

'Vigilance is the path which leads to immortality. Negligence is the path of death. Those who are vigilant do not die; the negligent are as if dead already.'

THE DIFFERENCES BETWEEN THE TECHNICAL AND THE PSYCHOLOGICAL MEMORIES

The vigilance we have just referred to is vigilance of attention and not vigilance of will or personal discipline.

The Zen Masters do not ask us to reject the process of memory-habit but to understand it. In fact they suggest that we see the 'false' as being really 'false' in the way that Krishnamurti proposes.

'To wash the living steel wire that we are' means that our mind should not get rid of the memory content itself but the identification and attachment to it. This is a very important distinction.

Memory is a natural and inevitable process. Were we to *lose* our memories completely we would no longer be able to find our way home. So we will resort to the distinctions suggested by Krishnamurti and which establish a difference between *technical or factual memory and psychological memories.*

The former are the result of the natural recording of FACTS. The latter originate from *identification and psychological association with them.*

We may remember someone's aggressiveness towards us (technical or factual memory), but wisdom consists of not feeling rancour (psychological memory) when on meeting the person in question the past incident rises in our mind. An engineer may with the aid of his formulae (technical memory) calculate the resistance of a concrete bridge. But if on passing over this bridge with some friends he boasts of the success of his calculations, he is abusing and going beyond the scope of his factual memory which is thereby degraded into the psychological memory which is identification.

To what factors may one attribute the power which the forces of memory-habits hold over mankind?

Reactions to the facts of everyday life determine privileged paths amongst the cerebral engrams. When similar facts are repeated our thoughts tend to develop along some of these privileged paths.

To identical circumstances we tend to react in an identical manner.

But still our memory is endowed with a remanence similar to that of the magnetized steel wire used as an example. This remanence is so strong that we have a tendency to be subject to our own past.

Professor G. Darwin said:

'I believe that . . . *The human mind is endowed with great inertia, and we could also say with a considerable viscosity.* It always passes sluggishly from one state of equilibrium to another.'

It is as a result of this *viscosity* that we literally 'stick' to our own past. Our accumulations of memories seem to attach themselves to us to such an extent that constant vigilance is necessary if we are to free ourselves from their clutches.

HABIT AND LIBERTY

It is important to realize that in so far as we are subject to the domination of our past memories, we do not in any way differ from the mechanical processes of a machine with complicated parts.

We react strongly and protest on being told the exact extent of our intellectual automatisms.

Still the facts are there and they are as stark as they are irrefutable and disappointing. The processes of thought of the average man and those of an erudite scholar offer few essential differences from the routine and repetition of a simple phonograph.

During a recording, the variations of acoustic pressure, according to their vibrational amplitude, have traced light or deep tracks on the surface of waxen discs. They do nothing but repeat indefinitely the same sound vibrations, known and recognized.

Likewise our brain records acquired or inherited, individual or collective, conscious or unconscious memories.

The essential difference lies in the complexity of the engrams, in their more fluid nature in comparison with the rigidity and rudimentary character of the track incised on the surface of a record.

Moreover, we are living processes with the faculty of arranging choosing and joining together the different memory recordings which constitute ourselves.

Nevertheless this does not in any way impede the essentially mechanical character of *our* mental functioning.

The gramophone record will repeat mechanically the song which has been recorded once and for all and, because it is a simple, single recording, the mechanical, repetitive and monotonous character of subsequent playings of the record becomes immediately apparent.

But the complexity of human memory recordings, the infinite combinations that are possible owing to their different registers and more fluid, less solid nature hinders us from being immediately aware of their mechanical and repetitive character.

Taken together these memory recordings take place within us to the sterile rhythm of simple habit, simple automatisms which are *rigorously inscribed within the confines of what is known*.

In our ordinary mental functioning there is no pure creation, no real innovation. Everything is merely the *mechanical* solution of infinitely complex equations whose data are borrowed from what is *known* from the *past*.

The fact that these lines startle most people is due to the lack of of information, which is perfectly normal.

These discoveries which have thrown a light on the processes of thought, memory and most psychological mechanisms are fairly recent.

Until now scientists have not had sufficiently delicate instruments to allow them to explore the frontier zones between the psychic and physical worlds.

They all felt that the enigma of life could not be solved by the discoveries of the old physico-chemistry alone. The research in macro-physics was followed by research in micro-physics. Ordinary chemistry was succeeded by micro-chemistry, biology by micro-biology and ordinary microscopes by the electronic and protonic ultra-microscopes.

Progress in electro-encephalography, and the ever more numerous methods in the new parapsychological sciences have given contemporary man means of research which can better inform him on the nature of the psychic processes.

In so far as we are able to observe their behaviour we are struck by their similarity with physical processes.

In the degree in which we were ignorant of their structure and processes we thought that our intellectual operations were immaterial or of a spiritual nature.

As we have already said, there is no creation or spirituality in the sterile round of our mental operations taking place within the limited cycle of 'known to known'. Every cause is linked to its effect. Everything follows on mechanically, just as an equation with complex given quantities has in it various possible solutions. That is what the electronic brains show us. The possible solutions to a mathematical problem are to be found virtually in its given quantities. The apparent separation between cause and effect, between the given quantities of the various problems and their solutions is just a matter of time. Thanks to their extreme specialization, electronic brains and robots can reduce the 'time factor' to the limits of the possible.

They help us to see more vividly the mechanical character of our mental operations.

If we apply strictly what has been said above to the processes of human intellectual operations we will see that in fact no real innovation or authentic creation exists in them.

In fact every so-called scientific or technical 'invention' or 'discovery' potentially existed in the ensemble of knowledge or data which preceded it.

The latest 'discoveries' in nuclear physics existed potentially in the first experiments and old theories of Bernouilli (the molecules) Dalton (atoms), Stoney (electrons), Einstein (photons), Planck (quanta) and Louis de Broglie (undulatory mechanics), etc.

On the technical plane man in general, invents very little or nothing. Essentially he bases himself on points of reference borrowed from the past. That which we call 'discovery' is really nothing but a process during which the whole history of humanity can be compared to the gropings of one man exploring ever more perfectly the structure of the things around him and that of himself and finally entering into 'direct contact' with the Real.

But until this 'perfect obedience to the Nature of things' has been realized, no true creation exists.

Those who examine things from the familiar dualistic point of view, see indeed a hierarchy of distinctions in the psychological values of our mental operations. The intellect capable of discovering the hidden solutions of a complex equation, of clearly apparent known quantities, is superior to the state of mind of an inwardly inert man who is content with mechanical repetition of acquired data without discerning any of their possible solutions.

But, in the mind of the great teachers, this hierarchy of values is inscribed within the rigidly limited framework of that which 'is known'. It bears the imprint of the processes of reference, deductions, inferences and inductions. Here the term 'to discover' takes on a different meaning.

According to the Zen Masters, to discover is to strip the mind of the false values which render it unable to 'see directly into its own nature' and which cover it up. The mind does not uncover anything . . . It covers.

From this particular point of view, the 'discoveries' of a physicist or team of physicists who are devoted to the study of many other recent discoveries, are not really discoveries.

They are one of the possible solutions which lie potentially in the complex equations which preceded them. A perfected electronic brain could do the same thing. Specialists in cybernetics and certain electronic robots are ready to build electro-magnetic and mechanical structures for 'discovering' the possible solutions to all the simple or complex given quantities, much more quickly than a whole team of mathematicians.

Between the processes of 'discovery' referred to above and that of fundamental and authentic discovery as conceived by the Zen Masters or by a Krishnamurti, there is no comparison. There, let us repeat, it is a question of a veritable psychological mutation, during the course of which the sterile circuit of 'known to known' is broken.

It is important to know that these are not gratuitous affirmations. The truth has just been demonstrated by electronic brains. Many materialists cried victory when they learnt of the extraordinary feats of cybernetics.

It appears that the exact meaning of the cybernetic experiments had escaped most of them.

The fact that the electronic brains have a memory and are able through this memory of the 'known' to effect associations and make deductions is quite natural.

Since psychical and physical processes are governed by the same laws, there was no reason why these thinking machines as we know them should not be made.

Recent progress in psychology and the study of the purely mechanical processes of the memory inevitably will end up in the construction of real thinking-machines.

Materialists seem to forget that these machines will always remain machines.

Their development cannot be beyond the limits of what is known, of deduction, and memory.

They will never be able to attain the Unknown.

Though from a structural point of view, LIFE is the very essence of forms both psychic and material, the realization of this life in [100] ourselves needs the transcendence of forms both psychic and material.

Life, God, is pure spontaneity, eternally renewed upsurging.

Physical and mental matter is governed by mechanical laws which bear the stamp of habit and repetition. There is the gulf between the integrated man and the machine: the former is completely open to the spontaneity and creative rhythm of LIFE, while the latter cannot go beyond the line of mechanical associations which goes from the known to the known.

The integrated man can reach the Unknown aspect of the divine. But the most extraordinary machine, the most subtle electronic brain can never reach the divine Unknown because their functioning derives essentially from known quantities which they are asked to solve; and above all, theirs are not living processes.

In other words the man who transcends the limits of his mind can really be free. Freedom can only exist from the moment when the sterile journey to and fro from 'known' to 'known' has ceased.

When the guiding principle of our existence slavishly follows certain ruts of our thoughts in the same way as a gramophone needle is guided by the grooves of a record, there is neither creation nor liberty.

Spiritual freedom only exists on the disappearance of our conformism, facile habits, logical deductions and mechanical automatisms.

What we need is a certain silence of the mind, an inner transparence, a mental relaxation, a freedom from all the interior dynamisms related to our habitual mechanical processes.

The meaning and value of this unknown have been pointed out by Rilke in his 'Letters to a young poet'.

'If it were possible for us to see a little further than our knowledge can reach, to see out a little farther over the outworks of our surmising, we should perhaps bear our griefs with greater confidence than our joys. For they are the moments when something new, something unknown enters into us. Our feelings are dumb with embarrassed shyness and everything in us retreats into the background. A stillness grows up, and the new thing that nobody knows, stands in the middle of it and is silent.

I believe that nearly all our griefs are moments of suspense which we experience as paralysis, because we cannot longer hear our estranged feelings living. Because we are alone with that foreign thing, which has entered into us; because everything in which we have confidence and to which we are accustomed is for a moment taken away from us; because we are in the midst of a state of transition, in which we cannot remain. The grief, too, passes. The new thing in us, that which has been added to us, has entered into our heart and penetrated to its innermost chamber, and is no longer there even — it is already in our blood. We do not experience what it was. We could easily be made to believe that nothing had happened, and yet we have changed just as a house changes into which a guest has entered. We cannot say who has come and perhaps we shall never know, but there are many signs to assure us that the future enters into us in this way, so as to transform itself in us long before it happens. The apparently eventless and motionless moment when our future enters into us is so much nearer to life than to that other manifestly chance point of time, when it actually happens to us as if from without. The quieter, the more patient, the more open we are in our grief, the deeper and the more unerringly does the new·thing enter into us. . . .'

CHAPTER XII

Tanha, or the Thirst for Becoming

ONCE again must we insist on the dualistic spirit in which the following lines are written. In fact Tanha or the craving to 'become' practically only exists for those who have fallen into the snare of the illusions of the 'I-process', of time and duration. These distinctions do not exist for the 'awakened'.

The avidity to 'become' springs from a fundamental force of habit.

And it is under its influence that *we oppose 'the will to live'* to the fact of *simply living*. The individual desire assuming the sole right to existence, is opposed to the 'non-desire' of a cosmic process which suffices unto itself.

Tanha is the inertia of force of habit which, maintained simply by acquired velocity, encloses the process of the 'flame of the ego' in a vicious circle. The flame burns and seeks avidly the elements which will assure it a pseudo-permanence. These elements are the basis of our daily existence: divers activities, the search for new sensations and enjoyment, desire for possession, instinct of domination, ambitions, endless plans suggested by the imagination, worldy vanities, and the search for a means to assure and develop prestige, etc.

The avidity of becoming, Tanha, comes from various fundamental factors which may be resumed as follows:

(1) Where there exists nothing but impersonal successions of thought and accumulations of memory, the illusion of a 'thinking' entity is born.

(2) This 'thinker' is in the habit of considering himself as a permanent 'entity', and wishes to safeguard his continuity at all cost.

(3) In order to do this, the pseudo-entity of the 'thinker' distinguishes himself from his thoughts and tries to influence them.

[101] The 'thinker' thus tries to affirm himself during innumerable transformations which need and create time.

(4) In the grip of the influence of the past, while looking only to the future, the mind of the 'thinker' is a prisoner of time. The present moment, with its riches, continually escapes him and is never lived in the fullness of that which, in the course of nature, it was destined to give him. The 'thinker' being incomplete in each present instant, seeks with all the greater ardour and despair the manifold possibilities of 'becoming', each as chimerical as the other and which he vainly hopes will assuage him.

(5) This thirst 'for becoming' is vigorously sustained by the ruses of the mind whose deeper layers do everything possible to hide from the 'thinker' the fundamentally illusory character of his existence and his search.

(6) Apart from these preceeding factors arising from a false vision of the 'I-process' itself, there are others which seem to encourage this error whilst all being exterior to the 'I-process'.

Amongst these we notice the universality of the process 'of becoming'.

Most of the processes in the world in the heart of which we are born, are processes of growth and of becoming. The seed sprouts and grows into a plant or a tree. Everything in our conception of the world is born, grows, develops, ages and dies. *It seems that on this biological 'becoming' by virtue of which living beings march onwards, there is superimposed a form of habit of 'becoming' and of 'growth'.*

Our biological past from time immemorial is a result of the processes of becoming and of growth. Our psychological structure tends to follow in the steps of habits which for so long have governed our material structures and those from which we are sprung. The error then consists in superimposing on to the impersonal becoming of facts, avidity, identification and psychological attachment.

(7) There is another factor which is outside the 'I-process' but is manifested in it and favours 'Tanha' or the 'thirst to become'. It is closely related to the preceding one. The history of a Universe is one of a process of continual associations. It seems that the moment privileged points appear, a desire for balance, a search for

complementarity, a nostalgia for a lost harmony and a 'fear of being nothing' appear simultaneously.

So atoms associate with atoms and form molecules. Molecules join forces with molecules and form the big molecules which are the bases of the first cells.

The mono-cellular creatures associate with one another and become pluricellular creatures. Thus a process of continued association can be observed from the atom through the amoeba, to man. This *associative force of habit* is continued in us by tendencies which are familiar to us. That which we call 'evolution' — in our dualistic image of the world — is really more psychic than physical. Consequently the associative force of habit throws out tendrils of its working process into the psychic world.

The 'thinker' associates himself with his material and spiritual possessions.

This process of association is so habitual that he does not realize the extent of its action. By it he identifies himself with 'his' name, the image he has made of 'his' own person, 'his' bank account, 'his' house. For as long as the 'thinker' thinks he 'possesses' all these things, he will be 'possessed' by them.

A more serious and subtle phase follows on to the process of association with material objects: the phase during which the 'thinker' identifies himself with 'his' ideas, 'his' beliefs, 'his' mental clichés, and above all 'his' accumulations of memory.

The force of associative habit is quite as strong as its opponent, 'disassociative force'.

As Carlo Suarès says:

'The 'I' is developed by successive association and dissociation. All psychological life is made up of oscillations of this nature. Desire is the sensation, felt by the permanence, of being in danger; assuagement is its feeling of not being in danger. Both these sensations tend, by their repetition, to establish themselves in the organism, and that is the awakening of consciousness. Thus each of the two poles works in the elaboration of consciousness and, by reason of this, the latter cannot at any moment pause, though it can "sleep"; *it is similar to an induced current that necessarily reinforces all the oscillations of the "I", these oscillations being experiences.* On maturity we see these oscillations diminishing more and more, finally dying because of the hardening, of the ossification of the "me", and consciousness slowly extinguishing itself in indifference or, on the contrary, we see these vibrations, by reason of their intensity, breaking the very instrument that made them and freeing consciousness itself, as a flower releases its perfume. Thus man will come to the point of refusing the experience through indifference, or *transcending it by smashing his own entity.*'

The 'I-process' in order to safeguard its continuity, develops a stratagem of transformations, innumerable modifications during which it oscillates from one extreme to the other. After having been associated with certain gains, it will leave them to try to win new ones. It will disassociate itself from the first ones in order to associate with the second. But amidst this process of successive associations and disassociations an 'entity' remains, a 'thinker' who in contrast to the alternative changes of 'surface', is building a permanence in depth in proportion to their intensity.

Still the day will dawn when the 'thinker' having wandered from enslavement to enslavement, will understand the vanity of all attempts to associate with anything whatsoever. He will become aware of the absurdity of the subtle game he has been playing with himself.

Nothing can fill up the unfathomable gulf of his inner contradiction. The mirage of the 'I-process' is like the sieve of the Danaides and can never be filled because it lacks real solidity.

From the moment when the 'thinker' understands, he is silent; stopping he looks more serenely within himself and into all things. Tanha, the thirst for 'becoming' is on the point of extinction. The tensions in order to 'become' are replaced by the relaxation of THAT WHICH IS. It is the hour of the 'letting go' of which the Zen Masters speak. The death of the entity of the 'thinker' is succeeded by the plenitude of Life.

CHAPTER XIII

Obedience to the Nature of Things

IN previous chapters we have spoken of the difficulties encountered in all attempts to define the nature of things. But though this cannot be defined nor 'known' as we generally know familiar objects, it can be experienced. At the same time let us make it clear that no duality of subject and experience exists in this paradoxical [104] process. The imperative necessity of transcending dualistic mental concepts has been expressed by Hui Neng:

'*As long as there is a dualistic way of looking at things there is no emancipation.* Light stands out against darkness; the passions stand against enlightenment. Unless these opposites are illuminated by Prajna so that the gap between the two is bridged, there is no understanding of the Mahayana. When you stay at one end of the bridge and are not able to grasp the one-ness of the Buddha-nature, you are not one of us. The Buddha-nature knows neither decrease nor increase, whether it is in the Buddha or in common mortals. When it is within the passions it is not defiled; when it is meditated upon it does not thereby become purer. The main point is not to think of things good and bad and thereby to be restricted, *but to let the mind move on as it is in itself and perform its inexhaustible functions. This is the way to be in accord with the Mind-essence*' (D. T. Suzuki – *The Zen Doctrine of No-Mind*, p. 36).

In order that the mind may function naturally and harmoniously – it must be freed from all attachment to oppositional notions such as good and evil, human and divine, relative and absolute, mobile and immobile. The mind which is caught in the snare of the apparent opposites loses sight of their essential identity in the reality which includes and dominates them.

'You must avoid such dualist notions and all liking or disliking, since everything is but universal mind', Hsi Yun tells us.

This 'monist' tendency in Zen thought has resulted in simplification of its mental representations of this world, rare as they are.

In order to understand the essential notions implied in the 'obedience to the nature of things', it is desirable to study some

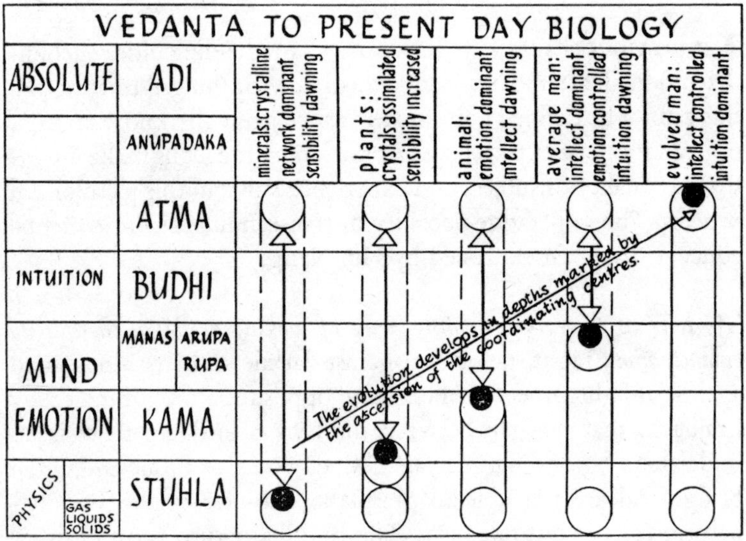

VEDANTA TO PRESENT DAY BIOLOGY		minerals:crystalline network dominant sensibility dawning	plants: crystals assimilated sensibility increased	animal: emotion dominant intellect dawning	average man: intellect dominant emotion controlled intuition dawning	evolved man: intellect controlled intuition dominant
ABSOLUTE	ADI					
	ANUPADAKA					
	ATMA					
INTUITION	BUDHI					
MIND	MANAS ARUPA / RUPA					
EMOTION	KAMA					
PHYSICS / GAS LIQUIDS SOLIDS	STUHLA					

The evolution develops in depths marked by the ascension of the coordinating centres.

Fig. 6

details of the psycho-physical anatomy of man and the world in general.

Most of the informative works have shown diagrams representing the Universe and man divided into a complex series of distinct planes. These works have been written by Occidentals whose outlook is basically dualistic.

They give an exact idea of the structure of man and the Universe as the Hindus see it. Their fertile imagination dwells with immense wealth of detail on the thousands of possible shades of emotion and thought and on the planes transcending them. This extreme division seems to have reached a climax in the work of the Indian thinker Sri Aurobindo. In his study of the psychological anatomy of man, Sri Aurobindo lays bare an extraordinarily complex sub-division of planes and levels of consciousness in the sector of the mind alone. There is a 'physical-mind', a 'vital-mind', an 'over-mind', and a 'supra-mind'.

The Zen presentation is far more simple.

Below are printed the two generally accepted methods of presentation.

Hindu presentation:

physical plane corresponds with the physical body

etheric plane corresponds to the etheric body (prana)

emotional plane corresponds to the emotional body (kama sharira)

lower mental plane corresponds to the lower mental body (rupa manas)

higher mental plane to correspond to the higher mental body (arupa manas)

plane of pure intuition to correspond to the intuitional body (Bodhi)

divine plane corresponding to the 'divine body' (atman) (see Fig. 6).

The higher forms of Buddhism, and particularly Zen, give a more homogeneous presentation of this structure in which we notice that the 'divine' plane is absent.

Totality-that-is-One of the $\left\{\begin{array}{l}\text{aspects or physical modes} \\ \text{aspects or the psychic modes}\end{array}\right.$
Real or the Cosmic Mind:

These aspects are sometimes presented as they appear in Figure 7.

The hierarchy or planes and levels of energy as presented by the Hindus seem more attractive to us because it corresponds more closely to our tendency to analyse and classify. At the same time it has certain drawbacks. It tends to oppose mind and matter, the divine and human. True, a certain link is suggested between the opposive aspects, but it still establishes the distinctions of an over-subtle hierarchy of values.

But it is not there that the essential difference lies between the mental outlook of the Zen Masters and the Indian classifications, or classifications under Indian influence. It resides especially in the fundamental fact that for the Indians, the planes of intuition and pure essence lie *beyond* and outside the mind.

In other words, 'spiritual' to most Indians, and as is the case with most of our ideas of spirituality, is beyond and outside the 'material' and the 'psychic'.

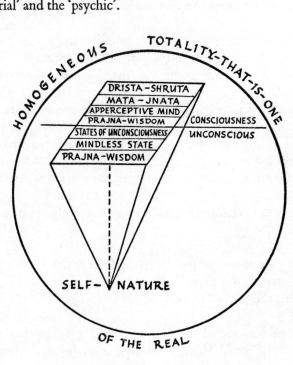

Fig. 7

Therefore, in order to discover the Real, we must seek it on the planes of cosnciousness beyond the mind.

This attitude is somewhat removed from the thought of the Zen Masters.

For they consider that the Real is the Totality-that-is-One of the physical and of the psychic, whose essential substance is cosmic mind. Everything is cosmic mind, including the physical and the psychic.

Both, however, recognize the existence of a complex superimposition of layers in our psychic structure. But Zen considers this to be part of Cosmic Mind.

The different layers of consciousness accepted by Zen Buddhism never imply a hierarchy of values as generally understood. That which we in the West call 'Divine' is represented in the eyes of the Zen masters by the psycho-physical Totality-that-is-One of man and the Universe. Outside this Totality-that-is-One nothing exists.

Madame A. David-Neel says: 'Nirvâna is Samsara; the individual, such as he is, formed by the five skandas, IS in fact exactly the Void, Reality, Nirvâna' (*Le Bouddhisme*).

Unless we insist on this fundamental unity of mind and matter, or ordinary and spiritual, we may lose ourselves in divers errors of interpretation.

This has been clearly stated by Hsi-Yun in a dialogue:

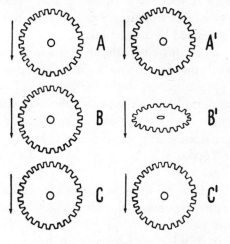

Fig. 8

Question: 'But is it the ordinary mind or the holy mind which is the Buddha?'
Answer: 'How can you have an ordinary mind and a holy mind?'
Question: 'According to the teaching of the Three Vehicles we have both. . . .'
Answer: 'If the Three Vehicles clearly distinguish these for you,

they are at variance with the truth. You still do not understand. All conceptions of an objective nature, such as that the "void" has actual existence must be at variance with the truth. It is from such [105] errors that ignorance arises. If only you would rid yourself of the concepts of "common" and "holy" (you would see that) apart from mind, there is no Buddha. Bodhi-Dharma, after his arrival from India, taught only that the substance of all men is the Buddha, but you still fail to understand, and thinking in terms of "common" and "holy", you allow your thoughts to gallop about in the world of form, thus beclouding your own mind . . . There are no things differing from each other. Hence (to understand this) is called attaining complete, perfect Enlightenment' (*The Huang-Po Doctrine of Universal Mind — Hsi-Yun*), p. 44.

[106] The profound nature of things is an absolutely homogeneous Unity, stripped of all distinctions and oppositional character.

Obedience to it requires a complete transformation of our mental perspective. The importance and nature of this transformation may be explained by an example.

Man can be compared with an extraordinarily complex mechanism made up of an infinite number of cog-wheels. These extend from physical matter to the last confines of the psyche.

It is impossible to localize the cosmic impulse which set these wheels in motion, for it is not only in matter, nor only in the psyche; neither outside nor above them. It is really the eternal rhythm of the Totality-that-is-One which includes and dominates all aspects at once.

By obedience to the nature of things we mean the realization of a physical and mental outlook which is completely adequate to the cosmic rhythm.

We can illustrate this point with a diagram.

However there is one error in it without which unfortunately, we would not be able to make ourselves understood.

A is the wheel representing the cosmic impulse, B the mind, and C the physical. Let us remember, however, that in reality A is not separate from B and C and that this is merely an artificial breaking up of a sole movement in order to facilitate the explanation (see Fig. 8).

First we shall deal with the example of obedience to the nature of things as realized by the man who has been integrated by the states of Satori or Nirvâna.

At each moment this man realizes an attitude that is completely adequate to the cosmic impulse. The latter, represented by wheel A, transmits the whole of its impulse to the mental wheel represented by B.

This wheel is completely available, for it is liberated from the routine movements of the force of habit. *As it is free from the grip of* [107] *the past and expects nothing further from the future, it adheres entirely to the present.* The cosmic impulse of A – which is renewed every instant – will therefore find in B a wheel *offering no resistance.* No longer will any sort of friction hinder the expression of the initial movement. Wheel C benefits directly from this inner harmony.

Let us now examine the case of the ordinary man. He 'disobeys' the nature of things and the process of his disobedience can be represented in the following manner: (see Fig. 8).

Accumulations of memory have gathered round B¹, the mental wheel, and have started off and given rise to secondary and 'parasitic' currents. That which was merely a wheel, believed itself to be an 'entity'. The instrument has identified itself with its function. Since then the mental wheel works 'on its own account'. It no longer submissively fulfils the task assigned to it. Instead of giving itself up to the cosmic impulse represented by the vertical wheel A¹, the mental wheel, caught in the snare of its own creations – duration and 'becoming' – finds itself in a totally *inadequate* position. It is placed 'edgeways', horizontally, and its position precludes all possibility of direct communion with the cosmic impulse of the present moment.

There remains wheel C¹ of the physical plane. Because wheel C¹ receives only indirectly the impulses inherent in the nature of things – it also tends to lose the normal harmony of its functioning.

By Correct Vision, thought or the mental wheel is freed of its mirages, resistances and cravings. It then reoccupies its place in the psychic function as a whole. The mental wheel then reassumes a vertical position by which the cogs of A and B interlock and turn smoothly.

CHAPTER XIV

Nirvâna or Satori

THE term Nirvâna is used in the divers schools of Buddhism.
The term Satori is found particularly in Zen.

Nirvâna means extinction, or more exactly, the movement of a
breath passing over the flame and snuffing it out. That is why the
first Western translators concluded too hastily that Buddhism was
nihilistic.

It is true that the term Nirvâna means extinction, but we must
first see what is being extinguished.

Nirvâna is the extinction of the flame of the 'I-process', to
which we have frequently referred. It is also the cessation of ignorance, the basic link in the chain of interdependent origins (Pratit-
yasamûtpada).

As it is said in the Samyutta-Nikaya IV 251-52: 'Whatever is the
extinction of passion, of aversion, of confusion, this is called
Nirvâna.'

Upon the cessation of false identifications, born of ignorance,
and the tensions inherent in the avidity of becoming, we become
integrated in the profound nature of things.

108   The experience of Nirvâna does not establish the realization of
a subtle desire of the 'I-process'. The conditions *sine qua non* of its
accomplishment are the elimination of all desire, all expectation, of
all *a priori* states of mind and all representation.

Nirvâna is not a supernatural or superhuman state. It is the
plenitude of the human. Nirvâna is the normal state of the mind
which is rid of all its egoistic conditioning, of attachment,
covetousness and ambition.

In this state we have not attained a reality outside us, nor have
we acquired anything new. We are simply revealed to ourselves
in the plenitude of that which we are.

'Between Nirvâna and Samsara there is not the slightest difference', Chandrakirti tells us, 'It must be understood, that nothing

is abolished, nothing is really annihilated in Nirvâna. Nirvâna simply consists of the complete suppression of all the erroneous constructions of our imagination' (Madame A. David-Neel — *Le Bouddhisme*).

When our mind is stripped of all its false accumulations it be-becomes transmuted into pure intelligence which has no relation- [100] ship with ordinary intellectuality. When our heart is freed from attachments and limitations of egoism and identification only the highest form of love remains. But Nirvâna goes beyond distinctions of love and intelligence. These two tendencies which to us are distinct and separate are integrated in a single apotheosis which is renewed from moment to moment to all eternity. That is why we believe that Nirvâna does not bring about the dehumanization of the human, but confirms the plenitude of its accomplishment. Only he who fulfills faithfully the requirements of his most profound and most real essence is worthy of the name of man.

CHAPTER XV

Nirvâna and the Void

MOST Buddhist texts teach us that the 'Void' is the profound nature of things. This most important idea should be studied in greater detail. The term 'Void' comes from the Sanscrit word 'Sunyata'. The study of the Sanscrit root of Sunyata shows that the notion of vacuity may be understood as being synonymous with 'Non-self'.

The Sanscrit word 'sunya' is derived from the root 'svi' (to swell). This notion implies the presence of a 'foreign' body apart and distinct from the original content. The Sanscrit 'svi' corresponds to the Greek 'ky'. As Professor E. Conze (London University) says:

'. . . You have the meaning *swollen* in such words as Latin *cumulus* (pile, heap) and *caulis* (stalk). You have the meaning *hollow*, from the same root, in Greek *Koilos*, Latin *cavus*. Thus our personality is *swollen* in so far as constituted by the five skandhas, but it is also *hollow* inside, because devoid of a central self. Furthermore "swollen" may mean "filled with something foreign". When a woman is "swollen" in pregnancy — and here again the Greeks use the same root in *kyo* — she is full of a foreign body, of something not herself. Similarly in this view, *the personality contains nothing that really belongs to it. It is swollen with foreign matter*' (*Buddhism*, p. 131).

That which has just been said clearly shows that the idea of vacuity does not in any way correspond to nothingness. When the 'foreign bodies' of our mental identifications, imaginative superimpositions and cravings to become have disappeared, the Self alone remains in its plenitude.

The Ratnamâlika (*Garland of Jewels*, attributed to Nagarjuna) says:

Nirvâna is not non-existence
How could you think such a thing?
We call Nirvâna the cessation
Of all thought of non-existence and existence.

'Void' is to be understood as the absence of our usual values, concepts of dualistic opposition, of our particular distinctions, cravings and attachments. These are the elements of the 'foreign bodies' which paralyse the harmonious functioning of the mind.

In the 'Path to Sudden Attainment', Hui Hai, a master of Zen during the T'ang dynasty, wrote:

'*When the mind is not attracted, there is* VOID. . . .' (p. 27)
'VOID *is simply non-attachment . . .*' (p. 25).
'*To understand the* VOIDNESS *of distinctions is to be delivered . . .*' (p. 17).

The continual requirement of such a rejection of distinctions surprises most people. They are used to the perception of opposites such as: black and white, heat and cold, good and evil.

The Western mind bears the mark of this comparison of the opposites to such a degree that it does not hesitate to pursue this into the domain of its mental representations of the divine. In the grip of this anthropomorphism we call God good and merciful, in a sense which shows that unconsciously we are opposing this to our concepts of evil. Zen masters tell us that God cannot be conceived. Moreover He has no opposite since He IS all things, and furthermore Nirvâna and Satori can only be realized when our mind has been freed of the last vestiges of our traditional notions of 'God'. All our usual distinction of values, both material and psychological, are literally transmuted in the nirvânic experience.

'Because your real nature is formless, *it is beyond perception.* Since it is intangible, we say that it cannot be perceived. While impossible to perceive, it remains profoundly still. . . .

'Because your real nature is formless, fundamentally there are no distinctions (between this and that) . . .' (*Path to Sudden Attainment*, p. 12).

Nirvâna goes beyond the process of perception, not only because of the inherent absence of form in our real nature but also because of its experience of the Totality-that-is-One in its complete homogeneity.

All processes of perception as we generally conceive them imply the duality of an entity perceiving an object and an entity distinct from that one.

Let us point out however, that the abolition of all distinctions, of all processes of perceptions as we understand them do not tacitly imply its impossibility of realization.

In fact, when the Zen master Hui Hai addresses his pupils he says:

'In speaking (thus) of no feeling, *I refer to common feelings and not to holy feeling.*'
Question: 'What is common feeling and what is holy feeling?'
Answer: 'If distinctions are made, that is (due to) common feeling. *Holy feeling implies the voidness of distinctions*' (p. 26) (*Path to Sudden Attainment*).

'The comprehension which takes place as a result of perception does not imply an understanding of the reality (of the thing perceived). *What you perceive without perceiving — that is Nirvâna*, also known as deliverance' (*Path to Sudden Attainment*, p. 13).

This paradoxical manner of looking upon the ultimate experience is not confined exclusively to Zen. Very similar statements are to be found in the oldest texts of Mahayanist Buddhism and especially in the famous 'Prajna Paramita Sûtras':

110 'Without special knowledge, supreme Wisdom understands all things and *without (special and distinct) perceptions it perceives all things.*'

We are faced here with a pure and supra-intellectual state of consciousness which is very far from the nihilism with which certain writers have qualified Buddhism.

The more attentively we study the texts of Mahayanist Buddhism and Zen the more it becomes apparent that the 'Void' of our familiar conception reveals an ineffable plenitude. The disappointments caused by the apparent negativity of the first approach, are succeeded by a positive sense which is as unexpected as it is extraordinary. That which appears in the form of an essentially destructive void becomes transformed into a highly creative vacuity. Finally in a serene and silent joy there emerges the vision of the supreme Reality Itself.

Earlier we have emphasized the absence of all solidity, all continuity, and all static substance in the very heart of matter. The same observations have been made in the domain of the mind.

The last vestiges of entities or 'things' have been finally effaced [111] and take only a second and derivative place before the dominant reality of universal flux, a kind of 'pure change without anything that changes'.

During the experience of Nirvâna the various ideas which we have just recalled – and until then they were only intellectual – are truly lived in the acuity of a non-mental perception.

From then on it seems that the 'I-process' has been emptied of its substance and all contents of self-identification. It loses its opacity and psychological solidity. In a way it is absent from itself and intensely present to the world. But the latter in its turn is equally freed of all opacity and all apparent solidity. The fragile limits which trace the definite contours of beings and things tend to become effaced. Everything seems to be bathed in a prodigous unity. *The 'Void' of habitual distinctions of the I-process coincides with the 'Void' of the things surrounding it.*

Let me quote here a paradoxical fragment from the 'Prajna Paramita Hridya Sûtra':

'There are five *skandas* and these should be regarded as "empty" by nature. Form and body are empty and their emptiness is indeed form. Emptiness is not different from form and form is not different from emptiness. . . .'

In this particular perspective when we see an object we penetrate it immediately by a kind of secret and silent resonance which is established spontaneously between our deeper nature and that of the object. This perception is of a supra-intellectual nature. It would be vain to seek to obtain an intuitive notion of it merely by any subtle process of imagination.

If we experiment in that direction we have the impression of being endowed – and in fact we are – with a progressive and permanent faculty of 'omnipenetrability'.

More and more, beyond superficial appearances, we are, by our basic nature, the basic nature of all things. This experience, to be authentic, cannot in any circumstances depend on fabrications elaborated by our minds.

112   This progressive stripping of opacity from things and from our own inner structure tends to *empty* our minds of their individual distinctions.

As our mental structure becomes more and more transparent the new perspective established in us tends to show us beings and things in ever closer conformity with their real nature; and they appear so transparent that they seem to be *emptied* of all the familiar and distinct values which we attributed to them before.

To conclude, we shall cite a text already referred to, from the Lankâvatâra Sûtra, in which the 'Void' is clearly assimilated with the highest meaning of 'final Reality'.

'What is meant by the "Void" in *the highest sense of final Reality* is that in the acquirement of an inner understanding by means of Wisdom there is no longer any trace of the force of habit engendered by *erroneous conceptions*.'

The notion of 'void' in connection with particular perceptions has been described in an original and suggestive manner in the work of the Zen master Hui Hai.

It is said there that the mind, caught in the trap of individual distinctions, 'abides' in them, and thereby cuts itself off from the totality of the Real.

The mind of the Sage, however, 'does not abide anywhere'.

The English translation of the Chinese text of Hui Hai is by John Blofeld, and expresses most clearly the notion of the 'non-abiding mind'.

★

Question: 'What is meant by the place of non-abiding?'
Answer: 'It means not abiding anywhere whatsoever.'
Question: 'What is not abiding anywhere whatsoever?'
Answer: 'Not abiding in goodness, evil, being, non-being, inside, outside or in the middle; nor in void, abstraction or non-abstraction — that is not abiding anywhere. The dwelling-place of the mind should be only this not abiding anywhere whatsoever. Whoever attains to this is said to have a non-abiding mind. The non-abiding mind is indeed the mind of a Buddha.'
Question: 'To what can this mind be likened?'
Answer: 'It is not blue nor yellow, red nor white, long nor short, coming nor going. It is not defiled nor pure, nor is it subject to birth or destruction. It remains profoundly and eternally still. *Such is the form of the real mind, which is also that of the body.* The real body is identical with that of a Buddha.'
Question: 'By what means can this body and this mind be perceived?'
Answer: '. . . They are to be perceived in your own real nature.'

Two essential notions stand out from these texts.

(1) Firstly, Nirvâna or Satori arise from the VOID of individual perceptions. This notion is expressed by the phrase 'the non-abiding mind', that is to say *the mind which is free from all distinct values.*

The Zen masters do not look upon the vision of Satori as the seeing of objects, things, or even definite principles. It comprises an exceptional purification which has been mentioned on several [113] occasions and which it may be well to repeat here.

Professor D. T. Suzuki defines its characteristics as follows:

'The seeing is not reflected on an object as if the seer had nothing to do with it. The seeing, on the contrary, brings the seer and the object seen together, not in mere identification but *in becoming conscious of itself, or rather of its working. The seeing is an active deed, involving the dynamic conception of self-being;* . . .'
'*The seeing is the result of* (his) *having nothing to stand upon.*'

★

From the moment when our vision alights upon an object its interference with it limits it. This very interference gives rise to secondary phenomena which hide from our eyes the first upsurging of essential Reality. Moreover such a process would rivet us to the domain of dualities, from which essentially we should free ourselves.

The perception of Satori, in spite of its power, is more vivid, ethereal and free than the familiar processes of perception. By contrast these seem weighed down by an extreme heaviness and monotony. In the degree in which we are oriented towards such a realization, all things, and even ourselves, seem to become impregnated with a new lightness and freshness.

(2) *The notion of 'real mind' assimilated to that of the 'Real Body', is very important in Zen.*

As we have already seen, the notion of 'void' should be understood as that of 'non-self'. The notion of 'void' implies an absence of all false values suggested by the thought of 'self'. These false values are the result of an identification with the sensory activities and their contacts with the material world.

Our notions of Reality unconsciously are linked with concepts or memories of our contacts with the solid world.

That which we think is substantial because of a superficial appearance of solidity is not really substantial. The things which appear to us as the most substantial are really these which are the most 'empty' of basic substance. There is an important difference (from the phenomenal point of view) between the apparent substance with which we are familiar and the fundamental substance.

A complete reversal of all our old notions of substance, 'body', time, space, movement and consciousness must take place in our mind. Most of these notions bear the indelible stamp of the universe of dualities created by our own mind. The sense of Reality should be seized in a completely different direction. It is revealed by the birth of a new dimension within ourselves. This dimension is new not because it is essentially different from those created by our mind, but because it both unites and dominates them. It is unthinkable but it can be lived.

It seems that as we approach Nirvâna or Satori, that which we call 'our' body becomes but an object amongst many others, as in the case of our mental representations. From the moment we are delivered from the illusion of living as distinct beings the part no longer mistakes itself for the Whole. Alone the awareness of the Whole, the very existence of the Whole appears from one instant to another in all its unfathomability and fundamental reality. From that moment our physical and mental life becomes secondary and derivative before the prestige of its common source. This prestige becomes so imperious that we cannot help attributing to it a degree of substantiality.

In the light of this new point of view the immense variety of beings and things is the multiple mode of expression of one sole substance called by Zen masters 'Cosmic Mind'.

We are 'Cosmic Mind' and know it not. Each being, each thing is an element of this eternal living God.

The substantial nature which we experience finally as a result of our purified mind, makes us believe that it is a '*body*'. This cosmic body is not only 'ours' but is the 'body of truth' or pure essence in which and by which all things and all beings move and exist. There is no longer here any difference between a physical and a so-called 'spiritual' body, between a physical and a so-called 'spiritual' substance. Moreover certain authorities consider that the term 'spiritual', as we conceive it, is not strictly adequate to the various forms of Buddhism.

Let us point out here that the expressions 'Body of truth' or 'Body of Buddha' (Dharmakaya), which are frequently used in the texts of Buddhism in general and Zen in particular, should never be taken in their usual meanings. *In no way is it a question of the body of a divine person* like that suggested by the anthropomorphic imagination of the West. The term 'body' is used because in our dualistic memories it is associated with positive and substantial reality.

Here we are just falling in with a linguistic convenience which, however, may easily betray us.

After Satori the reality which Zen calls 'Cosmic Mind' is revealed to us as the substantial, in-formal, impersonal and infinite basis of all things.

The notion of the 'body' of truth appeared for the first time in a treatise of the Buddhist sage Ashvaghosha entitled 'The Awakening of Faith in Mahayana'. This notion is one of three concepts known as 'tai' (the body), 'hsiang' (form), and 'yung' (use). The body corresponds to the fundamental substance, form to appearances and use to function. As D. T. Suzuki writes:

'. . . To be a real object these three concepts: Body, Form and Use, must be accounted for.

To apply these concepts to our object of discourse here, *self-nature is the Body and Prajna (supreme Wisdom) its Use*, whereas there is nothing here corresponding to form. There is the Buddha-nature, Hui-Neng would argue, which makes up the reason to Buddhahood; and this is present in all beings, constituting their self-nature. The object of Zen discipline is to recognize it, and to be released from error, which are the passions. How is the recognition possible, one may inquire? *It is possible because self-nature is self-knowledge. The Body is no-body without its Use, and the Body is the Use. To be itself is to know itself. By using itself, its being is demonstrated*, and this using is, in Hui-Neng's terminology, "seeing into one's own Nature" . . .'

In the foregoing a dynamic conception of Zen is immediately evident. 'The Body is no-body without its Use, and Body is the Use', is a thought which has immense consequences. It emphasizes the necessity of the process of experimental living. Satori can no longer be *only* a vision, it is *pure action*. Once again we can see the consequences of the total homogeneity of the Real. The function can no longer be separated from the substance, for it is itself substance, and vice-versa.

Hui-Neng's dynamic notion of Zen is radically opposed to that of Shen-Hsiu, defender of the Northern School, known as the School of Dhyana. The latter is of a considerably more static character than the Southern School of Hui-Neng.

The divergence between the two schools has been remarkably defined by Professor D. T. Suzuki:

'Shen-Hsiu's school pays more attention to the body aspect of self-nature, and tells its followers to concentrate their efforts on the clearing up of consciousness, so as to see in it the reflection of self-nature, pure and undefiled. They have evidently forgotten that *"self-nature"*, is not a somewhat whose Body can be reflected on *our consciousness in the way that a mountain can be seen reflected on the smooth surface of a lake. There is no such Body in self-nature, for the Body itself is the Use; besides the Use, there is no Body. And by this Use is meant the Body's seeing itself in itself. . . .'*

The divergence between Hui-Neng and Shen-Hsiu is generally illustrated by the reaction of the former on reading the poem (gatha) written by Shen-Hsiu. It runs as follows:

> 'Our body is the Bodhi-tree
> And our mind is a mirror bright;
> Carefully we wipe them hour by hour
> And let no dust alight.'

In answer to this 'gatha', Hui-Neng wrote one of his own and pinned it up discreetly in the meditation hall to the great consternation of the monks:

> 'There is no Bodhi-tree,
> Nor stand or mirror bright,
> Since all is void,
> Where can the dust alight?'

CHAPTER XVI

Nirvâna, Satori and Lucid Love

IN the state of Nirvâna our habitual distinctions of love and intelligence disappear like any other distinct values.

Basically the nature of things is a homogeneity in which all differentiated qualities of love, intelligence and consciousness are no longer relevant.

Once again we shall borrow an example from our dualistic methods of observation while making the usual reservations (see Fig. 9).

White light, streaming through a prism is split up into a spectrum of the seven basic colours. If they were to be transposed on to a swiftly turning disc, in the correct proportions, we would get an impression of whiteness.

We could consider this white light as a relatively homogeneous synthesis of all the separate colours which were revealed by the prism.

To combine this with the comparison drawn in the preceeding chapter we could say that this white light is neither blue, nor red, green, nor yellow. It is *void* of the distinctions inherent in particular colours, but is in itself the pure principle of brilliance.

The psycho-physical structure of man is a transforming medium of energy as a prism is of light.

In the same manner as white light is split up into seven basic colours on passing through a prism we regard the basic energy of our psycho-physical structure as separated in us, and by us, not into a coloured spectrum but into a range of varied psychical functions. The separate notes in this psychic scale are given the names of love, consciousness and intelligence.

There is identity between white light and its fundamental components on one hand, and the basic energy of our psycho-physical structure and the distinct qualities revealed by the complexity of our cellular and psychic composition on the other.

Looking at it in this way white light is as *void* of distinctions of blue, red and green, *as the energy or basic reality of our psycho-physical structure is void of the familiar distinctions of love, intelligence and consciousness.*

To say that white light is blue or red is as absurd as to attribute to the basic energy of our psycho-physical structure particular qualities of love, intelligence or consciousness, such as normally manifested by us.

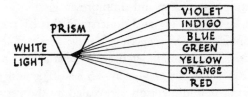

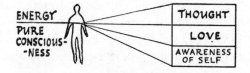

Fig. 9

N.B. The expression 'pure consciousness' should not be understood in its usual meaning. The reader should interpret it in the sense of the 'Zen Unconscious', that is to say, the principal of 'pure consciousness unconscious of itself'.
The white light is free of all separate colouring in the same way as the energy or basic reality of man and the Universe transcends our familiar qualities.

'God is Love', the affirmation used *ad nauseam* by most Occidentals on taking as a point of departure what they claim to know about love, has no meaning for the Sage. At most it expresses a very partial aspect of the total Reality.

From the 'Nirvânic' point of view, intelligence and love are no more separated in the Real than are the colours red and green in white light. Nirvâna is not only the summum of love, but also the summum of lucidity, expecially since distinctions no longer have any meaning for him who has attained it.

The term 'Cosmic Mind' should not be interpreted as meaning a supra-intellectual specialization established at the expense of a higher sense of love. The aspect of essential felicity in Satori is due to the element of love revealed therein. This felicity is not static, but is that of a dynamic equilibrium which is renewed at every instant. It is the felicity of perfect instantaneity.

It is both within and without things and beings, and takes no notice of their apparent superficial separateness.

It is this felicity which particularly at the beginning, gives the sense of omnipenetrability and omnipresence.

It would be vain to try and understand this by means of the ordinary mind. *The part cannot explain the whole. The omnipenetrability and omnipresence of Satori or Nirvâna are the result of the discovery of a dimension which — to us — is new.* The non-mental experience of this new dimension is revealed by the very nature of the eternal homogeneity of 'pure love-intelligence'.

By means of it we simply discover ourselves in the fundamental nature of what we were, are, and will be to all eternity. In so far as the content of the above has been actually lived it appears as the FACT, the POSITIVE FACT, above all others, and before the prestige of which the mirages of the 'I-process' vanish for ever.

The inner richness of this fundamental fact and its aspect of felicity have been expressed in an admirable poem by Sam Tchen Kham Pa (Dayalshanti Ghose):

Abide in This
Live only in This
Be self-effacing
And may your soul shine with Its Infinite Light, Its supreme
    peace,
O sublime immortality, I am ever in Thee.
I am no longer distinct from Thee,
Thy joy fills that which remains of 'my' soul,
Fires that which remains of 'my' heart
And incorporates me into the felicity of an eternal lightning-
    flash.

O Life immense and boundless!
Eternal and radiant splendour
Thou art henceforth my sole body
My sole dwelling. . . .
I am the divinity of things
Under this thick cloak of matter
I am the flame, silent and anonymous
Which unknown to all
Shines in the heart of outer darkness.

In the perpetual up-surging of my infinite vision
There are no more veils, no more darkness, no more light,
The nameless infinite, the Eternal that has no attribute are my
    sole dwellings, my sole Natural State.
It is in this Unicity that I see the infinite variety of things and of
    beings, melt into a common essence as pure water merges
    with pure water.
In the transluminous plenitude of an infinite reality
I am forever transfigured
As I transfigure all things,
By virtue of the Eternal Lightning-flash that I am.

I am . . . I am forever. . . .
That which was . . . That which IS . . . That which will be.

I am . . . I am forever. . . .
The infinite blessedness which, in its eternal rhythms,
Cradles the Universe and quickens the heart of things.

I am . . . I am forever. . . .
In my ultimate dwelling
— which is also that of all things —
Joy, harmony, the ecstasy of the world.

CHAPTER XVII

Lucidity without Ideation

I T is difficult for Western minds to admit the possibility of a *state of pure lucidity without ideas*. Our minds are so constituted that they love limited and definite notions. Consciousness to us is the result of the acuity of the perception of contrasts. We feel we do not know a thing if we are unable to name it or classify it in one of our categories of habitual values. Most of us measure intelligence by the skill with which symbols are manipulated.

The values on which our minds are based belong to the domain of established and recognized truths that can be demonstrated by the discursive intelligence. We only conceive a state of consciousness as intelligible in so far as the perceptions of which it consists refer to similar perceptions. In order to have rights of citizenship in our intellectual structure each value should have its title of nobility: it should be *known*, recognized, approved, tested and compared. Proof is to us the hall-mark of intellectual respectability. We lose sight of the fact that in the so-called spiritual domain the mind can never obtain the kind of proofs it is used to in the material field. To maintain that is so, is to impose inopportune extensions on the mechanical process which rules the material world in a field in which they have been proved to be totally inadequate.

Briefly, we have a horror of the unknown. A certain instinct of self-defence makes us fear everything that is not familiar and whose unexpected character might upset the routine of our mind.

We wish to pursue our existence protected by the shield of our certainties, our proofs and our assurances. All this shows the extent to which we are subjected to a basic fear.

The essential desire for security entailed in this fear of the unknown is derived from the instinct of preservation fundamental to the 'I-process'.

The mechanical character of the process is proved by the experiments of cybernetics. The intellect of the ordinary man functions within the limited framework of the 'known' just as do electronic brains. True creativeness can only be realized in the Unknown of the given instant.

Our bewilderment on hearing Zen or Krishnamurtian thought, suggesting to us the possibility of a state of lucidity without ideation, is a result of the instinct of self-defence of the 'I-process'.

Most of us seem to have the feeling that, once stripped of our certainties, our symbols and mental habits, we would sink into incoherence and nothingness.

We are forced to admit, however, that the highest forms of lucidity and intelligence are only realized in so far as our minds [114] are freed from the grip of symbols, images and ideas of whatever kind they may be.

We can moreover try by ourselves the possibility of realizing a state of silent observation which is perfectly clear and intense, without ideas or distinct thoughts, without forms or symbols or words.

The acuteness of pure lucidity of a given intsant is in direct proportion to the absence of ideas and memory-automatisms crowding our mind. In other words, in as far as the 'force of habit' ceases to work on our mind, the latter will recover the unfathomable peace of its eternal nature. Such is the state of Nirvâna.

Later we hope to develop the reasons for which this silence of the mind, and inner transparence cannot be the outcome of an act of discipline. The absence of fabrication and objectivation by the mind cannot be the effect of the will of the 'I-process', but arises from an informal and transcendent understanding of an intuitive nature.

Man has *understood* the fatal role staged by identifications, and his attachment to the memory-clichés that clutter up his mind. He has seen and felt the corruption introduced by automatisms which cause the memory to give a name to anything that comes into the mind from moment to moment. The importance of this process [115] can be illustrated by an example borrowed from physics. In fact we could say that a *relationship exists on the one hand between the electron and the perturbation of the photon which lights it up, and on*

the other between the mental state of a given instant and the perturbation
induced by the 'word' projected by the memory.

So, as Krishnamurti suggested, the full comprehension of this
process brings about a silence of the mind. From then on, the
Intemporal is fully realized.

CHAPTER XVIII

Nirvâna, Satori and the Present

LET us understand that the state of Nirvâna or Satori is manifested in us by a total obedience to the nature of things. We have pointed out repeatedly the eternally dynamic presence of the Real. *The supreme awakening can only be realized by a perfect coincidence between the Present of the nature of things within us, and the Present of the environment.* (Let us point out, however, that a concession has been made to our dualistic language, since, in the Real, there is no longer a distinction between ourselves and our environment.)

Whenever an idea arises between ourselves and an external fact, the coincidence of the two Presents is thereby prevented. The force of memory-habit projects between each new instant and ourselves this [116] *fatidical echo of the past which is the word.* The mind cannot support the burden of a conscious or unconscious attachment to words and at the same time realize a total adherence to the present. We can see that there are no half-measures in this process. That is why the Zen masters insist on the sudden character of Satori. The mind cannot be either slightly or greatly influenced by the past. The slightest trace of the latter hinders adherence to the Present. But we all know the extent to which the all-powerful automatisms of memory instantly crowd the mind with a multitude of words from moment by moment. If we watch ourselves closely we can see how difficult it is to think without words.

As long as the word, this echo of the past, is projected between us and the fact, we will be unable to realize an attitude of perfect adequacy. Thus consciously or unconsciously we reveal our *preference* for the past. Something within us holds back and will not welcome the plenitude of the Present.

We shall recall some words of Zen:

'*The Perfect Way knows no difficulties except that it refuses to make preference . . . A tenth of an inch's difference and Heaven and Earth are set apart.'*

[117] This quotation finds its full significance when we see the extent to which the subtle, imperceptible and rapid recollection of a word can corrupt the freshness of each new instant.

That is why at the moment of an authentic experience the terms Nirvâna, Satori, Body of Buddha, Cosmic Mind, or any others should be dismissed from the mind.

Bearing in mind what has been said, we understand better the full import of the words of Chao-Chou, a Zen master who reacted sharply against the continual use of the word 'Buddha'.

'I do not like to hear the word Buddha. . . .'

'When you pronounce the word Buddha clean your mouth for three years to get rid of the filth you thereby breath. . . .'

Let us point out, however, that the cessation of our practice of verbalization and the state of mental serenity do not merely result from an understanding of what has just been explained.

In the state of Nirvâna or Satori, man no longer has an agitated mind, not because he tries to obtain any kind of immobility, but rather because, in a certain sense, *he can no longer do otherwise.*

The man who has realized Nirvâna or Satori thinks with his heart and loves with his brain. These two functions are no longer distinct, and in fact they have never been so. Satori is intelligence of the heart.

During an interview with Professor D. T. Suzuki, we asked him whether the very arduous mental training of Zen did not hold certain dangers.

The master answered by placing his hand on his forehead and saying: 'There is danger if you try to understand by means of this only'; then, indicating his heart, he continued: 'But if you grasp Zen here, then health, peace and equilibrium shall be yours.' The same day the Professor quoted a Zen 'Koan' which ran as follows: 'When I hear I see, and when I see I hear.'

[118] This shows us to what extent in the realization of Nirvâna or Satori, the specific and distinct characters of our sense-perceptions

fade out in the presence of the realization of a state of fundamental integration.

When I hear the sound of a distant bell I am, in a manner of speaking, this bell; I am the molecules of air which it has caused to vibrate, and I am this sound-wave which is spreading in space. Being attentive to the deeper nature of my being, which is the nature of all things, all external events, all sound, all movement, allow me to vibrate in perfect accord with the common essence by means of a secret resonance which is renewed from moment to moment.

All that which I see I perceive 'through' this deeper reality. All that to which I listen I hear through this identity which is as unfathomable as it is unlimited. In the end in my eyes it assumes such an important place that it remains the dominating note of all distinct perceptions, whether they be visual, olfactory, tactile or auditive.

By the end of this process I can effectively say that when I see I hear, and when I hear I see.

One should also say that in so far as we really approach such an experience it assumes, despite its formal purification, a power in the light of which all distinct perceptions disappear as the shadows of night are dissipated in the light of the rising sun.

The realization which fulfills us from instant to instant becomes the normal from that moment on.

Each sense, which heretofore impeded Correct Vision by means of identification and avidity, undergoes a metamorphosis as wonderful as unexpected. It co-operates with the basic harmony of the outer and inner Universe. It seems to be the impersonal auxiliary of a process both individual and cosmic which is entirely free of personal identification and all cravings for permanence whatever they be.

In the light of this we can better understand the meaning of an apparently paradoxical text of Hsi-Yun.

'People are often hindered by their sense perceptions from perceiving their own minds and by phenomena from perceiving (underlying) principles, *so they frequently try to escape the former in order to still their minds* and reject the latter in order to preserve their grasp of principles. They do not realize that this is to obscure phenomena with principles. . . .

. . . *The foolish man eschews phenomena but not mentation, while the wise man eschews mentation and not phenomena'* (*The Huang Po Doctrine of Universal Mind* – Hsi-Yun, p. 35).

The same language is used by Hui-Neng.

'When used the Samadhi of Prajna, which is MUNEN (no-thought-ness), it pervades everywhere, and yet shows no attachment anywhere. Only keep your original Mind pure and *let the six senses run out of the six portals into the six dust(-worlds)*. Free from stain, free from confusion (the mind), in its coming and going is master itself, in its functioning knows no pause. This is the Samadhi of Prajna, a masterly emancipation, and known as the deed of no-thought-ness' (D. T. Suzuki – *The Zen Doctrine of No-Mind*).

The experience of Nirvâna or Satori does not, as some people think, separate us from the world; on the contrary, as a result of it, we are totally present to the world, for it gives us the possibility of bringing together an admirable spiritual symbiosis, that which we in the language of the West would call the fullness of our hidden divinity and our humanity. We shall not be able to participate fully in the Great Drama of the Universe until we cease to identify ourselves with each of our functions.

The processes of the total visible and invisible Universe are comparable to the perpetually varying harmonies of a cosmic symphony of which we are the apparently separate notes. The symphony is a whole, and the notes are not independent. When, dying to ourselves, we obey the nature of things, we enrich the total harmony by the perfectly natural resonance of our particular note. From then on the individuality of our particular sound is no longer a result of personal choice but simply the impersonal result of the cosmic impulse at a privileged point, changing from instant to instant according to circumstances. Such are the bases of the perfect adequacy taught by the Zen master.

The notion of Satori as a coincidence between the Present that lies in the depths and that of the 'surface', explains the symbolism of the Tibetan 'Dorje' (see Fig. 10).

The 'Dorje' is a cylindrical or tubular object bulbous at either end. It is used to direct on to the congregation the magnetism or spiritual radiation of the officiating monk in certain Tibetan rites.

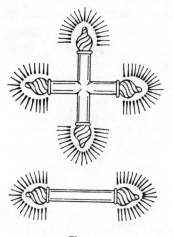

Fig. 10

It can also be represented by two bars, formed like a cross ending in four points and giving the impression of a quadruple sword. These are the 'exoteric' aspects of the 'Dorje', and as such, they have little interest for us.

To certain masters the term 'Dorje' means thunderbolt, and symbolizes the state of Nirvâna in all the power and light that it may have.

When the memory-habits of the 'I-process' cease, a possibility occurs of coinciding in perfect adequacy with the secret eternity of the instant. The creative impulse of 'Cosmic Mind' is compared to the lightning-flash of an Eternal Present. From the moment when a certain inner transparence is established in us we realize perfect availability to this cosmic impulse. When we are totally absent to ourselves the coincidence of the Present that lies in the depths and of the surface present is established.

It is comparable to being struck, spiritually, by lightning whereby we are definitely wrested from the dream of ignorance.

This is the profound symbolism of the 'Dorje', thunderbolt of the Eternal Lightning. 'Dorje' corresponds to the Sanscrit 'Vajra'. The notion of the Real, assimilated to that of an eternal lightning-flash, is at the basis of the purest teachings of Buddhism. The Vajracchedikâ Sûtra, as its name implies, is the teaching of the lightning or the thunderbolt of the eternal diamond.

Pure Buddhism and Zen are the doctrines of perfect instantaneity; the full power of the Eternal Lightning can only be received in the instant.

Such is the true nature of our being, to the vision of which the masters beckon us.

CHAPTER XIX

Satori and the Zen Unconscious

THE ideas of the Zen Unconscious and of Satori are closely linked. The Chinese root expressing this state is 'Wu-Nien' or 'Wu-hsin'. The character 'hsin' originally symbolizes the heart. The character 'nien' has 'chien' above the heart, which means 'now'.

Hui-Neng proposes three fundamental concepts for Zen and they are closely interrelated.

The notion of the Unconscious is one of the essential bases of Zen. This Unconscious should not be confused with that of the psychologists. It should be understood as a basic cosmic principal in which both the highest characters of the heart 'hsin' and those of lucidity are represented. We shall develop later the entirely homogeneous characteristics of this Unconscious in which all distinctions are eliminated.

The Zen Unconscious is a state of pure and infinite consciousness which is unconscious of itself. This state is free of all particularization. [110]

Another characteristic of Zen is its 'non-fixation'.

English translators call it the 'non-abiding mind', the mind that has no dwelling.

By this term the Zen masters insist on the absolute ubiquity of the Unconscious. It ignores our limitations and our distinctions. It is not to be found more in one being or one object than in any other. A third characteristic of the Zen Unconscious is its 'absence of form'. Hui-Neng defines it as follows:

'By formlessness is meant to be in form and yet to be detached from it; by the unconscious is meant to have thoughts and yet not to have them; as to non-abiding, it is the primary nature of man.'

'O good friends, not to have the mind tainted while in contact with all conditions of life this is to be Unconscious. It is to be always detached from objective conditions in one's own consciousness. . . .' (Suzuki – *Zen Doctrine of No-Mind*, p. 57).

The characteristic of 'non-fixation' of the Zen Unconscious is applied equally to space but it is quite as much lacking in fixity in time. It is always in the Present, and is renewed every instant. It is this which distinguishes it from the unconscious of psychologists, which bears traces of the force of individual and collective memory-habit.

The notion of 'non-fixation' in time and space is closely bound up with the absence of 'consciousness of self'. The constitutive elements of the 'I-process' or 'consciousness of self' are in fact the result of a continuous accumulation of engrams round a fixed point. If we suppress all fixity and all continuity at the imaginary point of our example, we thereby eliminate all possibility of memory-habit. The past bases of reference being absent, the central point which records them and accumulates them is bereft of all faculty of objectivation. And it is nothing but a process of pure movement freed of all personal identification. Its plenitude is entirely in the instant without duration of the Eternal Present. That is why the Unconscious can be defined as pure consciousness unconscious of itself. Renewing itself at every instant, it dies to its past and is deprived of any possibility of reference. It is sufficient unto itself.

The search for a point of reference or support betrays a fear, an unconscious disequilibrium, a desire for continuity deriving from this fear, and an instinct of preservation which is none other than the fear of losing itself. These various symptoms are inherent in the reign of the 'I-process' which has identified itself solely with its personal and distinct aspects.

Consciousness of self implies a duality, the objectivation of a subject which is reflected on an object distinct from itself or which it creates as such.

The absence of fixation removes any static or dynamic point of support. Finding no support or duality on to which to objectify itself, the Zen Unconscious escapes all our dualistic mental representations. By means of thought all that we grasp of the Zen Unconscious is that which it is no longer.

The mind, as a prisoner of its particular function, will always come up against the limits and forms which it has itself created.

Nevertheless a possibility exists of breaking this vicious circle which imprisons us.

While our ordinary consciousness bears the stamp of fixity of habits, *the Zen Unconscious is the dawning state above all else*. It is the state of perfect instantaneity, without duration, past, or future.

We could give it the characteristics admirably defined by Dr. Roger Godel:

'Consciousness is reborn as the fire of the sun is born each morning as it climbs over the horizon. This dawn is a point without dimension yet its fan, on opening, invisibly annihilates the shadows of the surrounding sky. So intense is the brilliance of this unique moment of consciousness that all feeling of duration vanishes; the past, memory, thought of the "I-process", and its future are consumed in the flame of the dawning state.

The web of time is rent. The sun is new each day, says Heraclitus. This intuition is correct. *To pure consciousness the instant lived is without duration because it is free from all incorporation with memory; it springs up in the heart of eternity, in the flash that reveals it.*

Each needle-point of dawning consciousness is new, a unique reality which could not be repeated, which could not be compared with any other' (*Expérience Libératrice*, p. 173).

A fairly simple comparison which has all the weaknesses of comparisons — especially in this domain — may suggest an intuitive vision of the Zen Unconscious. Let us not forget, however, that in order to conform strictly to the requirements of the fundamental nature of things, no imaginative activity can survive in the mind.

Having made these reservations we will compare the personal 'consciousness of self' to the water in a vase, and the Zen Unconscious to the unlimited waters of the infinite and unfathomable ocean. The sides of vase are formed by the accumulations of memory and the resistances set up by auto-identification. We know that all liquids exert pressure on the sides of the vase in

which they are. In the same way, consciousness, a prisoner of the
limitations and resistances created by identification with memories
exerts a certain pressure. It is 'under tension'. Such is the general
outline of the objectivation process. The pressure of water on the
sides of a vase explains by analogy the crucial factor of pure
consciousness which objectivizes itself while limiting itself and
which limits itself while objectivizing itself.

The process of Satori consists in smashing the sides of the vase
of the 'I-process'. From then on, there only remains the boundless
waters of an infinite ocean.

Consciousness of the 'I-process' is a result of an identification
with the apparently continuous and external succession of fleeting
moments. The realization of perfect instantaneity or Zen Unconscious is reached when we live each present moment to the
full, freed of past reminiscences which try to suggest to us the
external, and natural succession of phenomena.

The absence of sides and limits prevents all objectivization and
all possibility of perceiving oneself. Let us note, however, that the
water still remains. It is the principal, essential and eternally
dynamic element.

Humanity can be compared to two and a half thousand million
'pseudo-entities' enclosed in sealed vases. The total of memory-
accumulations being different for each individual, the 'walls' of
each vase are of dissimilar shape.

The 'pressures' of each individualized consciousness will therefore be different and will determine the characteristics of the
individual unicity.

The Zen Unconscious is realized from the moment of cessation
of identification of each particular consciousness with the portion
of water lying within the apparent limits of its 'vase'.

Certain authorities will say that in the spirit of the Zen masters
there is no 'vase' nor 'walls', nor 'particular pressures' and that
these elements belong to the 'mirage' of the 'I-process'.

The Zen masters do not deny the 'vases' or 'forms', but they
bid us free ourselves from identification with particular aspects.
When these identifications with particular forms cease the limits
of the ordinary consciousness of self vanish. Alone the Uncon-

scious remains in its infinitude. Let us not forget, however, that the breaking of the walls of the vase is a matter of secondary importance.

It is true that *for us* this breaking of the vase is important, but is not the content more important than the container?

CHAPTER XX

Characteristics of Satori
according to the Zen Masters

THE term 'Satori' corresponds to the Mahayana term 'paravritti'. It means 'awakening', 'turning over' of the mind or
conversion in the highest meaning of the word. This inner turning
over engenders a complete recasting of all the bases of thought,
for these depended on the reality of the 'I-process' before the
experience of revelation, and after Satori they undergo a considerable metamorphosis. It is a veritable psychological mutation
of thought which all the means available to ordinary intelligence
are incapable of expressing and analysing.

The fundamental characteristics of Satori are generally defined in the following manner:

(1) *Irrationality*

The experience of Satori is not the result of any rational process.
On the contrary, discursive activities, imaginative anticipations
and prefigurations are obstacles making unrealizable any authentic
Satori experience.

(2) *Intuitive Vision*

In Satori there is an element of intuitive vision which is beyond
all mental representation. It is a process of experience which transcends all the familiar dualities of 'spectacle and spectator' or
'vision of things seen and of subject who observes'. Satori is not
an annihilation.

During this experience we are delivered from the snares laid by
apparent distinctions of things and beings. We see them as they are
but are incapable of feeling any kind of attachment where they
are concerned.

As Professor D. T. Suzuki said:

'It is noteworthy that the knowledge contained in Satori is concerned with something universal and at the same time with the individual aspects of existence' (*Essays in Zen Buddhism*, vol. 2, p. 29).

Bodhi-Dharma for his part declared:

'As for my Satori, it is not a total annihilation, but knowledge of the most adequate kind; only it cannot be expressed in words.'

(3) Categorical Authority

By this the Zen masters mean that no authority whatsoever, no logical agent can refute the experience of Satori.

Referring to this, D. T. Suzuki writes:

'Satori is thus a form of inner perception, which takes place in [121] the most inward part of consciousness. Hence the sense of authoritativeness, which means finality.'

It should be noted here that the adversaries of Zen, or Buddhism and gnosticism in general, try to diminish the value of the experience by taxing it with subjectivity. They lose sight of the fact that the condition *sine qua non* of Satori is the elimination of all thought, all imagery, all memory-automatism of the past, briefly all that which forms the 'I-process'.

All that remains of the 'I-process' is that which lies within the apparent limits of the physical, corporeal form. But the latter is freed of all self-identification and attachment whatsoever. There is no longer any psychological, mental, and affective superimposition to corrupt the total adequacy of the instant.

So if Satori is realized in the heart of a 'pseudo-entity' whose superficial aspects are personal and finite, the essence of its inspiration, of its very reality, is drawn from the infinite and impersonal source in the depths. Only to inattentive and ill-informed minds can the experience of Satori appear to be subjective.

(4) Positive and creative sense

Though the living reality of Satori can only be defined negatively

[122] in relation to our habitual values and individual perceptions, it remains nevertheless the POSITIVE and CREATIVE FACT above all others. Our inability to define this fact — because of its very nature — is not sufficient reason to tax it with negativity or unreality. From the moment when we discern or effectively live the profound reality of beings and things we endow all our actions with a harmony and creativity which they could not have within the limits of egoism.

(5) *The sense of 'returning home'*

The realization of Satori brings with it simultaneously feelings of inner peace, security, rest and deliverance; and the tensions due to the craving to 'become' being absent, only the peace of the Being remains.

[123]   We have not acquired anything new, but we have been fully reavealed to ourselves. Such is the meaning of the expression 'Returning home' which is frequently used by the Zen masters, while reminding us that the 'home' is not static.

[124]   'Zen calls that to "return home". *You have found yourself now*; from the beginning nothing has been hidden from you: it was yourself who shut your eyes to reality' (Dr. H. Benoit — *Supreme Doctrine*, p. 31).

The fact that we are Reality, and that we have never ceased so to be, and that in consequence the realization is but liberation from a mirage, is frequently brought out in all works on Zen. Because a mirage is in a certain sense non-existent the fact of being delivered from it is — from the point of view of the Sage (and not of the layman) — non-existent. That is the deeper meaning of the following text which is an answer made by Zen master Hui Hai to his disciple:

'The knowledge that the mind is formless and intangible is the Law Body expressed in void. To understand the meaning of this is to know that there is no realization (of Nirvâna, etc.). The realization of the Supreme Body of the Buddha's Law lies in no attainment and no realization. If there were realization and attainment, those who considered themselves to have realized (Nirvâna) would be persons holding false views and arrogant (on account of their superiority) ... The Vimalakirti Sûtra says: "Sariputra asked Devakanya, 'What have you attained?' Devakanya answered, 'I have attained nothing and realized nothing to reach my present state. If I had attained anything, or realized anything, I should have to become a person arrogant in the Law'.'" (*The Path to Sudden Attainment*, p. 22).

That is why the Buddha himself said:

'I have truly obtained nothing from complete, unexcelled Enlightenment.'

(6) *Impersonal tone*

The experience of Satori is devoid of all personal character.

The essential reality which it allows one to experience is totally impersonal. Every perception is an occasion for Satori. Elsewhere we have gone into the details of this impersonality.

(7) *Feeling of exaltation*

The vision of boundless and infinite vision of Satori is in singular contrast with the cramped aspect of the limits of personal consciousness.

When the experience is effective it reveals itself by a considerable exteriorization of potentiality. The Zen masters avoid describing its modalities for obvious reasons. Nevertheless the true state of Satori delivers the intelligence and heart from the limitations which confined them. The pure lucidity, without idea, of the Zen Unconscious is more than a mere unit of vision. It is impregnated with an ineffable something which is beyond that which we call 'Love'. But, as we have explained elsewhere, this state of 'Love' is no longer separated from the pure homogeneity of Cosmic Mind. The state of 'Satori' reveals to man the plenitude of his existential felicity.

(8) *Instantaneity*

Zen masters also insist on the sudden and abrupt nature of Satori.

Professor D. T. Suzuki says the following about this:

'Satori comes upon us abruptly; it is an instantaneous experience. Therefore, if it is not abrupt and instantaneous, it is not Satori.'

It could not be otherwise, for Reality is from instant to instant. We have several times examined its upsurging, spontaneity, instantaneity and Eternal Presence.

Therefore the experience of Satori needs a complete liberation from the grip of the past, from all mental habits, and all attachment to our memories. Its intensity may be grasped from this remarkable passage by the writer Carlo Suarès (without any reference to Zen thought) in his *Comédie Psychologique*.

'If this "me" is not afraid of losing itself, of no longer having anywhere to lay its head, in short, when, pushed by the magnificent dynamism of absolute doubt, it is not afraid of disassociating itself from everything; of rejecting its old associations, and rejecting the new snares laid by the objects of the world in order to bind it to them; of destroying the new entity which is being rebuilt on the ruins of the crumbling entity, when this "me" transformed into an incandescent torch, mercilessly burns all that is itself then one day, *becoming supremely conscious* and no longer finding anything with which to associate, that which remains of it leaps all together into the eternal flame which consumes all, except the Eternal, and being dead as an entity, it is nothing but life.'

The perfect 'instantaneity' is a result of a continual psychological dissociation which delivers us from the clutches of our own past.

The sense of the 'I-process' and the notion of a static entity are strengthened the moment we fall into the trap of the chain of external phenomena.

By total presence of the Present and perfect instantaneity we cast off the memory-accumulations which isolate us by differentiating us continually.

CHAPTER XXI

Zen Buddhism and Everyday Life

125 $\mathbf{M}$OST writers agree on the fact that Zen is not to be understood but to be lived; and far from being incompatible with the requirements of everyday life, Zen confers on it its own full revealing value. There are no actions which we should consider as 'ordinary' in contrast to others which we regard as 'exceptional' or extraordinary. Zen asks us to bring to bear the intensity of an extraordinary attention in the midst of all so-called 'ordinary' circumstances. Reality is where we are from moment to moment. *The determining factor of our realization depends on the mental attitude in which we approach external and internal circumstances and phenomena.* The quality or kind of happening is secondary. Each incident of daily life, each perception of the concrete world, can be an occasion for 'Satori'.

We may recall the thought of a Zen master who insisted on the fact that the 'Infinite is in the finite of each instant.' This is how Professor D. T. Suzuki expresses it:

'*Mystics are thus all practical men*; they are far from being visionaries whose souls are too absorbed in things unearthly or of the **126** other world to be concerned with their daily life. The common notion that mystics are dreamers and star-gazers ought to be corrected, as it has no foundation in fact . . . If mysticism is true, its truth must a be practical one, verifying itself in every act of ours, and most decidedly, not a logical one, to be true only in our dialectics. Sings a Zen poet known as Hokoji:

> How wondrously supernatural,
> And how miraculous this!
> I draw water, and I carry fuel!'

Such a disposition of mind leads the Zen disciple on towards a more attentive technique of action during which thoughts, words and gestures tend to take on a character of full responsibility which destiny has a right to expect of human nature.

In Zen monasteries the monks participate in manual work and perform various mundane tasks, but they are required to accomplish them to perfection.

Amongst the practical advantages of the Zen attitude we will mention perfect objectivity, constructive activity, perfect adequacy, compassionate detachment, rapidity of the reflexes in relaxation and eternal inner youth.

(1) *Perfect objectivity*

It is generally admitted that all errors of judgment, blunders, 'failures' come from a too subjective inner attitude impregnated with attachment, cravings and personal passions.

Buddhism in general and Zen in particular prompts an attitude of wide-awakeness and constant vigilance, in which the 'force of habit' of the 'I-process' gives way to the state of pure and impersonal lucidity of 'Cosmic Mind'.

In so far as we die to ourselves and become no longer anything but an impersonal centre of pure perception, we have a consciousness of beings and things which is no longer misrepresented by preferences or personal dislikes.

Intense and silent observation, far from all preconceived ideas, from memory-projections of the past, gives us the possibility of approaching the content of each new instant in a manner that is totally adequate to its requirements.

From the moment at which our thought dissociates itself from the history of its own past, it is no longer only *'our'* thought in the same way that 'our' intelligence is no longer *only* in such a circumstance 'our' intelligence.

When the mind is freed from the hold of its memory-habits it realizes a state of extraordinary flexibility and sensibility in which it experiences the plenitude of its natural power of penetration.

In this particular perspective the clear vision of the mind is sufficient unto itself. A man living such a process is *freed from choice*.

Perfect objectivity is attained in the state without choice.

[127] All choice implies a preference, and all preference conditions the freedom of movement of the mind. Zen suggests an impersonal objectivity of a superior kind of which we can give a concrete example.

Moreover this has already been used by several authorities: we should observe all that is presented to us in an accurate, impersonal and objective manner as would a camera perfectly adjusted.

Let us suppose for a moment that we are looking in the window of a large store where a multitude of articles and great variety of objects are displayed.

If we are biologists or astronomers, our attention is immediately drawn to the microscope or telescope which lies amongst a number of other objects. If a child is with us, he will only have eyes for the doll or electric train while we would not have noticed them. Unnoticed by any of us a choice has been effected with the speed of lightning. It is a result of our memory-associations. The sight of certain objects or people spontaneously causes preferential reactions in our memory-associations which are determined by the privileged progress of our thought. Once again we have come across the action of force of habit.

Zen suggests, as does Krishnamurti also that we look in this shop-window in an impersonal manner as a camera would. Nothing escapes the lens of a perfectly focused camera. It does not *choose*.

We are forgetting that the preferential attention given to one object is made to the detriment of that which might be given to others. The impersonality and absence of choice in the attention

[128] which Zen suggests that we realize, second after second during daily life, raises human existence to its highest degree of efficiency and gives it the character of supreme wide-awakeness.

(2) *Constructive activity*

That which has been said above not only shows the practical aspect of Zen, but also its constructive aspect.

[129] 'Nirvâna and Samsara' are one and the same thing, Zen masters

tell us. Everything is 'Cosmic Mind'. Matter is spiritual and spirit is material. It follows therefore that any new inner attitude tends irresistibly to materialize in action on the external plane. The riches of the mind should express themselves in matter and by matter.

The 'I-process' being dead to itself, the actions it accomplishes are no longer specifically its own. If the external gestures by which they are expressed are similar to those which it has made hitherto, the deeper motives behind these gestures will no longer convey the forces of habit of the egoism. The 'apparent' actions of the 'I-process' are now an expression of Life that is perfectly adequate to the particular circumstances. These actions are therefore eminently constructive and positive.

Any action which bears the imprint of the avidity of the 'I-process', its instinct for possession and domination, is a negative and incomplete action. It can only engender slavery, misery and conflict both for the individual and the community.

An eminently positive and constructive action is that in which the fullness of life is expressed at the very instant of its emergence. It is sufficient unto itself. It requires nothing and awaits nothing. It is [130] just such a discrete, silent and anonymous process which sustains the whole Universe, from the infinitely small world of the atom to the distant nebulae of the infinitely great.

We can seize it within ourselves in the full power of its plenitude from the moment the tensions of avidity cease.

Our difficulty lies in the fact that the tensions of our avidities are generally situated in the deep zones of our unconscious. We often think that we are relaxed and perfectly present to the present, when in fact a host of tensions and secret aspirations remain buried in the innermost recesses of our mind. Therefore our actions are never fully lived, for they perpetually bear the imprint of a secret call and of a subtle anticipation.

We will quote an important passage from D. T. Suzuki which confirms what has just been said.

'Life delineates itself on the canvas called time, and time never repeats; once gone, forever gone; *and so is* an act once done, it is never undone. Life is a sumiye-painting which must be executed once and for all time and without hesitation, without intellection, and no corrections are permissible or possible. Life is not like an oil-painting, which can be rubbed out and done over time and again until the artist is satisfied. With a sumiye-painting any brush-stroke painted over a second time results in a smudge; the life has left it. All corrections show when the ink dries. So is life. *We can never retract what we have committed to deeds; Zen therefore ought to be caught while the thing is going, neither before nor after. It is an act of one instant. This fleeting, unrepeatable and ungraspable character of life is delineated graphically by Zen masters who have compared it to lightning or sparks produced by the percussion of stones.*

The idea of direct method appealed to by the masters *is to get hold of this fleeting life as it flees and not after it has flown'* (D. T. Suzuki, *Essays in Zen Buddhism*, vol. I, p. 298).

Amongst the positive and constructive elements of Zen we will also mention correct attention, the elimination of imaginative dreams.

Those in the West who hastily accuse Buddhism of dreaminess lose sight of the fact that the true dreamers are not precisely those of whom they are thinking. The true dreamers are those who are literally 'possessed' by their agitations, their desires, their passions and the disordered fantasies of their imaginations. Such is the situation of nearly all present-day men who pride themselves on their realism and positive sense. Most of their actions arise from confusion and total irresponsibility.

¹³¹ Into this great inner disorder Zen suggests that we bring a measure of order and clarity by bidding us be less agitated, more concentrated and more attentive. The practice of 'Correct Vision' consists in devoting ourselves entirely to the work which falls to us. We should be totally present to that which we are doing without any intervention of the imagination.

This was the meaning of the answer given by a Zen master to a pupil when the latter asked him the secret of the method which had led him to 'Satori'. The Master answered: 'When I am hungry I eat, when I am tired I rest.' The pupil, surprised and disappointed with such a paradoxical answer replied in his turn: 'But everyone eats when he is hungry, and rests when he is tired.' ... 'No', answered the Master, 'when you eat, you are not attending to what you eat, and when you lie down you are not attending to your rest; your mind is elsewhere, and your imaginative activities are given free rein. When you are hungry, you do not eat. ...'

We can see immediately that an active life, far from being incompatible with Zen thought, offers on the contrary, an extraordinarily fertile field of experience. The essential of Zen thought consists, as we have said elsewhere, in suppressing mental activity which comes between us and the facts. Contemplative life deprives us of continual contacts and unexpected frictions between the external events and ourselves, and moreover it tends to develop in most people certain subtle forms of mental activity that are particularly harmful and which can result in auto-hypnosis. Among many contemplatives a marked schism is established between mind and matter, between the abstract and the concrete. Zen, on the other hand, is essentially a return to the concrete.

The intensity and frequency of experience arising from modern life do not only have their undoubted negative side: they may allow some people to realize the validity of their inner experiences.

We can live in the world while remaining free from the attachment which generally binds those who are slaves to the outer appearances of the world. The great art is to play the game of Life without identifying ourselves with the evanescent masks of form, for only when we are freed from forms can we appreciate the hidden Reality which they express.

(3) *Perfect adequacy*

Perfect adequacy consists of an attitude of attentive, vigilant and impersonal lucidity, which permits an adequate response to all circumstances occurring on any plane. When our mind is filled with an idea to which it feels an attachment we find ourselves unable to respond completely to the requirements of a given moment.

For as long as we tackle *actual* facts while thinking what similar facts in the *past* have done to us, we shall be incapable of grasping the exact relationship between these new facts and ourselves in their actuality. This relationship changes continually because, though the facts presented seem identical, the observer who perceives them is being transformed continually. Moreover, each instant has a unique character; it has never been and never will be again that which it is. Zen insists very much on this character of unicity in our relationship with circumstances during each instant. In trying to solve the problem of the present moment by basing ourselves on acquired knowledge of the past we are literally killing creative life. We are letting the 'force of habit' work in us, and this cuts us off from the Real.

Hsi-Yun says in his doctrine:

'When everything within and without, bodily and mental, has been relinquished; when there are left absolutely no objects of attachment, as in the void; when all action is dictated purely by place and circumstance and the concepts of subjectivity and objectivity no longer held – that is the highest form of relinquishment' (*Huang-Po Doctrine of Universal Mind*, p. 36).

We can give a fairly simple example to illustrate what we have just said. If, while driving a car, we are preoccupied by family, business or emotional worries, we will not have sufficiently swift reflexes to avoid an unexpected obstacle.

Perfect adequacy requires us to be both fully and impersonally attentive to circumstances. That is where the difficulty lies. In so far as we are fully attentive we have a tendency to attach ourselves to objects, things or beings to which our attention has been directed. Only the process of Life with its contacts, frictions, frustrations, can reveal to us through the severity of the experience just undergone the way to detachment and dispossession which will lead us to the highest accomplishment of our nature.

Perfect adequacy teaches us to transcend ourselves in order to respond to the inner requirements of the beings around us without, however, binding ourselves to them by means of some kind of attachment.

The mind which has been freed from attachment and the static tendencies of habit, conceals extraordinary flexibility and agility, and returns to its eternal norm which is pure Liberty. The realization of such an inner attitude gives us a superior sensibility, which helps us to understand others better, and to love them more, as they are and not as we would like them to be. This sensibility turns us towards a new attitude which is imbued with a higher form of forbearance.

Perfect adequacy reveals the pure existential felicity which is inherent in the most impersonal heights of Love.

(4) 'Compassionate' detachment

Zen substitutes an atmosphere of relaxation, serenity and simplicity for the tensions created by our strivings to 'become', to possess and to dominate.

By analogy certain images may help us to understand the notion of 'letting go', proposed by the Zen masters.

When we raise a heavy burden our muscles are stretched in the effort until we feel tired. The moment the burden is put down our muscular fatigue disappears and is replaced by the euphoria of relaxation. In fact we are in a state of continuous psychic tension. Our mental musculature is contracted by the fundamental avidity of the 'I-process' (Tanha). This mental musculative is stretched, tensed to the utmost by our desires and fears. This 'I-process' is a 'becoming', and this 'becoming' inevitably implies the *tensions* inherent in the *efforts* realized in order to reach what we deem desirable to become.

The moment we become aware of the falseness of such an attitude we 'let go', and the suffering inherent in our inner tensions are succeeded by the felicity and relaxation of *Being*.

True detachment is not the result of spiritual discipline.

If we simply reject, by an act of will, things and beings for which we feel attachment, we are merely evading the problem, for the Sage would ask us immediately: 'Who is rejecting this or that?' We should recognize that, subjacent to the alternative processes of attachment and detachment, the permanence of an 'I-process' remains secretly which, far from excluding itself, feeds essentially on our oppositions.

'Compassionate' detachment cannot come about through *choice* on the part of the 'I-process' but from a non-mental comprehension of the illusion of its very existence.

When resistances, the avidities of accumulations of the 'I-process' cease, the nature of things is revealed in the plenitude of its riches.

The man who has realized Satori has not decided to be detached, but, being intensely aware of the infinite riches of his nature, he can no longer be attached to anything. He can no longer feel desire or attachment because his awakening has revealed to him that *he is at the heart of the beings and things of the whole Universe, at the heart of that which is most precious and irreplaceable in these beings* [132] *and things. In other words, affective detachment is not a means, it is a consequence.*

The Zen masters teach us that one should not train oneself in meditation or detachment. They only formulate one requirement: that of a vigilance, an attention, a wide-awakeness of every moment, because the flame of life lies in the heart of each passing second.

Humanity could be compared to two and a half thousand million greyhounds rushing in pursuit of a mechanical hare on a vast race-track. These 'human greyhounds' are taut, over-tense, avid and violent, but Zen tries to teach them that what they think is a real hare is only a mechanical hoax. The moment man fully realizes what is implied by this truth he 'lets go', and the bitterness of his struggles and violence are succeeded by relaxation, peace, harmony and love.

The consequences of such a release are immense, not only for the physical, nervous and mental health of man as an individual, but also for humanity as a whole.

Such are the essential bases of effective non-violence, compassion and kindliness as taught by Buddhism in general and Zen in particular.

(5) *Rapidity of the reflexes in relaxation*

We all know that in most animals fear paralyses their instinctive reflexes. That which is true for animals applies also to man from certain points of view. Most of the mistakes we make, as well as our indiscretions and blunders arise directly or indirectly from our fear and greed.

When the mind has 'let go' and is free from the 'tensions' of becoming, the body and the nervous system both undergo an extremely beneficial transformation. Recent progress in psycho-somatics has shown the important modifications occurring in the degree of alkalinity of the blood and in divers hormonal secretions as a result of our emotional states.

Relaxation of the body along with relaxation and silence of the mind can be coupled with the highest lucidity, both mental and physical.

What strikes us when we observe authentically integrated be-ings, or men who have 'realized' themselves, is the astonishing adequacy to circumstances which they reveal at all times, and the extraordinary agility with which they can at certain moments take action themselves in order to avert a danger threatening others. There is a striking difference between this attitude and that revealed in Hindu Samadhis, for in most of the latter the acuity of inner contemplation tends to dissassociate the mystic from the external universe and to make them oblivious to the world.

Such is the case of the 'Nirvikalpa Samadhi', a mystical ecstasy during which the worshipper is literally ravished from the outside world and is subjected to the exclusively unilateral domination of the pure essence.

Perfect adequacy is only realized in the Sahaja Samadhi which is the state of contemplation or pure vision in the waking state. In this state consciousness on the material plane persists parallel with an awakening in the highest spheres of 'cosmic mind'.

Moreover from that instant distinctions between one and the other are non-existent.

Attention, though external and concrete is *involuntarily* carried to its highest point. This does not diminish in any way the [133] authentically cosmic state of being, but is on the contrary a result of its realization.

This attitude confers rapidity on the reflexes in relaxation. The body finds again its natural and instinctive wisdom, which is no longer perverted by false mental values, but spontaneously obeys the requirements of its highest nature.

The rapidity of the reflexes in relaxation facilitates our adaptability to the needs of an active life. Without it we would literally lose our foot-hold as a result of the precipitation of the changing circumstances in which we become involved. It arises from our presence in the Present, our vigilance of every moment, and the impersonality of an observation without choice.

(6) *Simplification of needs*

Amongst the direct consequences of effective experience of Zen, we should mention progressive simplification of existence.

The discovery of our true nature, or even approach to the inexhaustible riches which it conceals, delivers us from most of our needs such as possessions, worldly vanities and thirst for varied enjoyments.

In so far as we are capable of discovering the hidden treasure which lies in our own depths, as in the depths of all things, the external values tend to lose their attraction. By this we should not jump hastily to conclusions regarding the anti-social character of the integrated man or of the man who is on the way to such a state.

An anti-social man is one whose fundamental egoism only engenders passions, violence, possessiveness, jealousy, domination and continual demands.

When we are 'dying' to ourselves these various sources of misery, conflict and suffering dry up automatically.

Again we should point out that *the simplification of needs is not a means but a consequence.*

How far should this be applied? What are the minimum or

maximum needs appropriate to each person? No one can define them or draw up a system around them. That is where we should exercise our judgment, these problems force us to the 'Use of the Great Body' of which the Zen masters speak; and this Use depends for each one of us on the place and circumstances. If we were to codify the laws concerning it they might soon become a great bondage for us.

The keenness of perception inherent in 'correct' attention automatically mobilizes a considerable quantity of nervous and psychic energies. This process spontaneously brings about the transmutation of part of the sexual energies whose demands become less imperious. The inner transformation is also expressed by similar modifications in the alimentary domain. The intensity of perception and vigilance of the mind required in correct attention are incompatible with too copious and rich a diet.

These concrete details show us that there is no so-called spiritual problem which is distinct from daily behaviour. The absence of needs and the simplification of life are expressed as much in mind as in matter, since these two aspects are linked by a fundamental unity.

(7) Eternal youth

True youth is much more psychological than physical.

We can see people who biologically are young, but who psychologically are characterized by a lack of inner life which is akin to death.

In so far as we are freed from the 'force of habit' we accede to the creative dynamism of an intense inner life. The controlling factors of psychological ageing are routine, sterile repetition of identical habits and the accentuation of divers forms of egoism.

When the illusion of the 'I-process' is unmasked all our desires, mental routines and memory-automatisms disappear. We are renewed from instant to instant. Each day is veritable re-birth to us, for every morning we awaken freed from the grip of the innumerable yesterdays of our existence. We begin again at zero, and we leave behind all danger of mental fossilization. We are freed from our fundamental fear by virtue of which we were clinging to our inner certainties and carefully protected routines of thought. The atmosphere of anxiety of the past, with its unjustified fears, gives way to the infinitely serene confidence of Reality Itself.

From then life takes on for us spontaneity and freshness. Each second seems to beat the rhythms of an eternal spring. The heart, freed from its bonds, vibrates in the limitless plenitude of a state beyond Love. In this plenitude of perpetual resurgence there will be discovered the ineffable charm of eternal youth.

CHAPTER XXII

The Inadequacies

THE inadequacies are the attitudes of mind which hinder us from seeing the profound nature of our being and of things, and which therefore render us incapable of responding adequately to the demands of varied circumstances and situations arising in the course of our lives.

Amongst them we shall draw attention particularly to false methods of concentration, processes of imitation and attachment.

(1) *False methods of concentration*

A whole literature popularizing yoga upholds the merit of mental concentration. Certain writers, having understood the need for inner calm, propose that we immobilize the continuous procession of our thoughts by an act of will. They advise us to fix our minds on one point to the exclusion of all others. Some compare the process of concentration with the action of a magnifying glass which causes the sun's rays to converge on one single point, thus setting fire to any inflammable material. Others propose the systematic rejection of images rising in our mind and aspire towards a complete vacuity.

All these practises should be condemned, for they lead nowhere except to disequilibrium and inner death.

When mental activity is disciplined as a result of an act of will a considerable state of psychic tension is engendered. Such a proceeding is doubly wrong.

Firstly, the Sage would ask us 'Who disciplines this or that?' And we shall have to recognize that it is the 'pseudo-entity' of the 'I-process' that is resorting to such a stratagem in order to affirm itself. The 'I-process' is a fact, but, as it is perceived, it is an illusion. Any action undertaken in such an attitude of psychological illusion only strengthens the illusory notion of the 'I-process' having a separate existence.

Secondly, the essential process which Wisdom suggests, consists in a liberation from all our inner tensions. We have nothing to build, but we have to destroy. The state of tension caused by the false methods of concentration which we have just described prevents all possibility of spiritual realization. Satori or Nirvâna demands from us a certain receptivity, an availability, an inner transparence and a complete relaxation. The methods of concentration presented in most systems of Yoga, and by certain Buddhist writers are radically opposed to the correct attitude. All discipline arising out of an act of will makes us incapable of 'dying to ourselves' and strengthens the 'forces of habit' from which it is essential that we free ourselves.

If, then, we examine the attitude of the man who systematically rejects the images arising in his mind, we will see that it also is false.

The true masters have never said that anything whatever is to be 'rejected', and they would immediately pose the classical question of the Hindu advaitists: 'Who' rejects? We would then have to admit that, beyond the successive oppositions of our rejections and acquisions, an 'I-process' remains which draws its sustenance from the tensions inherent in these oppositions themselves.

It is not a question of *rejecting* anything whatsoever, but of *understanding profoundly* the process of one's own existence. This deep understanding, or 'Correct Vision', frees the 'thinker' from the illusion of being an entity. From that moment all his disciplines, achievements, ambitions and avidities disappear and are replaced by the vision of the Real. The Sages have pointed out that all rejection is the result of an act of choice, and that by the process of choosing, the 'I-process' cannot be freed from its limitations. It is simply transformed and takes on other aspects. The Sages clearly denounce the stratagem: the 'I-process' is preserved throughout its successive modifications. Wisdom consists in unmasking the deeper motives of egoistic avidity which govern all acts of choosing.

(2) *The processes of imitation*

By processes of imitation we mean all physical or mental conformisms that tend to condition the human mind. By adhering to a particular system of thought, beliefs and dogmas, we are conditioning our minds. The great strength of Zen on the one hand, and of the Krishnamurtian stand-point on the other, lies in the fact that they are not systems of thought, but statements of a way of living freed of all ideation.

A world of difference exists between the attitude of the Christian who gives himself to the keeper of his conscience, the Hindu [134] who submits to the instructions of his 'guru', and the strictly individual process of auto-revelation proposed by Zen. In the first two examples we are faced with practices of imitation which are as harmful as can be on account of the serious damage they do to the spiritual integrity of the subject, which latter requires emancipation from all outside authority and above all from any kind of conformism.

The cult of images, symbols and mental clichés of all kinds falls within the framework of imitative practice.

In proportion to their fervour, Christian mystics who meditate on an image of the Virgin, end by falling into a self-hypnosis during which they contemplate not the virgin, but a materialization of their own mental projection. The same can be said for those Buddhists who concentrate with fervour on a given image of the Buddha.

All fixing of thought on an image, symbol, or any idea, gives rise to phenomena which are not a cause for rejoicing as many seekers, whose sincerity is in no way to be doubted, seem to suppose. A study of the inner life of certain Sages shows us the struggle which they had to endure against images whose cult they had cherished hitherto. The part played by 'japas', which are very current in India and extolled by both Hindu and Western writers, is also negative.

The act of pronouncing indefinitely certain identical syllables chosen by the master, and often differing for each disciple, leads to a kind of magnetic torpor akin to auto-hypnosis. It is a question there of real mental intoxications ending in minor ecstasies which have no relationship with real spirituality. They are more harmful on the spiritual plane than alcohol, drugs and narcotics could be on the physical plane. It is urgently necessary loudly to insist on the spiritual degeneracy of these practices for very reason of the success which attends their easy realization. It is inconceivable that serious people, or supposedly serious people should use such puerile procedures in the secret hope of a spiritual realization, for this can only be achieved in so far as we have thrown off the influence of such narcotics. It is an awakening and not a state of torpor caused by some inner or outer magic practice.

The imitative processes do not only cover the adherence to images or ideas suggested by others, but the whole of the memory-habits of the past, and, consequently, the accumulations in our own minds.

By way of example we could mention the inner attitude of the reader enraptured by the notion of 'Cosmic Mind' or that of a universal unity of essence. This enthusiasm would automatically lead him to the effective experience of reality whose grandeur and authenticity he had intuitively already felt. But let us suppose that such a man decides to turn to nature and try to find in a more suitable place that which he has glimpsed in a flash. It is most likely that he will feel again all that which appears before him as bathed in 'Cosmic Mind'.

It may be that he thinks of the presence of the 'Cosmic Mind' in the earth of the path he is treading, in the air he breathes, or hear it through and beyond the singing of the birds and the whispering of the wind in the trees. If he persists in such an attitude sooner or later he will see that he has come to a dead end. *For as long as he has the idea of 'Cosmic Mind', memory-automatisms intervening every moment between him and the circumstances, calling everything 'Cosmic Mind', he will be unable to reach effectively the actual experience of the Real.* The mental image of the Real which he has unconsciously built up in his mind will perpetually come between him and Reality.

[135]   The experience will only take on its full authenticity when: (1) it has been freed from memory-automatisms which 'name' the states; (2) the absence of any expectation of any kind whatsoever has freed his mind from the tensions which oppose its perfect plasticity.

Silent observation, lucidity without ideation, attention without 'verbal thought', vigilance in the moment, are the fundamental elements of 'Correct Vision'.

By means of their denunciation of the harmful role of the 'forces of habit', the processes of gross or subtle imagery, the higher forms of Buddhism and Zen allow human nature to develop its highest creative possibilities.

(3) *The attachments*

By attachments we do not only refer to psychological attachments, such as the dependence in which we find ourselves in respect to particular persons or certain objects, but also attachment to ourselves. This means attachment as much to our own thoughts as to our bodies.

In so far as we lean on others we are evading the central reality of our being, and we are turning away from the Real. Attachment [136] to particular beings or definite objects prevents us from experiencing the real nature of things. All fixing of the mind on a particular point implies a mobilization of energy to the detriment of the vision of the whole. The localization of our psychical energies round a privileged point tends to limit us to the specialization of an exclusive perception. The experience of the real only surges up in us when our mind is freed from attachment to all preferences, distinct perceptions, particular values and all points of privilege.

A true mental despecialization is in question.

We should add that this does not lead to any incoherence, nor amorphous rhythm of inner life steeped in monotony. Transcendence of points of privilege and detachment from beings and particular objects, especially on the emotional plane, should not be confused with the mortal inertia of a glacial indifference. We have pointed out elsewhere that detachment is not indifference. The higher forms of love and compassion are realized solely in detachment from the egoistical demands of the 'I-process'.

Finally amongst the obvious attachments of the 'I-process' we will mention identification with the body.

A certain control over the body is necessary in order that the riches of the mind may be expressed. Undue sexual and alimentary indulgence renders impossible acuity of spiritual perception.

The different points on which we have laid emphasis, such as the influence of memory-automatisms and secret inner expectations, require in order to be perceived clearly, a vigilance, a flexibility and an acuity of perception that are incompatible with a lack of control of the body's demands.

Many Buddhist monasteries attach great importance to discipline where eating is concerned. In certain brotherhoods the monks only eat once a day, at noon; and they are strictly forbidden to eat in the evening. Others can never eat after sunset. The reasons are obvious. Because of the inter-connection between physical and psychic factors late meals hinder the normal process of sleep, not only from the physiological point of view but above all from the psychological.

Digestion being a question of nerves, the nervous energy mobilized by the assimilation of a heavy meal at night reduces the possibility of psychological receptivity and true rest during sleep. The nervous system is in fact the only intermediary between the physical and the psychic.

The triumph over the attachment to our bodily demands is one of the first indispensable materializations which prelude our complete liberation.

(4) Meditation 'in compartments'

137   We mean by 'meditation in compartments' the exercise of meditation at set hours which many men of religion practice at certain times of the day. This process tends to establish a scission between 'ordinary' life and so-called 'spiritual' life.

138   The plenitude of life is here from instant to instant, and we should seize it at the heart of every passing second by means of vigilant attention.

The process of meditation 'in compartments' leads to serious deviations with the drawback of over-estimating our real possibilities.

In fact if we train ourselves in contemplation we may obtain divers anterior joys through certain cultivated experiences.

We often give full rein to the projections unleashed by our unconscious which correspond to forms and tendencies arising from our hidden desires. As daily life never offers such a total adequacy to the fantasies of our 'I-process', we tend to tackle it by constraint and force, with ill will. We allow ourselves to enjoy in anticipation the few instants of meditation during which our imagination, unleashed, carries us over the incidents of the outside world. In this way we sink slowly into a process of evasion and auto-hypnosis which acts as a veritable spiritual narcotic.

Zen masters insist much on the constant nature of meditation. Hsi-Yun advises us as follows:

'Every day, in between walking, standing, sitting or lying, and in all your speech, exhibit no attachment to things of the phenomenal sphere. Whether you speak, or merely blink an eye, let everything you do be utterly dispassionate (Huang-Po, *Doctrine of Universal Mind*, p. 4).

Another Zen master, Shen-Hui, upbraided his disciple Teng for the artificiality of his 'prepared' meditations.

Teng: 'First of all it is necessary to practise meditation by quietly sitting cross-legged. . . .'

Shen-Hui: '*When one is engaged in meditation is there not a specifically contrived exercise?*'

Teng: 'It is so.' [139]

Shen-Hui: 'If so, this specific contrivance is an act of limited consciousness, and how could it lead to the seeing of one's self-nature . . .? This exercising in meditation owes its function ultimately to an erroneous way of viewing the truth; and as long as this is the case, exercises of such nature would never issue in (true) meditation' (Suzuki, *Zen Doctrine of No-Mind*).

It is important to bear in mind that one does not 'train' for Satori. Training can be useful in material or technical fields; one goes 'into training' for boxing, football, fencing or tennis . . . It is even possible 'to train' in order to pass an examination on mathematics or history. In these fields a preparation or accumulation of facts is necessary.

¹⁴⁰   But each type of work needs the right tools; strong heavy work needs strong heavy tools, and delicate light work needs delicate refined instruments. The idea of spiritual 'training' implies something 'gross and heavy' in contrast with the quality of lightness, spontaneity and freedom appertaining to 'Satori'.

Most of the Zen masters insist on the sudden nature of Satori.
¹⁴¹ In meditating we are consciously or unconsciously in an attitude of secret expectation. In other words we are putting ourselves into a state of receptivity, but this preparation is stamped with a subtle avidity and with prefiguration, and is too conscious of itself.

Satori arrives unexpectedly, with a spontaneous up-surging that is incompatible with painstaking preparation. Its spiritual explosion can only penetrate a completely relaxed mind freed from expectations and secret hopes.

The advantage of continuous meditation, inseparable from life itself, lies in the inner relaxation which it brings to whomsoever practices it. In the beginning the results are less spectacular, but they are more in accord with the nature of things. If they are slower they last longer, like the processes of nature.

There is no particular instant that deserves more attention than any other. Eternity is there, in its entirety, from moment to moment.

Therefore we should be present to the Present, from moment to moment without any preference.

(5) *Erroneous interpretations of the 'Void'*

As we have already several times pointed out, the notion of the 'Void' often gives rise to confusion. There are many who interpret it literally and try to realize 'emptiness of mind' by means of intense concentration. Such vacuity is absolutely negative and does not contain any possibilities of revelation.

Mental activity is part of the processes of life. *So the aim should not be to suppress it but to assign it a different method of functioning which shall be in keeping with the profound nature of things.*

Mental functions, as they are, are inadequate because of their identifications and attachments. 'Void' should be understood as the absence of false values arising from attachment and identification. All other interpretation can lead to serious errors. Moreover this attitude is confirmed by the commentaries in the doctrine of Hsi-Yun:

'Just making the slight response suitable to the occasion . . . So many people, including a large number of Chinese Buddhists, *have made the mistake of supposing that Dhyana practice aims at making the mind a complete blank.* This doctrine has been thoroughly refuted by Yeh Ch'i, a contemporary monk now living in Yunnan, who points to the obvious fact that *a state of blankness cannot be* maintained permanently . . . The aim of Dhyana *is to eliminate from mental process all feelings of attachment or revulsion which arises from the belief that things have independent and permanent entities of their own. Permanent blankness of mind would lead to many absurdities,* such as having to be forcibly fed by a nurse, and would probably end in lunacy. According to the Dhyana Buddhists, however, it is possible to react to the circumstances of daily life in a way which will enable one to deal with them satisfactorily *while remaining entirely dispassionate and fundamentally unaffected by them* (Huang-Po, *Doctrine of Universal Mind,* p. 49).

The divers forms of the 'Void', obtained through concentration and by discipline of the 'I-process' are a kind of *refusal of life,* imbued with an element of self-defence and evasion when faced with the problems of existence. To flee is to solve nothing, and the true solution of our problems can only be found by facing them instead of running away.

(6) *Lack of discernment*

The most striking example of the contradictions inherent in the lack of discernment has been furnished by theologians.

While admitting that the 'deity infinitely surpasses any tangible image' and that in order that we may see it 'it has to show itself *without any intermediary*', (1) the Church not only sets itself up as an intermediary but also claims the exclusiveness of the role and imposes adherence to dogmas, beliefs and ritual which constitute the absolute negation of the essential truths it seems otherwise to admit.

112   We have also seen St. Thomas recognize that the gift of intelligence 'while not helping us to see the divine essence, it does show us what it is not'. (2) Then he says that 'we on earth know God all the more perfectly in that we understand that he is beyond everything our mind could grasp'. Why, therefore, not only propose but also impose on young minds from their tenderest years a set of notions and attributes which will henceforward paralyse all possibility of
113   approach to the divine.

When we pose such questions to those who are inured to the obscure disciplines of theology we find the answers to our queries in their reactions. The clarity of the direct, non-mental experience is absent, and its place has been taken by intellectual speculation and adroit interpretation of the texts.

The exact place of the division between the living reality itself and the evermore erroneous interpretations given by contemporary theology *is to be found at the very root of the mind.* Once again we understand the full significance of the Zen thought which says 'A tenth of an inch's difference and Heaven and Earth are set apart.' The slightest lack of attention, the faintest lack of discernment lead us imperceptibly on the fatal downward path of false values.

If we say that the 'people' cannot rise to these abstract teachings, that they need concrete symbols, we are making a somewhat serious mistake.

Firstly, Zen is not an 'abstract teaching', for it is essentially practical and on the contrary tends to clear our minds of all abstraction. Secondly, we would be admitting to a disquieting state of degeneration of present-day civilization in comparison with that existing between the time of Buddha's death and the coming of Christianity. In fact history has shown that at the time of the Buddha and of Asoka the pure teachings of the doctrine were easily understood by the people.

Therefore it is through a lack of judgment and as a result of a form of cowardice that the organizers of most of the great religions have encouraged the mental laziness of the 'masses' by trying to lower Truth to their level instead of doing everything to raise the people to the heights of the pure teachings proclaimed by the Masters.

The strength of the position of Buddhism in general and Zen in particular lies precisely in their freedom from metaphysical speculations. The term 'God' is non-existent in the divers forms of Buddhism. Only 'Cosmic Mind' exists, of which all beings are an integral part. This Reality is self-sufficient, and its realization within ourselves, and by ourselves, delivers us from all lack of discernment.

CHAPTER XXIII

Buddhism and Social Problems

THE events of the twentieth century have proclaimed more eloquently than any speeches the failure of the social, economic, political and religious systems. Innumerable economists, sociologists and moralists, of all schools of thought, have tried to find a remedy and have drawn up plans, but the sickness of the world has only worsened. International conferences multiply their sessions with a futility which would make us smile if it were not so tragic. At a time when the criminal explosions of atomic and thermo-nuclear bombs threaten the whole of the planet it is of the greatest urgency to establish healthier bases for a new civilization.

Twenty centuries of Western culture resulted in a civilization of which egoism and money are the masters. If modern man has supersonic aeroplanes, television sets, radar, electronic brains, etc., he also has the weapons for his own destruction. Some, however, will point out that the legal edifice has evolved in two thousand years, and that the technical progress has developed at a dizzy speed. Perhaps in this lies one of the fundamental causes of the present drama, for there is a considerable disparity between technical and moral development. Modern man, as a certain Dutch philosopher pointed out, is only a refined barbarian.

By a 'barbarian' we mean all men in whom the avidities of the 'I-process', and the violence arising from them, are in the fullness of their expression.

These are precisely the qualities which are active in the individual, the constitutive element of the world.

All our social, religious and moral structures are based on the reality of the 'I-process' whose expression in all domains they encourage. Such is the fundamental drama of so-called 'Christian' civilization.

Were the absolute reality of the 'I-process' to be assumed as the point of departure it is inevitable that it affirm itself with the violence and cruelty of which we are suffering the consequences in the tragic events of the present time.

In radical opposition to the above, the basic idea of Buddhism is the impermanence of the 'I-process' and of all things.

With such an outlook it is inevitable that Buddhist civilizations display this highly pacific attitude and are free from most of the civil disputes from which the present-day nations have suffered and still endure.

The fundamental notion of the impermanence of the 'I-process' leads man to an attitude of detachment, both from himself and from outer things. The appetites, greed for gain, violence and spirit of conquest and domination were completely absent among the peoples who lived under the influence of Buddhism between the fifth and second centuries B.C. Moreover the notion of the impermanence of the 'I-process' has as a direct counter-part, that of fundamental natural unity, by which distinctions, separations between beings and things, take on a secondary importance. This vision of unity is expressed by an infinite respect for life in all its forms, whether animal or human, and is responsible for a kindliness, true clarity of outlook and unfailing forbearance.

It is obvious that the moment an individual becomes aware of the impermanence of his 'I-process', and of all things, he will turn towards a way of life which is free of cravings and the innumerable desires which still clutter up the mind of modern man. History has convincingly shown what can be achieved by a civilization that is truly pacific because not based on the 'I-process'. No one can deny the eminently social character of Buddhism. It is the only religion which has never started a war, because, if avidity and egoism are removed from the heart of man as an individual, these negative tendencies also disappear from the actions undertaken by communities which are the sum of these individuals.

Rarely has history known such a convincing example as that offered by the Buddhist Emperor Asoka. During the thirty-seven years of his reign he was able to prove that *the purest spiritual values could serve as helm governing all political action*. The emperor mingled with the people and asked them questions without distinction of belief or of social position. He learnt about their suffering, their needs and their hopes, and helped his subjects not only with his gold but also by constantly spreading in person the teaching of the Buddha. He constituted a body of officials to whom he taught the real significance of their role, for he insisted that they should not regard themselves merely as officials, but also as instructors of the people, and who, by the example of their lives should give the teaching of Buddhism its full meaning.

Asoka had many amphitheatres built in which the masses received instruction. He watched carefully over the prices of goods in order to avoid abuses and unlawful profits. *There was no privileged class.* The emperor himself was a constant example of a life of simplicity and of service, from which pomp was absent. As he respected life in all its forms, he forbade hunting and animal combats; he concentrated especially on the development of family life in an atmosphere of peace.

On the economic plane the problems were very simple: as there were no longer any military conquests taxation was light, and the proceeds were devoted to the progress of social life, education, medicine, the building of hospitals and the encouragement of the arts. The latter, in fact, during the reign of Asoka received an extraordinary impulse and were powerfully affected by exchanges with Greece.

Most historians agree that during the reign of this marvellous emperor India enjoyed a peerless glory.

Everywhere along the roads wells and reservoirs were made available to travellers. In the smallest villages as in the towns, joy reigned. Crimes and robbery were exceptional. It would seem that the emperor wanted to create a kind of paradise on earth. Human relationships were marked by kindliness, fraternity and gentleness. Exploitation did not exist and work was a joy. The inner riches which shone in the hearts freed all men from envy, over-weening ambition, intrigue and violence. A considerable encouragement was given to architecture. The ancient grottos were transformed into sanctuaries whose decorations have been admired by the whole world. Over 80,000 buildings of all kinds were erected.

In order that his prodigious work of social regeneration might continue for centuries, the Emperor Asoka had pillars and large columns set throughout his empire on which were engraved his principal edicts.

Let us give a few extracts from them:

'There is no higher duty than the well-being of the whole world; and my small effort is an attempt to redeem my debt towards my fellow-creatures so that I may make some of them happy here below and that they may go to heaven in the other world. All men are my children, and from me they shall receive happiness not suffering.

It is with this sole aim that I have raised these religious columns, and created guardians of the Faith. By the roadsides I have planted nyagrodhas to give shade to both man and beast; I have planted mango-groves, and have had wells dug; in many places I have had caravanserais built for the benefit of man and beast.

By order of the king, beloved of the deva, the officers of Tosadi who are set over the administration of the town, must know the following: you are set over hundreds of thousands of creatures in order to gain the affection of good men. Every man is my child; just as I wish my children to enjoy every kind of success and happiness in this world and in the next, so do I wish for all men.

For centuries in the past, murder of living beings, violence towards fellow-creatures and lack of respect for parents were rampant; but today, King Piyadasi, beloved of the devas, faithful follower of religion, has made the voices of the drums sound in such a manner that it is like the voice of religion itself.'

The grandeur with which these edicts are imbued needs no comment.

In conclusion we would like to stress the highly social nature of Buddhism and the urgent necessity for our present leaders to draw upon it for inspiration. . . .

Some opponents who wish at all price to ignore the weaknesses of the Christian civilization and diminish the merits of the Buddhist civilizations think that they have found their 'weapon' by dwelling on the poverty which is to be found in China and the East in general. They forget that civilizations, like people, have their cycles of birth, growth and decline. The cycle of Buddhism occurred between the fifth and first centuries B.C., and at the time of its apogee, it became the most illustrious and exceptional period in history.

CHAPTER XXIV

Buddhism and Christianity

WE have no intention of exhausting the numerous possibilities of elucidation which lie in the comparisons of [145] Buddhism and Christianity. Amongst their varied similarities and differences we shall confine ourselves to mentioning those aspects which are relevant to our preoccupations. Obviously the divergencies seem more important than the similarities. Moreover it is very difficult to establish with exactitude which are the one or the other on account of later alterations in the teaching of the Masters which occurred in the course of centuries. Elsewhere we have mentioned our profound conviction of the identity of the experiences of all human beings, accomplished according to the highest possibilities of their nature. We shall draw our inspiration from this basic identity in order to rediscover in the little that remains of the first teachings, the common splendour of their original inspiration.

Both Pagan and Christian writers have made it clear to us how Christianity in the early centuries betrayed the purity of Jesus's [146] message. During their constant quarrels, we see the early Christians endlessly occupied in correcting, interpreting and smoothing out the Scriptures.*

In his letter to Pope Damasus, St. Jerome naively states he only altered in the Gospels what seemed to him to modify the sense. He suppressed the first Gospel of St. Matthew (Hebrew version known as the Ebionite version) because 'this Gospel presented Jesus as born from the seed of man'.

St. Jerome adds with disconcerting simplicity that he has 'destroyed everything'.

This example, taken from thousands of others, shows how difficult it is to know the exact content of the teaching of Jesus himself, who in fact spoke Aramaic, as did his disciple John.

* *Témoignage d'un pèlerin d'absolu*, P. d'Angkor, p. 116.

From Aramaic to Greek, and especially from Greek to Latin, lies a whole series of deformations and errors.

As Dr. Edouard Szekely says: 'To say that the New Testament, as the basis of all the Christian Churches, is deformed and falsified would be to assume a heavy responsibility, but there is no higher religion than the truth.'*

HISTORICAL FACTORS OF INTERDEPENDENCE BETWEEN BUDDHISM AND CHRISTIANITY

These factors are numerous though generally not well known.

We are forgetting what our civilization owes to Greece. Greece inherited much from the old cultures of Egypt, Mesopotamia and Crete. But that which Greece received from Egypt was acquired in its turn from India by way of the Persian conquerors.

Contacts between East and West have always existed, and they were closer and more constant than we generally suppose. This applies in particular to the historical periods preceding Christianity.

The impression of a lack of intercourse between East and West is due to the fact that after the fall of the Roman Empire all communication between them was severed.

The West, devastated by the barbarian invasions, lived in a sort of drowsiness, withdrawn within itself and knowing only itself during the dark period of the Middle Ages.

The Occidentals had so completely lost all notion of the rest of the world that many thought that, by opening the sea-route to India and China, the Portuguese and Spaniards had really discovered a new world.

This illusion should be dispelled. Moreover it would appear that this was carefully fostered by those who wanted at all costs to conceal the true oriental origins of Christianity.

We now know beyond all doubt that India and China had, during many centuries, from the dawn of historical times if not

* *Evangile de la Paix de Jésus-Christ selon St. Jean*, E. Székely

before, maintained frequent commercial, cultural and artistic relations with the West.

A great number of authentic proofs of these exchanges are to be found in the ancient writings of Greece, Egypt, Chaldea, as well as India.

Greek, an Indo-European language, bears a great similarity in its roots with Sanscrit, the sacred language of the Hindus. Both have a common origin.

Relations between East and West, independently of those mentioned above, have existed from 2000 B.C.

They were first established on the steppes of southern Asia and formed the basis of the common Indo-European language. The Indo-Europeans had the privilege of benefiting from a sensational discovery of that time: the use of horses for chariots of war. This technical revolution helped them to conquer Asia Minor, Iran and northern India.

Fifteen centuries before Christ, the Egyptians used to go to India by sea in search of perfumes and divers precious things.   147

Solomon, in building the temple at Jerusalem, used certain materials brought from India.

Darius, King of the Persians, sent his troops as far as the north-western regions of India.

Other contacts were established between East and West during the reign of Alexander the Great (356-323 B.C.), King of Macedonia, whose conquests stretched as far as the Indus.

He founded colonies up to the borders of Russian Turkestan, at Khodjend in the Ferghana, at the foot of the T'ien Chan Mountains, and also at Samarkand near the boundaries of India and eastern Asia.

Seleucus Nicator, who was conquered by Chandragoupta (Sandracottos) Emperor of India, sent the Greek historian Megasthenes as ambassador to the court of the Hindu monarch.

The sovereigns of the Greek kingdom of Bactria were not

alone in maintaining cultural and commercial relations with the successors of Chandragoupta, but also many other princes living even farther away.

Indisputable proofs of these frequent contacts are to be found in the edicts chiselled on stone columns and rocks during the reign of Asoka, the great Buddhist emperor.

Particularly fruitful relations between Buddhism and Greek thought were established in Afghanistan where until the Christian era Greek kings, successors of Alexander the Great, reigned.

They were succeeded in their turn by the Indo-Scythian kings, one of whom was the famous Kanishka. They ruled for over two centuries.

Rene Grousset has written the following about them:

[148] 'The rule of the Greek kings who succeeded Alexander, and after them that of the hellenized Scythians, was to last some centuries in Afghanistan. The result was that *these Indo-Greek or Indo-Scythian kings finally became converted to Buddhism.* The famous Buddhist text, the Milindapanha, tells us of the conversion of Milinda, who was the Greek king Menandros who ruled over the Punjab about 150 B.C. As regards Kanishka, an Indo-Scythian king, he was a Buddhist saint who presided over the Councils' (Revue *France-Asie*, September 1953, p. 768).

There the tendency to objectivity dear to the Greeks frequently met with the more introspective, less demonstrative character of the Asiatics.

As a result of their cult of form the Greeks were the first to attempt a sculptural representation of the Buddha. The early Buddhists would probably have considered this sacrilege, but this does not prevent us in any way from appreciating the profoundly moving character of the splendours of the Indo-Hellenic or Greco-Buddhist art.

King Asoka who ruled between 274 and 236 B.C. made of Buddhism a universal religion. He caused it to spread throughout India and to Ceylon, Cashmere and Gandhara. Due to him, many

Greek princes living at that time received Buddhist missionaries whose influence was considerable in various centres where, later, Christianity was established and developed.

Antiochus, King of Syria between the years 261 and 246 B.C. gave a warm welcome to the Buddhist messengers.

Ptolomy II Philadelphus, King of Egypt between the years 284 and 246 B.C. was a scholar with great influence. King Asoka [149] sent him, too, some Buddhist monks in whose teaching he was greatly interested.

Antigonus Gonatas, King of Macedonia, who lived between 318 and 240 B.C., also showed a keen liking for the teaching of the Buddha.

Margas of Cyrene and Alexander of Epirus were amongst the Western notabilities in frequent contact with Buddhist thought.

After the reign of Asoka, other pillars of Buddhism were not only the Indo-Scythian King Kanishka (A.D. 78-103) but also Harshavardhana (A.D. 606-647) and the Pala dynasty (750-1150) which ruled over Bengal.

We think it worth while recalling that the Roman Empire traded as far afield as China, which they called the 'land of the Seres'.

The Chinese for their part, called the Roman Empire Ta-Tsing.

Finally, farther back, at a certain period around the fifth or sixth centuries B.C., the Indians knew the Greeks whom they called 'Yavanas'.

This term was later extended to include the Romans.

These far-off contacts are derived from a common ancestry mentioned before which goes back to between 2000 and 1500 years before Christ.

Sylvain Levy in his interesting study (*Le Bouddhisme et les Grecs*), points out that at the end of the fourth century B.C., Buddhists and Brahmans were to be found in Athens.

Buddhist writings show that from the third century B.C., many Buddhist missionaries travelled far from India in order to spread the wise words of the Buddha.

The accounts of the third Buddhist Council at Patalipoutra in 242 B.C., held during the reign of the Emperor Asoka, mention the names of some of the most illustrious of these missionaries.

One, called Yavana Dharma, was sent to Bactria, and the other, Maha-Rakshita, had considerable influence in Alassada, the capital of the Greek Empire, which corresponds to the present Alexandria in Egypt. It was later in this very place that one of the most active centres of Christianity was established, and indeed Clement of Alexandria mentions that he had often met Buddhist missionaries and Brahmans.

It is particularly interesting to note that the Essene communities and the sect of the Therapeutae, the forerunners in Egypt of the Thebaid hermits, had frequent contacts with Buddhist thought.

Their precepts seem to have almost entirely drawn their inspiration from the teaching and the practices of Buddhist asceticism.

Buddhist thought spread as far afield as the shores of the Dead Sea, where the historian Pliny speaks of the passage of a number of missionaries.

To conclude, we will point out that there is a possibility of Jesus having gone to Tibet during his ten or fifteen years of adolescence, of which we know nothing. In an account of his journey which has been violently attacked by the Vatican, and considered as a fantasy by many writers, Nicolas Notovitch claims to have found traces of the presence of Jesus in Tibet. Tibetan texts refer to the existence of 'Saint Issa' and mention that he was crucified between two evil-doers.*

A close study of the history of Brahmanism, Buddhism and Christianity reveals a striking identity in the processes of progressive degeneration of these religions.

The fundamental element responsible for this degeneration lies in a certain quality of inertia inherent in the human mind.

This inertia leads men to seek easy and comfortable solutions which save them from effort and initiative.

Most men refuse to follow the teaching, originally pure and

---

* *La Vie Inconnue de Jesus*, Nicolas Notovitch.

distilled, of the great masters, for the latter have always demanded a profoundly individual work of inner transformation.

Consequently the greater number prefer to limit themselves to the easy adoration of an image of the person of the Master rather than effect the profound awakening which the latter had advised them to realize.

The process of the deification of the Master itself arises from different factors of a somewhat complex nature. During his life his human character is evident and only his teaching counts. The man matters less although he is always surrounded by affection and respect but, the moment he dies, legends spring up and undertake their debasing work.

The Master is no longer a man but becomes a veritable 'God', and because it seemed unacceptable for such a God to be born from an act of human love, the mind invents the subtle stratagem of a spiritual conception.

Sri Krishna and the Buddha himself have not escaped this process of deification. Both have been so announced by Sages and 'seers'.

Legends present them as the fruit of a spiritual conception, and the circumstances of their death are accompanied by numerous miracles: cascades of flowers, earthquakes, etc.

In his remarkable study on the oriental origins of Christianity Professor Albert Metzger has compared the elements of the deification-process in Brahmanism, Buddhism and Christianity.

CHRISTIAN TEXTS EVOKING RENEWAL OR INNER RE-BIRTH [150]

We will compare these texts with those in Buddhist teaching, which evoke the necessity of freeing ourselves of the 'force of [151] habit'.

The Gospels and the Epistle to the Corinthians contain numerous illusions to spiritual re-birth. They tell us that 'one must die to be born again'. Obviously this death is of a psychological nature and applies to what is definite in the domain of the inner life.

¹⁵²   To die to oneself is to die to one's *habits; for the essence of the 'I-process' is habit.*

We may cite here the words of Jesus to Nicodemus (Gospel of
¹⁵³ St. John, chap. III, 3-4-5-6-7):

'Verily, verily, I say unto thee, *Except a man be born again, he cannot see the kingdom of God.*'

A similar demand for renewal is voiced in the allusions to the *purifying of the old man.* The 'old man' represents everything in us that is ancient, rigid, all that is lacking in creative life, and is *habitual.*

St. Paul is quite categorical on this point in his Epistle to the Galatians:

'For in Jesus Christ neither circumcision availeth anything, nor uncircumcision, *but a new creature.*'

In his Epistle to the Philippians:

'Brethren, I count not myself to have apprehended; but this one thing I do, *forgetting those things which are behind* and reaching forth unto those things which are before, I press toward the mark.'

TEXTS EVOKING THE SENSE OF LIBERTY IN THE
EARLY CHRISTIANS

In the Epistle to the Galatians (chap. v, verses 1-18) it is written:

'Stand fast therefore in the *liberty* wherewith Christ hath made us free, and be not entangled again with the yoke of bondage. Behold I Paul say unto you . . . Ye are called unto *liberty* . . . But if ye be led of the Spirit, ye are not under the law.'

The liberty in question here is of a spiritual nature. The allusion to the yoke of a new bondage is — taking into account the circumstances – a warning to the Judeo-Christians to be on their guard against the spiritual danger of conformism and exaggerated fear of the Law.

Jesus never ceased to inveigh against the theologians of the established religion and the doctors of the Law whom he accused of having stolen from their people the keys of true knowledge. This key was none other than Freedom of thought.

That is why He cried:

'Woe unto you, lawyers! For ye have taken away the key of knowledge: ye entered not in yourselves, and them that were entering in, ye hindered (St. Luke, chap. XI, v. 52).

The destructive action of respect for the dead letter was also denounced by St. Paul:

'But even unto this day, when Moses is read, *the veil is upon their heart*. Nevertheless when it shall turn to the Lord, the veil shall be taken away. Now the Lord is that Spirit: and where the Spirit of the Lord is, there is *Liberty*' (Epistle to the Corinthians, chap. III, vv. 15-17).

Buddhists should understand the term 'Lord' as the profound Being or the 'real nature of things and of beings'.

It corresponds, though rather distantly, to the Dharmakaya or Body of Truth.

NEED OF THE KNOWLEDGE OF SELF IN CHRISTIAN TEXTS

We may recall once again the central notion arising from Zen: we are the Reality, but we do not know it. A mental veil hinders us from becoming aware of our real nature. In fact *we are Gods*.

When Jesus was stoned by the Jews who accused him of presenting himself as a God, he replied: 'Is it not written in your law, I said, Ye are gods?' (Gospel of St. John, chap. X, v. 34).

Old writings dating from the second century tell us 'Christianus alter Christus' that is to say that every 'christian is another Christ'.★

Some may ask how is it possible if we are gods that any veil could hide from our eyes fundamental reality of our being.

In fact, the illusion of the 'I-process' is a mirage but this mirage does not in any way affect the plenitude of our real nature. But *for us* who live in this instant under the yoke of mental habits, which have engendered this mirage, an urgent task is called for: that of *knowing* ourselves.

The necessity of this fundamental knowledge, which is the basis of Buddhism, is repeated by Jesus after the Last Supper when he speaks thus: 'But Eternal life consists in *knowing yourselves.*'

The process of this knowledge is totally alien to the study of the sacred texts. Did not St. Paul write that we are:

'The temple of God, and that the Spirit of God dwelleth in us' (First Epistle to the Corinthians, chap. III, v. 16).

and also that:

'The Law was not engraved in tables of stone, but in the fleshy tables of the heart' (Second Epistle to the Corinthians, chap. III, v. 3).

CHRISTIAN TEXTS EVOKING THE DIRECT APPROACH TO THE DIVINE

The non-ritualistic position of Jesus is reflected in the words used to the Samaritan woman who was worshipping on the mountain. Jesus said to her:

'Woman, believe me, the hour cometh *when ye shall neither in this mountain, nor yet at Jerusalem, worship the Father.*'
'But the hour cometh, and now is, *when the true worshippers shall worship the Father in spirit and in truth*: for the Father seeketh such to worship him.'

★ *Le Christianism Césarien*, Dr. Alta, p. 132.

'*God is a Spirit: and they that worship him must worship him in spirit and in truth*' (Gospel of St. John, chap. IV, vv. 21-23-24).

To adore in Spirit and in Truth means that only the Spirit in us can know the Spirit; but, for the Spirit in us to be able to know the Spirit, it must be 'born again'. The Spirit which is a slave to the 'force of habit' cannot recognize its fundamental reality. To 'worship in Truth' the Spirit must be freed of lies suggested to it by false mental values. That is the reason the Sages teach us that the approach to the divine (or discovery of ourselves) requires a transparent mind which has been purified of its accumulations of memory.

Unfortunately we lose sight of all that is implied in such a purification and only follow its exterior aspects.

The man whose outward conduct might conform to the traditional concepts of purity, but whose mind is still under the sway of dogmas, beliefs, ritual or ideas, does not 'worship' God in Spirit and in Truth.

To worship God in Spirit and in Truth is certainly not to adore him through the images we make of him, nor by repeating the names by which we generally call Him. *To think God in this manner is the same as denying Him effectively.* God can neither be thought nor named.

As Buddhism in general and Zen in particular teach us, only *the 'void' of our particular perceptions*, of our distinct values, allows the divine spirit in us to recognize itself in all things. Such is the essence of Zen thought, translated into Christian language.

It is to this fundamental 'poverty' of spirit that Jesus makes allusion in his Sermon on the Mount.

'*Blessed are the poor in spirit, for theirs is the Kingdom of Heaven*' (St. Matthew, chap. V, v. 3).

The 'poor in spirit' are those whose mental clarity has not been darkened by false intellectual knowledge and petty preoccupations of the 'I-process'.

If we are 'poor' in these personal elements, we will be infinitely *rich*, but this new wealth will no longer be specifically ours.

We shall simply realize a state of inner transparence which will give us a direct vision of our real nature. Such is the significance of the words of Jesus:

'*Blessed are the pure in heart, for they shall see God*' (Gospel of St. Matthew, chap. v, v. 8).

St. John of the Cross uses similar language in his Nights:

'Spiritual people in fact accomplish much by practising patience. Their only occupation should be to *leave the soul free and at rest, divested of all distinct knowledge and thought,* without thinking to what their mind and meditation might be applied.

As soon as the soul succeeds in *carefully purifying itself of tangible forms and images, it will bathe in this pure light*' (The Ascent of Mount Carmel, I-II, chap. XIII).

This passage shows certain similarities with the Buddhist texts which evoke the 'void of all distinct knowledge and thought'.

CHRISTIAN TEXTS EVOKING THE ABSENCE OF FORM AND THE INABILITY OF THOUGHT TO SOLVE THE PROBLEM OF GOD

'That which my soul sees', said Angela of Foligno, 'can neither be conceived by thought, nor expressed by word. *I see nothing and I see all*; the more this infinite good is seen in the darkness, the more it is certain and the more it exceeds all things' (St. John of the Cross, Les Cahiers de la Vie Spirituelle).

The expression 'I see nothing, and I see all', is specifically Zen.

The 'Void' of our distinct perceptions is, to the Zen master, the plenitude of a total perception which defies all attempts of expression in ordinary language.

Angela of Foligno in the following lines emphasizes this point [154] of view by placing less value on the vision of the 'divine power and divine wisdom than on that of darkness':

'When the soul sees the divine power, divine wisdom, and divine will, as has happened to me in a miraculous manner, *that seems less than this (darkness)* . . . what I see now is a whole: the rest could be called parts . . . All the grace which has been granted me *is little beside the infinite good which I see in the divine darkness.'*

The Rev. Father Garrigou-Lagrange writes the following when commenting on the reasons for which infused light manifests itself as a darkness:*

'*The deity or inmost life of God is infinitely beyond any tangible image* or any intellectual idea which has been created or could be created; to see it "sicuti est" it must reveal itself *without any intermediary.'*

This is precisely the direct method of approach suggested by the higher forms of Buddhism, Zen and Krishnamurtian teaching.

'The more we understand the inability of any idea to reveal to us the uncreated and infinite light, the more that appears inaccessible to us and *obscure, but not of an infra-intellectual obscurity, like that of matter, but of a translucent obscurity, that of the supreme truth,* which is too unintelligible to us.'

Let us point out that Tibetan Buddhism often speaks of the 'uncreated and infinite light'. The need for liberation from the hold exercised on us by images, symbols and mental clichés taken from the outer world, has been pointed out by St. Thomas in his commentaries on the 'gift of intelligence'.†

'This gift of intelligence', he says, 'purifies our mind from ties with palpable images . . . It does indeed not help us see the divine essence, but it shows us that which it is not; *we know God here below all the more perfectly in that we know that he transcends all that our mind can grasp.*

We notice immediately the similarity of the negative approach to the Real, which is familiar in Zen and somewhat rare amongst Christians. The essential technique of approach in Buddhism consists rather in saying that which the 'Body of Truth is not', since Reality escapes all positive description.

---

* *Saint Jean de la Croix,* pp. 76-7.
† St. Thomas, II-II-q-8-a-8.

TEXTS EVOKING THE SIMPLICITY OF WISDOM

From the moment the mind is cleared of its mental complexities attachments and memories, it realizes a state of fundamental simplicity. This state of simplicity, which is very familiar to the Buddhist spirit, has been expressed in another way by St. John of the Cross. In order to appreciate this similarity too much importance should not be attached to the concepts of 'Son of God' and of the 'soul' which are evoked in texts of the Christian saint, especially as it is highly probable that he transcended them.

'Take away these forms and drop the veils altogether so that the soul *may be established in pure nakedness and poverty of spirit, and as soon as this has become pure and simple it is transformed into the simple and pure divine Wisdom* which is the Son of God' (The Ascent of Mount Carmel, I-II, chap. XIII, ed. Vie Spirituelle, p. 132).

The same idea of simplicity is expressed by Jesus in these words:

'Verily, I say unto ye, he who receives not the kingdom of God *as a little child*, shall not enter therein.'

The fundamental simplicity inherent in the state of wisdom should be preceded by a harmonization of the psychical functions: equilibrium between reason and love, and abolition of the oppositional distinctions with which we are familiar.

This transcendence of the oppositions of good and evil, of left and right, intellectuality and emotivity, is expressed by a kind of interior levelling. The words of St. John the Baptist re-echo our thoughts:

'Prepare ye the way of the Lord', he said, 'Make his path straight . . . Every valley shall be exalted and every hill shall be made low. . . .'

This advice applies to the work of harmonization which we have to effect within ourselves. Modern psychologists, and Dr.

C. G. Jung in particular, dwell on the necessity of establishing a balance between the axes of our rational and irrational functions.

All excessive specialization upsets the harmony of the whole. It is practically impossible for us to transcend the affective and mental spheres unless we have previously established their reciprocal equilibrium.

THE IDEAS OF THE 'BODY OF BUDDHA' AND THE 'BODY OF CHRIST'

Certain common ground exists between Buddhism in general, Zen in particular and Christianity with regard to the frequently expressed notions of 'Body of Truth' or 'Body of Buddha' (Dharmakaya) of the Buddhist and the 'Glorious Body' or 'Body of Christ' of the Gospels.

It is written in the *Path to Sudden Attainment* by Hui Hai (p. 11):

'The mind with no particular abode is calm. Such is the form of the real mind which is also that of the *real body. The real body is identical with that of a Buddha.*'

The citations from this work of Zen dwell on the fact that this *'real body is void of all our distinctions of opposition'*. It should, however be considered as a plenitude triumphing over the limits inherent in separate things and beings, but before the resplendent Unity of the 'Body of Truth' the illusion of the separateness of being vanishes forever.

According to Zen, all beings and all things are the 'Body of Truth' but we can only perceive it by freeing our mind of its habitual method of dualistic perception. An echo of this condition is to be found in the following passage of Hui Hai:

'Not to perceive things as existing or not-existing is to perceive the true body of Buddha.'

We particularly draw the attention of the Western reader to the fact that the notion of the 'Body of Buddha' is not connected with that of a *person*. It designates something which we could rather inadequately define as a 'cosmic principle' which covers the whole of the visible and invisible aspects of the Universe.

If we suppress in the following quotations the word 'Buddha' in 'Body of Buddha' and word 'Christ' in 'Body of Christ' we shall have taken yet another step towards the pure comprehension of an eternal Truth which does not depend on particular systems. We shall thus be nearer the direct teaching of the Sages in whose names these systems have been established.

Having made these reservations here we shall reproduce certain fragments from the text of St. Paul in his Epistle to the Corinthians:

'Now there are diversities of gifts but the same Spirit. And there are differences of administrations but the same Lord. And there are diversities of operations, but it is the same God which worketh all in all. *For us the body is one, and hath many members, and all the members of that one body, being many, are one body*; so also is Christ.

Now ye are the body of Christ, and members in particular' (I Corinthians, chap. XII, vv. 4-5-6-12-27).

During the Last Supper, Jesus took some bread, broke it, and gave it to his disciples saying, 'Take, eat, *this is my body*', and then He passed round the cup saying 'Drink ye all of it for this is my blood'. The Zen masters interpret these words in a manner different from that of the Christians: to the former *everything is the 'Body of Buddha'*, so if Jesus said 'the bread is my body' it was because *all things without distinction* are the 'real Body', that of the Totality-that-is-One of the Universe; not a single grain of dust lies outside this Reality.

Here is how the Dutch writer J. Vanderleeuw expresses it:

'When we enter the world of Reality desire becomes superfluous, *since we are all that is*, and there is nothing to desire outside Reality. *How can we want a thing when we are all things, and experi-*

ence all things as our own being? When we have seen Reality, there is not a grain of dust which has not a sublime meaning, since it is for ever part of the Eternal' (*The Conquest of Illusion*, by J. Vanderleeuw, pp. 232 and 234).

CHRISTIAN TEXTS WHICH EVOKE SPIRITUAL LIGHT

These texts are very numerous. The early Christians, like most [155] mystics had a cult for spiritual light. St. John says:

'And the Light shineth in Darkness: and the Darkness comprehended it not' (St. John, chap. 1, v. 5).

St. Paul, when he addressed the Ephesians, described God to them as 'Father of Glory' (Bright Light).

St. John of the Cross said that from the moment the soul was [156] purified of tangible forms and images, it was bathed in *pure and simple light*.

Even if Zen does not allude to spiritual light, Tibetan Buddhism on the contrary is rich in works devoted to 'Bright Light'.

'Tibetan Yoga' commenting on the 'Doctrine of Bright Light', tells us that:

'The Real State of the Mind, the true identity of all things, inseparable from the Void, beyond the domain of phenomena, while [157] one experiences the great happiness of thought which transcends, is "primordial Bright Light".'

Primordial Bright Light, the visual condition of the mind in its primordial state, the *True State*, unsullied by the process of the thought of Samsara, this experiencing as a *Natural State* an ineffable spiritual happiness which is inseparable from the realization of the Void, the ' "THAT which IS" of all things'.

The void alluded to in this quotation is not only the absence of all particular distinctions that we have so often mentioned.

It is also the state of interstitial silence which exists between two [158] thoughts.

It occurs when the mind ceases to be in the grip of memory-automatisms and is therefore linked with the absence of distinct ideas.

The stanzas of the Doctrine of the Bright Light express the aforegoing in other terms:

'The realization of Bright Light must take place in *the interval existing between the cessation of one thought and the birth of the following thought.*'

The Bright Light is approached here by the practice of the six [159] rules of Tilopa which are well-known in Tibet:

'Do not think, do not imagine, do not analyse.
Do not meditate, do not reflect.
Abide in the Natural State.'

In reading these stanzas we can see a certain difference in nuance between Zen and Tibetan Buddhism. Where texts evoking spiritual light are concerned, the latter is closer to Christianity. In the eyes of Zen masters the vision of the Bright Light should be transcended.

Professor D. T. Suzuki says the following on this subject:

'So long as the seeing is something to see, it is not the real one; the seeing is no-seeing — *that is, when the seeing is not a specific act of seeing into a definitely circumscribed state of consciousness* — is it the seeing into one's self-nature' (*The Zen Doctrine of No-Mind*, p. 42).

It should be useful to point out here that, inasmuch as the integrated men reach the vision of the infinite depths of the Universe and themselves, *the notion of spiritual light appears to them to have to give way* to a translucent reality.

In fact spiritual light is the result of an interference between the world of pure translucent essence and the world of phenomena. We can evoke once again a similarity in the processes of mind and matter. In fact it is common knowledge that the sunlight, with which we are familiar, is not as we know it except at the low altitudes at which we pursue our daily life. Astronomers and alpinists know that at great altitudes the sky becomes deep violet and finally completely black. 'Potential' light, in proportion to interference on the part of matter appears as real light. On the spiritual plane a similar process occurs.

Nevertheless there exist in Buddhist thought certain tendencies which establish a distinction between Spirit and Light. In his comparative study of gnosticism and Buddhist thought, Lassen (quoted by Garbe) writes:

'Buddhism in general establishes a very marked distinction between Spirit and Light, and does not consider the latter as at all immaterial. Nevertheless a teaching is to be found in this religion which is very similar to the gnostic doctrine; according to it Light is the manifestation of Spirit in Matter: Intelligence thus imbued with Light enters into relationship with matter, in which relationship Light can be reduced and finally completely obscured.

'*It is said of the Supreme Intelligence that it is neither Light nor non-Light, neither obscurity nor non-obscurity, since all these expressions imply relations between Intelligence and Light, relations which did not exist in the beginning.*'

Certain neo-platonists and Egyptian mystics have commented on the nature of the supreme essence in very similar terms.

Some speak of the ever constant brilliance of the more than light. It conceals such a character of purity that most of those who approach it describe it as 'darkness'.

We repeat here the interesting record of the Christian mystic Angela of Foligno:

'All the grace which has been granted me is little beside the infinite good which I see in the divine darkness.

I see nothing and I see all; the more this infinite good is seen *in the darkness, the more it is certain and the more it exceeds all things.*'

We shall conclude this rapid survey of the points of contact existing between Buddhism and Christianity with a commentary on the symbolism of original sin, of baptism and resurrection as envisaged by certain Buddhists.

To most of them 'original Sin' is the result of a defect in the working of the mind. The allusion to the forbidden fruit refers to the wrong use of the intellectual faculties. It is not so much thought, as a natural function, which is 'forbidden', but the wrong uses and abuses which are made of it.

Genesis tells us that man ate of the fruit of the Tree of Knowledge.

By eating this 'fruit of the Tree of Knowledge' he fell into the trap of *identification*. *The mental function, which was only a partial function in a vast ensemble of processes, became identified with its particular role.* This identification is responsible for the illusion of the consciousness of self. Original sin is nothing other than this illusion. The origin of our bondage begins the instant we imagine we are separate entities. It is the drama of the part which thinks it is whole. Man has sometimes been called a 'rebel angel' or a 'fallen angel' on account of the imposture to which he resorts when unlawfully assuming the sole right to existence.

He is a 'rebel angel' because he resists the law of life, and he is fallen as a result of degradation caused by the 'force of habit'.

Only one thing can deliver him from this disgrace: direct vision of his deeper nature. From this moment the world of opposites gives place to the Ocean of Bright Light. *'Baptism is nothing other than the symbol of the immersion of the "I-process" in the Ocean of Bright Light.'* The moment a being is immersed in the plenitude of the common essence of all things, his old egoistical values are totally overthrown; and he is henceforth delivered from the illusion of being a distinct entity and he feels permanently and indissociably integrated in the totality of the Universe.

Having been delivered from 'original sin', he is in what the Christians call a 'state of grace'. The death of the 'old man' is not essentially an annihilation; through his death comes resurrection; though not the resurrection of the earthly body, but of the 'Glorious Body', the Christian 'Body of Christ' and the Buddhist 'Body of Buddha'.

The symbolism of the Resurrection and Crucifixion has been interpreted in a most interesting manner by Professor D. T. Suzuki. Let us remember, however, that the word 'will', used by this eminent Japanese scholar should be devoid of a personal sense. The Zen masters imply more particularly the manifestation in man of an impersonal cosmic principle.

'The awakening of a thought marks the beginning of Ignorance and is its condition, when this is vanquished, "a thought" is reduced to the will, which is Enlightenment. . . .

In this respect Christianity is more symbolic than Buddhism. The story of Creation, the Fall from the Garden of Eden, God's sending Christ to compensate for the ancestral sins, his Crucifixion and Resurrection – they are symbolic. To be more explicit, Creation is the awakening of consciousness, or the "awakening of a thought"; the Fall is consciousness going astray from the original path; God's idea of sending his own son among us is the desire of the will to see itself through its own offspring, consciousness; Crucifixion is transcending the dualism of acting and knowing, which comes from the awakening of the intellect; and finally Resurrection means the will's triumph over the intellect, in other words, the will seeing itself in and through consciousness' (*Essays in Zen Buddhism*, vol. I, p. 153).

DIVERGENCIES BETWEEN BUDDHISM AND CHRISTIANITY

The divergencies between Buddhism and Christianity are more numerous than their similarities. If we examine the essence of Zen Buddhism in particular, we find ourselves faced with radical incompatibilities.

At certain points, not only is the basis different, but also the methods of approach diverge markedly.

A study of these aspects would require several volumes, so we [160] shall confine ourselves to summarizing the most striking points.

BUDDHISM: RELIGION OF NON-CREATION

In contrast to Christianity, Buddhism in general and Zen in particular are not what might be called religions based on a 'creation'. Nevertheless some forms of Buddhism have inherited from India the notion of cycles of activity and rest applied to Universes; but, even in this case, there is no 'creation', no absolute beginning. The Manvantara, or periods of activity, succeed 'Pralayas', or periods of rest, much as day follows night. These are arbitrary divisions which our mind makes in the heart of a Totality-that-is-One, which has neither beginning nor end.

According to the Zen Masters an attitude which distinguishes a creator from his creatures arises from ignorance. Because we, in our apparent individuality, have a beginning and an end, we believe we are justified in applying the process which imprisons us to the Universe as a whole. It is obvious that none of our concepts of time, creation, beginning, end and purpose apply to the Real.

The position of the religions based on a 'creation' comes up against various obstacles. If God created the world from nothingness, as some say, he was fulfilling a need for objectivization. If He was fulfilling a need for objectivization, He is not absolute; if He is not absolute, He is not God.

Moreover if creation has a beginning, this in some sort is added to the pre-existence of God. But if anything whatever can be added to God, He is not infinite, He is not absolute, and therefore He is not God.

Lastly, if God has created immortal souls, endowed with a life *eternally distinct from Him*, his attributes of *eternal* Omnipresence and perfect Ubiquity would be *eternally limited* by his creatures who are *eternally distinct from Him*.

If God is limited He is no longer God.

These distinctions are non-existent in Buddhism. There remains only the Totality-that-is-One of the Universe, without beginning and without end. It is complete in itself, and exists by itself. There is no God outside it. This Totality is in no wise the emanation of a divine essence distinguished from it by any kind of transcendence.

To our dualistic vision it appears as a succession of innumerable transformations in which there is no intervention of finality, search, or purpose, such as we conceive them. It is the great 'Body of Buddha', 'void' of our individual values.

The evolution which we note in our image of the world on the biological scale of phenomena is only a partial process. It must be envisaged in a space-time totality, which includes it and dominates it. In this wider perspective considerations of growth, progress, evolution and relativity in general appear insignificant.

But this does not in any way diminish their *relative significance for us.*

To understand it we should place ourselves momentarily outside our familiar divisions of time: into past, present and future. That which we call 'evolved', is the object of active transformations in a complex organization realizing great physical and psychical flexibility. This allows the 'fluidity of the depths' to materialize on the 'surface'. That which we consider evolved, in our perspective, does not have to evolve much more in order to express the creative dynamism of Life. On the other hand that which we consider as having evolved little, is considered by us as having a long evolutive ascension before it in order to attain more flexibility and creativity.

Let us take A as the highly evolved individual, and B as the evolutive work we believe is necessary for him in order to attain his integration.

C is the individual we consider very slightly evolved, and D is the important task which is incumbent on him in order that he may realize his liberation.

The sums of A+B and C+D are identical. They represent a fundamental constant which governs the psycho-physical aspects of the Totality-that-is-One.

INEXISTENCE OF THE IMMORTAL SOUL IN BUDDHISM

The problems raised by the existence of the individual soul and its immortality are considered as pseudo-problems by all the masters of Buddhism in general and Zen in particular. The very fact that each human being is included in the Totality-that-is-One is sufficient in itself. But the infinite possibilities inherent in our veritable situation are not perceptible to us. From instant to instant we have the possibility of participating in the unfathomable character of Eternity, which we not only carry within ourselves, but which we *are*. Ever since a veil has fallen over our minds, we try to prove to ourselves the absolute existence and the permanence of our separate individuality.

These attempts are judged somewhat severely by the Sages. They form an essential part of the ignorance by virtue of which our 'permanent pseudo-entity' is built up. Briefly, we are faced with a closed cycle, whose essential motor is mental activity. If we are able to situate the mental function in the correct place it should occupy, in the complex hierarchy of psychic functions, the closed cycle of the 'I-process' is broken. The notion of the ego is a result of the privileged position occupied by mental activity in our actual psychic structure. If we succeed in modifying the situation, by that very act we dissolve the illusion of the ego which resulted from it.

The Christian idea of the permanence of the individual soul, and of the eternal co-existence of this soul at the side of a God distinct from itself, is totally opposed to the spirit of Buddhism.

Most forms of Buddhism and of Zen admit that a complex of psychic energies exists in man, which express themselves as emotional and mental activities. To most forms of occidental spirituality, the ensemble of emotional and mental activities constitutes a permanent soul.

To the Zen masters, on the contrary, the human psychic makeup is devoid of all continuity. All their efforts are concentrated in systematically exposing the notions of the permanence or reality of itself which the 'I-process' may have.

REINCARNATION

Some people ask what happens, in the light of this hypothesis, to belief in reincarnation which is so familiar to Buddhist thought.

Generally we think that reincarnation automatically implies the permanence of a soul remaining identical with itself during the complete cycle of successive lives.

Even though most forms of Buddhism accept reincarnation, the higher forms, such as Tibetan Buddhism and Zen, see the problem in manner rather different from that which we suppose.

That which we call 'soul' in their eyes is only a 'series of causes and effects' of a psychical nature, which follow each other at a prodigious speed, swift as lightning. We literally 'burn', we are told frequently by the masters of Buddhist thought. Our appearance of continuity is as lacking in foundation as is the continuity of a flame. The 'I-process' is recreated, reconstructed and transformed from instant to instant. There where our casual glance thinks it sees a permanent individuality, there is really only a rapid succession of moments of a consciousness, and evanescent thoughts.

Indeed each apparent individuality – being the result of a sum total of extraordinarily complex causes and effect – takes on provisionally certain characteristics of unicity. But from the moment when the clear vision of Nirvâna supervenes the cycle of cause and effect of the 'I-process' is broken. The flame of personal consciousness is extinguished. There is no defeat, but a victory. But let us repeat once again, that in the eyes of the Zen masters, 'nothing has happened' since really all that has taken place is the sudden disappearance of a mirage.

The inexistence of the ego or permanent soul reduces to nothing the ideas of Redemption, Salvation as taught by most present-day Christian churches.

It is inconceivable that so much effort be expended to 'save' an entity, which from *certain* points of view is inexistent. At the very most it can be torn away from its dream, although only itself can do that.

The true process of liberation is that of self-enlightenment and 'self-awakening'. The veritable masters are just 'catalysers'.

Their effect simply depends on their presence; thereafter the process of self-revelation can only be strictly individual.

That is why the monks or masters of Buddhism never consider themselves as intermediaries or 'ministers of God'.

We are eternally the Real, and we have nothing to acquire.

There is only one thing which we must do: look very clearly, so as to discover 'that which is'.

These notions are very different from those suggested by most Christian churches by their acquisitions of virtues. For Zen, virtues are not a means but a *consequence*.

The inexistence of a God distinct from ourselves and of a permanent ego, eliminates all ideas of merit, pardon, remission of sins, salvation and prayer which are the bases of present-day Christianity.

From the moment when our notions of merit cease, we see that a complete metamorphosis takes place in our inner values. Ritual, sacrifices to 'please God', and prayers appear to us clearly in all their uselessness. Indeed, ritual and prayers can have a certain efficacy but this derives from ceremonial magic and the power of thought. These practices exist in all religions, not only Christian, but also in the Hindu and Buddhist 'Tantra'. The Sages consider them as belonging to the occult — a domain which, in their eyes, is completely alien to the essential realities. The man who has 'Correct Vision' does not practice any ritual, nor does he pray. He IS, quite simply, and that alone is enough. That alone is enough for such a man is truly the 'salt of the earth', because of the richness of his love, and the lucidity and harmony which he radiates from moment to moment.   Such a man does not pray any more. He asks for nothing.

He gives, simply and spontaneously.

As religions grow older, we notice that they tend irresistibly to become attracted to the world of form. This process of degradation towards the 'superficial' is a consequence of an inherent tendency to inertia in the human mind. The deviations of the mental nature of man are identical in all climates, at all epochs, and produce similar effects. Whether the law of mental inertia operates amongst white or yellow races, it expresses itself by a call to exterior decorum, magic and spectacular displays of religious pomp. Nevertheless it seems obvious that the West has been subjected to these influences more fully than the East. The all-pervading technical progress of the West has placed the emphasis on the material and exterior aspects of the world. Its conquests of time and space have been so spectacular, that it is almost inevitable that the consequences should be expressed in the superficiality of our interests. The prestige of the external has dimmed the interest in so-called spiritual things, and, should the latter reveal itself, the little energy left to deal with it barely enables us to triumph over the limitations of form. In fact, by a strange paradox, in so far as technical progress has triumphed over the barriers set by time, modern man has less and less time at his disposal. The Oriental, on the other hand, takes his time. This attitude allows him to effect a psychic decantation during which he frees himself more easily from the magic of forms.

THE IDEA OF 'SAVIOUR' AND 'SALVATION'

In the teaching of Zen there is neither an external 'saviour', salvation nor special ways. Each cause set in movement simply has its corresponding effect. When we have fallen into the pitfall of the illusion of time, cause and effect seem to us to be separate. To the Sages, they are inseparable.

No one has the right to interfere in the process of cause and effect which govern the inner life of others. Nevertheless, the Zen masters will try spontaneously to enlighten those whom they meet on the fundamental nature of the processes which govern their existence and are responsible for their miseries, conflicts and sufferings.

The idea of atonement or the remission of sins cannot enter the mind of the true Sage. It may just arise in the imagination or the heart of a generous soul which still identifies itself with the exterior aspects of things.

This idea, which everybody thinks is sublime, has however a fundamental flaw. The spiritual romanticism with which it is imbued hinders us from seeing that, in fact, the notion of atonement or remission of sins encourages cowardice, contributes to ignorance and strengthens the inner inertia of man.

Moreover, if anyone took upon himself to assume the responsability, the effects of the causes which we have set in motion, we would be completely unable to make progress towards the light. If we do not respect the laws of nature, we are not long in suffering the consequences.

The suffering resulting from this will enable us to correct ourselves. The role of the Sage is not to undergo all this in our stead but to enlighten us in such a way that the ignorance which lies at its origin may be dispelled for ever.

Progress in psychology has demonstrated that we cannot experiment 'by proxy'. The fire of experience completely undergone leaves the acuity of perception that is inherent in psychological maturity. The best examples and the most weighed advice cannot afford help to man that is as valuable as a personal experience which has been profoundly lived.

We are not unaware of the fact that there are certain yogis or Hindu 'gurus' who follow the dangerous and terrible path which consists in taking on themselves the 'karma' of their disciples. The result of such a process is that the disciple is plunged into complete psychological dependence on the Master. In the eyes of the true Sages such an attitude ends in the state of mutual servitude which is all the more dangerous in that it is subtle and idealized. Neither the disciple or the Master is aware of the dangerous impasse they have entered. In most cases the Master depends unconsciously on the whole-hearted adoration which the disciple professes for him. The total acceptance of his system of thought or his method of spiritual training, and the esteem with which he feels himself surrounded, are so many elements which give his 'I-process' prestige and authority, unconsciously desired. Reciprocally the disciple, who is no longer used to thinking for himself, depends psychologically on the presence of the Master, on his affection, his advice, themes for meditation or divers exercises prescribed by him. The moment the falseness of this process of mutual gratification becomes evident they both find themselves on the threshold of particularly poignant but highly revealing and salutary personal dramas.

'THE TREE SHALL BE KNOWN BY ITS FRUIT. . . .'

The idea of 'salvation', which is so familiar to Christians, is at the root of the worst forms of spiritual imperialism.

Dr. Hubert Benoit says:

'If I believe that I *must* achieve my "salvation" I cannot avoid believing that I *must* lead others to do the same' (Dr. H. Benoit, *Supreme Doctrine*, p. 16).

This attitude is made still worse by the addition of the notion of merit. Most Christians subtly hope to please God by wresting from heresy the souls of the unfortunate unbelievers who do not share their way of thinking. This attitude leads to the direst cruelties.

The atrocities of the Inquisition, the crimes and brutalities of the Dragonnades, the tortures endured by the martyrs of free-thought, illustrate the harmful violence inherent in the idolatry of salvation. Yet violence does not result exclusively from the idolatry of salvation. *Attachment to any ideal, whatever it may be, is virtually a violence*; but it happens that unfortunately most idealists are not willing to admit this.

The atmosphere of Buddhism is much more serene and peaceful, for it does not depend on the cult of an idea but, on the contrary, tries to free the mind from all false ideation.

Buddhism has had no religious wars or bloody crusades. It merely sent out peaceful monks, whenever it was possible, who taught universal brotherhood, detachment from material possessions, the impermanence of all things and of the 'I-process', and infinite respect for life in all its forms.

The masters of Buddhism in general and Zen in particular always had a profound sense of liberty. The essential basis of their methods of investigation is freedom of thought. *Never do they impose their views.*

As Dr. Hubert Benoit expresses it:

'A clear understanding on the other hand, neither forbids the teaching of others nor obliges one to take it. But the man who has understood that his own realization is not in any manner his duty, contents himself with replying if asked, that if he takes the initiative in speaking, it will be only to propose such ideas with discretion, without experiencing any need of being understood. He is like a man who, possessing good food in excess, opens his door. . . .' (Dr. H. Benoit, *Supreme Doctrine*, p. 17).

The idolatry of salvation and the idea of redemption of sins arise from a double fundamental error.

(1) There is an *identification* of the mind with the external aspects of things in general and suffering in particular. Even if, in Satori, we are in a *certain sense* all things, we cease to identify ourselves with their superficial appearances alone. The identity which unites us with other beings is well beyond their corporeal forms but this nevertheless does not hide them from our eyes. In a certain way we are, in the very heart of the being who suffers, that which remains unaltered by their suffering. In this new perspective a profound change takes place in our familiar values.

Before the experience of Satori we identify ourselves with suffering. The balance-sheet of our attitude is negative. One suffering is added to another. After Satori, we respond to the sight of suffering by Love, inner peace, and the understanding of correct values. In this case the balance sheet is positive: darkness is answered by light.

(2) The other basic error which is responsible for the idea of redemption of sins, should be sought in the general tendencies of our mind. We are so much corrupted by interest and calculation, that we have acquired the habit of believing that all pain and suffering should be *rewarded, paid for*. Therefore, in our eyes, the immense suffering of Jesus should be compensated for by the 'redemption of sins'. By its exclusive deification of the person of Christ, Christian thought tends to give this compensation an exceptional importance.

ZEN IMPERSONALITY

A fundamental difference in atmosphere exists between the impersonality of Zen and the personal sentimentality of many Christian mystics.

Numerous texts of Christian mysticism contain such expressions as spiritual marriage, the bridegroom, the bride, impassioned lover, the flame of love, embrace, beloved, the Father, Son of God, etc. We can see immediately the weaknesses of such an anthropomorphism of which no trace can be detected in Zen.

Basing itself on the reality of the 'I-process', Christian thought bears the deep imprint of personal values. It rarely transcends the plane of dualities: subject and object, spectacle and spectator, worshipper and object of his adoration. Christian saints transcending this plane are exceptional.

While Buddhism in general and Zen in particular aim at an *integration, abolishing all duality*, Christianity remains in the dualist *communion* existing between worshipper and the Divine.

The sense of simplicity and scant spiritual romanticism of Zen is illustrated most strikingly in an example cited by Professor D. T. Suzuki:

'Chao-pien, a great government officer was a lay disciple of Fach'uan of Chiang-shan. One day after his official duties were over, he found himself leisurely sitting in his office, when all of a sudden a clash of thunder burst on his ear, and he realized a state of Satori. The poem he then composed depicts one aspect of the Zen experience:
Devoid of all thought, I sat quietly by the desk in my official room,
With my fountain-mind undisturbed, as serene as water;
A sudden clash of thunder, the mind-doors burst open,
And lo, there sitteth the old man in all his homeliness.'

We can see that whatever personal element remains in this account of the experience is very limited. We can measure the distance between the prosaic image of the 'old man in all his homeliness' and the exaltation of Christian expressions such as the 'omnipotence of Christ the King', or 'God in all His Glory'.

Indeed a certain enthusiasm can help us in the conquest of the mirages we have created, but we should have to rid ourselves absolutely of the exaltation so that there would only remain existential felicity which is sufficient unto itself.

BUDDHISM AND THE MEMORY OF THE BUDDHA

Many Sutras teach that:

[162] 'The Sage seeks in his own mind and not in that of the Buddha, while the ignorant seeks in the Buddha and not in his own mind.'

This attitude is radically opposed to that of Christianity, in which that of the practical outlook draws inspiration from the person of Christ.

Christians invoke the words which Jesus is said to have uttered at the Last Supper: 'Do this in memory of me.' No true Sage would take the responsibility of recommending the faithful of all peoples throughout the ages, to do anything whatsoever in *his memory*. He would be paralysing for ever all possibility of deliverance for minds who drew inspiration from such a servitude. Memory is the greatest obstacle to the spiritual flowering of man. Inexorably memory-automatisms prevent our perception of the Divine. Never could we admit that a Sage or messenger of 'God' could by words so contrary to the truth, enslave the human soul for centuries to come. We shall have to choose between alternatives: either Jesus said these words and is not a Sage, or those who followed him, through an excess of love for him, committed the imprudence of adding this obligation of remembering.

Errors as serious as these, on account of their enslaving influence, seem to support the thesis of P. L. Couchoud, who tried to prove the mythical character of Jesus in his work entitled *Jesus, Le Dieu Fait-Homme*, p. 352.

'The god made man,' he says, 'is the divine companion who tears man away from the anguish of his loneliness. Basically he is nothing but the heart of man mysteriously perceiving himself in the agony of his infinite weakness and in the exaltation of his infinite strength.'

In the eyes of the Buddhist masters that which is known as 'evil' is merely the force of habit, and particularly its manifestation in the routine of memory. The moment any man demands that anything whatever be done in 'memory' of him, he is conditioning the minds of those listening to him. He encourages and strengthens the hold of the forces of habit. He is inciting us to plunge into the dead past and thereby rendering impossible perfect adherence to the present.

CHAPTER XXV

Similarities between Zen and Krishnamurti

Points of contact between Buddhism, Zen thought and the teaching of Krishnamurti are many; so many in fact that dozens of volumes would be necessary to explain them in detail. We shall limit ourselves here to mentioning merely some important similarities without, however, following their highly interesting developments to the extent that they deserve. Most enlightened readers will have often noticed the parallelism existing between these two ways of life.

For Zen and Krishnamurtian thought have this in common: they are not philosophies in the general sense of the word, but rather a way of living.

We come up against the same obstacles in both when trying to define them, as they are outside the categories of habitual values.

To begin with we shall say briefly what both *are not*.

Neither Zen nor Krishnamurtian thought can be considered systems of ideas or metaphysics.

Neither have dogmas, beliefs, obvious or subtle symbols, ritual, temples, disciplines, or principles.

Both oppose spiritual authority ('Do not place any head above your own', Seng-T'san, Zen), and condemn attachment to texts ('If you are upset by the Sûtra, upset the Sûtra yourself.')

There is no 'method' for either of them. (There is no method for, as Zen tells us, we ourselves are Reality.) Krishnamurti develops exactly the same point of view in a work with the significant title of *Pathless Reality*.

Both Krishnamurti and Zen insist on the fundamental *fact that we have nothing to do*, that we have no spiritual edifice to raise.

We do not have to 'become' anything else, but be fully conscious of what we are.

We shall examine here more carefully some points of greater importance:

(1) *The inexistence of the 'I-process' or 'thinker' in Zen and Krishna-murti*

We apologize for re-printing here certain texts which have served as points of departure for other commentaries.

'Nobody performs the action, and nobody tastes its fruit; only the succession of actions and their fruits revolves in a continual circle, like the cycle of tree and seed, without anyone being able to tell where it began.

Those who do not perceive this succession believe in the existence of an ego' (*Le Bouddhisme*, A. David-Neel, p. 33).

Krishnamurti expresses the same truth in other words:

'*Without his thoughts, the thinker does not exist* . . . This separation of thinker and his thoughts is a stratagem of the "thinker" in order to assure himself security and permanence' (Krishnamurti, *Connaissance de Soi*).

One of the essential bases of Krishnamurtian thought is defined in this phrase. There is no 'thinker' as a static entity, but simply a succession of thoughts whose rapidity, following each other, gives an appearance of continuity. Thereafter, Krishnamurti tells us, all our attention should be brought to bear on the process of thought itself and not on the thinker. It is vain to pay undue attention to a mirage as such. It is wiser to learn as a result of what processes the mirage has appeared. If we succeed, all the problems raised by the mirage change and become pseudo-problems. Such is the reason for which Krishnamurti suggests that we do not seek to solve the problems in the particular circumstances in which they generally arise, *but study what within us has created all these problems*. Here, too, Krishnamurti and Zen insist in the same way on knowledge of self.

(2) *The operations of the 'I-process' in Zen and Krishnamurti*

The texts below are not only inspired by Zen but also by Buddhism in general. In his *Apologie du Bouddhisme*, C. Formichi writes:

'The immanent force in each individual is conceived only in strict dependence on the materials it elaborates and which Buddha calls the skandas. There are five of them: body, sensations, perceptions, discernment and consciousness' (p. 84).

Krishnamurti says almost the same thing:

'All life is energy; it conditions and is conditioned, and this energy in its auto-active development creates its own materials, the body with its cells and senses, perception, judgment and consciousness '(Krishnamurti, *Ommen*, 1936).

C. Formichi, writing on the energy which feeds the 'I-process' according to Buddhism, says:

'Processes in action exist by virtue of an inner energy which becomes perceptible to us as consciousness during a spontaneously active evolution. The essence of the auto-agent consists exactly in this. The auto-agent is that which is able to maintain itself by itself and this maintenance by itself takes the form of an automatic recharging. . . .

Expressions of will are always new points of support which the "me" creates for itself.

Just as the rubbing of one piece of wood against another gives off heat which increases with each rubbing so, from the friction of the processes of the "me" against the outside world, against things, other expressions of will always spring up afresh.

This reaction of the processes of the "me" in contact with the outside world is what keeps the process itself in motion.

The process of the "me" is the thirst for living, the impulse towards life, life itself, as the heat of the flame, is the flame itself.

The process of the "me" cannot have any principle if, like the flame, it is a process which feeds itself.

But the "me" is not produced, it acts by its own impulsion . . . it burns *ab aeterno* because it is ceaselessly renewed.

The consciousness that no "me" exists, stops the Karma like a charm, the thirst of living, which like a flame, uses any fuel and burns spontaneously and perpetually, enclosing us in the intolerable prison of world suffering.' C. Formichi (*Apologie du Bouddhism*, pp. 87-97 *passim*).

The thoughts expressed in these fragments drawn from this interesting work by C. Formichi are also expressed with striking similarity by Krishnamurti in his talks at Ommen in 1936.

He invokes the existence of a sole self-acting process living on its own activities.

During his lectures at Ojai, 1936, he compares the 'I-process' to a flame. He says that '*this flame maintains itself by its own heat, and the heat is itself the flame*. In exactly the same way, the ego is maintained through its desires and ignorance' (Krishnamurti, *Ojai*, 1936, p. 34).

'When the mind completely discerns this process,' he says, 'it sees itself as being this process, and sees that it uses every action to feed itself.'

This clear vision of the process of thought is one of the fundamental elements of Krishnamurtian thought.

Therefore the two teachings concur perfectly in this particular field.

(3) *Identity of methods*

The methods proposed by Krishnamurti are closer to Zen thought than to the other forms of Buddhism.

Krishnamurtian thought could be defined as a statement of the manifold conditionings of the mind.

In fact Krishnamurti teaches us that Truth is free and unconditioned; and we have to place ourselves in a position that we can approach this freedom and non-conditioning. Therefore we must effectively free our own mind from its conditioning if it is to reveal to us its full richness.

Amongst these conditioning factors Krishnamurti and Zen both enumerate the following elements:

(a) memory-habits or mental automatisms.
(b) distinct or exclusive perceptions.

    (c) partitioned or set meditations.
    (d) attachment to ideas, beliefs and images.
    (e) dualistic vision of divers opposites.
    (f) the craving for 'becoming'.
    (g) techniques, methods or means.
    (h) cult of authority and disciplines.
    (i) search for virtues.

(a) *Memory-habits*

We have placed the accent on the word 'habit', as this is an underlying theme in most Buddhist texts. We shall not cite again the texts dealing with the 'force of habit' which have already been commented upon in this work.

We shall merely bear in mind that most of them teach us that the 'I-process' is the result of a constellation of memory-habits which condition each other. Their succession and their complexity produce in consciousness the illusory appearance of continuity.

Krishnamurti considers memory-habits as the most formidable obstacle to the perception of the Real. He continually condemns their static and restrictive character. Reality for him is in the instant. It is perpetually new. If we wish to perceive it we must free ourselves from memory-habits.

'We do not approach our experiences anew. And our experience is not really new unless we put in to it an immense interest and a great love. Then it is something new at every second, and not an accumulation of anything that is old' (Krishnamurti, *Madras, Benares*).

Concerning the conditioning inherent in mental habits, Krishnamurti says:

'You will see that wherever there is continuity, habits, thought-processes passing from one continuity to another, there is always servitude, friction and pain . . . this memory, we give it life by incessant accumulations and constant reminders . . . Habit is a dead thing to which we give life' (Krishnamurti, *Madras, Benares*).

(b) *Distinct or exclusive perceptions*

In the eyes of the Zen master distinct or exclusive perceptions entail the fixing of the mind on a particular point. This localization of mental energy on a privileged point hinders its freedom of movement, conditions and limits it. *Mental activity can nevertheless exercise its attention on particular beings and things although remaining entirely free of attachment to them.* This nuance is of the greatest importance. Perfect attention is realized in total adequacy to place and circumstance but since these change from instant to instant the mind should be freed from the past during each present moment which it encounters. It can then see and treat the facts which arise but this must be done in an attitude devoid of all fixity, tension and attachment.

This is clearly set forth in the conversations of Zen master Hui Hai with his disciple:

Question: 'Explain what is meant by true perception.'
Answer: 'To perceive that there is nothing to be perceived is called true perception.'
Question: 'Explain what is meant by saying that there is nothing to be perceived.'
Answer: 'It means that at the *moment of perceiving the various kinds of phenomena, sensual attachment does not arise.* Not allowing yourself to be moved, or love or hatred to dwell in the mind, is called perceiving that there is nothing to be perceived' (*The Path to Sudden Attainment*, p. 16).

Krishnamurti repeats exactly the same fundamental truths when he invokes the necessity of a de-specialization of the mind. He teaches us that exclusive perceptions damage the inner adaptability without which we cannot be fully revealed to ourselves.

'A mind imprisoned in an exclusive concentration can never find the truth,' he says, 'but a mind that understands each movement of thought, that is conscious of each sentiment, being extremely supple and swift, is capable of seeing that which is . . .' (Krishnamurti, *Madras, Benares*).

(c) *Partitioned or set meditations*

Zen masters insist on the artificial nature of 'meditations at set hours'. Zen is inseparable from Life itself. Therefore it is from instant to instant that perfect attention in all circumstances should be realized. This is expressed in the conversations of Hui Hai.

Question: 'Should we exert ourselves only when we are sitting in meditation or also when we are moving about?'

Answer: 'I spoke of exerting yourselves, not just sitting. Walking, standing, sitting, lying, whatever you are doing and at all times continually exert yourselves without interruption. This is called forever dwelling (in Enlightenment)'.

The same idea was voiced by Zen master Shen-Hui:

'. . . when we talk of "seeing into one's self-nature", this seeing has also a binding effect on us if it is construed as having something in it specifically set up; that is if *the seeing is a specific state of consciousness*. For this is binding' (D. T. Suzuki, *The Zen Doctrine of No-Mind*, p. 27).

The whole of Krishnamurtian thought is steeped in an infinite respect for the spontaneity and renewal of the Real. To Krishnamurti this Reality is something completely unknown. We can only approach it when we are rid of all our certainties, references and land-marks.

Any preparation conceals an artificiality which is imbued with secret expectation. That is why Krishnamurti says:

'To meditate is to live from moment to moment, and not to shut oneself up in a room or in a cave, because by so doing it is impossible to find out the truth. The truth is to be found in the course of contacts with our daily life.

To meditate is, where thought is concerned, to free oneself from time, because in duration, the Intemporal can never be apprehended' (Krishnamurti, *Madras, Benares*).

In the spirit of Zen as in that of Krishnamurti, meditation is alien to all prayer, cult of a being or a symbol, discipline or devotion. For both it is knowledge in action.

(d) *Attachment to ideas, beliefs*

Attachment to certain forms of thought and beliefs, is, in the eyes of the Zen masters and Krishnamurti, one of the major conditioning factors of the mind.

A striking example of this is to be found in the dialogue between the Zen master Hsi-Yun and his disciple P'ei Hsin.

Question: 'Upon what principles is all that your Reverence has said based?'
Answer: 'What are these principals that you seek? *As soon as a principle is established a departure from universal mind takes place.*'
Question: 'But what is the principle which you mentioned just now about the past which stretches backward into eternity not being different from the present?'
Answer: 'It is only on account of your seeking (for a principle) that you yourself differentiate between them. If you were to stop seeking, how could there be any difference?' (*The Huang-Po Doctrine of Universal Mind*, p. 45).

Zen master Te-shan expressed the same idea when in one of his sermons he denounced the danger of attachment to the least thought or value:

'Cherish but one iota of thought, and lo, karma is at work and you are on the wrong path. Allow one flash of imagination to cross your mind, and lo, you are a slave. . . .'

Throughout the work of Krishnamurti, we notice allusions to the destructive role of ideas which, far from uniting men, have set them against one another throughout the ages. 'Belief paralyses experience', Krishnamurti tells us and he does not hesitate to denounce 'learning' as an 'obstacle to wisdom' (Krishnamurti, *Madras*).

The answers of the Master Hsi Yun to the questions of his disciple are strikingly parallel to the Krishnamurtian attitude towards mind and learning.

'If you now set about using your mind to seek mind and,
[164] relying on others, hope to find only through learning, when will you ever succeed? In former times men's minds were sharp. Upon hearing a single sentence, they abandoned study and so came to be called 'the sages who, abandoning learning, rest in spontaneity'. In these days, people only seek to stuff themselves with knowledge and deductions ... They do not know that *so much learning and deduction, on the contrary, become obstacles.*
When so-called knowledge and deductions are undigested, they are both poisons' (*Huang-Po Doctrine of Universal Mind*, p. 43).

Krishnamurti often uses similar language when he says that any imperfectly understood experience remains engraved on our mind and, in a certain sense, increases the burden of its accumulations of memory.

(e) *Dualistic vision of divers opposites.*

[165]   We have already commented this portion of a discourse of Hui-Neng the Sixth Patriarch:

'As long as there is a dualistic way of looking at things, there is no emancipation. Light stands against darkness; the passions stand against enlightenment. Unless these opposites are illuminated by Prajna, there is no understanding of Mahayana' (Suzuki, *Zen Doctrine of No-Mind*, p. 37).

Krishnamurti dwells continually on the conflict of opposites in whose clutches the 'I-process' is caught. The 'I-process' turns from vice to virtue, from evil to good, from activity to non-activity, from wealth to poverty. Under cover of these superficial changes, which Krishnamurti intentionally calls 'modified continuities', the 'I-process' attributes to itself permanence. What is more, it feeds on the tensions, which it creates entirely between the oppositional values built up by the mind. Thus the sterile and dolorous pilgrimage of life wends its way, to which only keen discernment can put an end.

(f) The craving for 'becoming'.

In Buddhism in general and Zen in particular, the craving for 'becoming' or Tanha, is considered as the dominating element in [166] our bondage. All aspirations towards a 'becoming' lead us to inextricable impasses. Buddhist Scriptures tell us that we are of-the-nature-Buddha. The only task which is incumbent upon us is that of becoming aware of it. As Krishnamurti expresses it 'If we understood the difference between "to become" and "to be", perhaps then we would understand the meaning of happiness . . . To become is continuous and have you not noticed that that which is continuous always imprisons?' (Krishnamurti, *Madras*).

(g) Techniques, methods and means

The correct approach to the Real can only be negative. Buddhism in general, Zen in particular and Krishnamurtian thought are imbued with this apparent negativity. It could not be otherwise. The reality they are trying to discover cannot be described. All technique, any set project for realization, inevitably conditions the mind of him who draws inspiration from it, and prevents him from all possibility of effective experience.

The essential of what has just been said is taught by all the Zen masters.

In the *The Path to Sudden Attainment* by Hui Hai, we read the following:

'*The absence of a positive method of abstraction is called complete Enlightenment.*'

In another Zen work there is an account of a disciple questioning the Master Hsi Yun on the subject of the 'means' or methods of realization. He obtained the following answer:

'*As long as you are concerned with "by means of" you will always be depending on false media*' (*Huang-Po Doctrine of Universal Mind*, p. 47).

In these answers to requests for 'methods', or so-called 'practical' receipts, we find exactly the same point of view as when we read the works of Krishnamurti.

'Happiness', Krishnamurti tells us, 'cannot be found by the use of any "means", but only by abandoning the idea that we are chosen people walking along a particular path.

The means creates the end. The end is fabricated by you, therefore it is conditioned' (Krishnamurti, *Madras*).

(h) *Cult of authority and disciplines.*

The spirit of Zen, like that of Krishnamurti, can be defined as 'spiritual anarchy'. This definition should be understood to exclude any derogatory sense of the term, as evoking negativity.

We do not have to resort to the cult of any spiritual authority for the reason that, from all eternity, we have been and we shall ever be the Real.

That is why Zen says:

'Place no head above your own.'

Krishnamurti uses similar language when he denounces the danger of the authority of the masters, traditions and disciplines:

[167] 'You are destroying yourself in following another. When, blindly, you follow a tradition, a leader, or a party, by disciplining yourself, are you not destroying your own process of thought? (Krishnamurti, *Madras*).

(i) *The Search for virtues.*

All research of whatever kind leads to the conditioning of the mind.

Krishnamurti and Zen condemn the vanity of the pursuit of

moral qualities. Virtue, purity and detachment are not means but consequences.

Hui-Neng says:

'When you cherish the notion of purity and cling to it you turn purity into falsehood ... Purity has neither form nor shape, and when you claim an achievement establishing a form to be known as purity, you obstruct your own self-nature, you are purity-bound' (D. T. Suzuki, *Zen Doctrine of No-Mind*, p. 26).

In answer to the questions which his disciple asks him, concerning the putting into practice of his teaching and of virtues, Hsi-Yun clearly defines the position of the Zen masters:

'Words that are used to attract the dull witted should not be relied upon.'
Question: 'If these teachings are meant to attract the dull-witted, I have not heard the Dharma which is intended for people of the highest capacity.'
Answer: 'If they are really people of the highest capacity *where can they find others to be followed by them?*
If they seek from within themselves they will still find nothing tangible; how much less can they do so from elsewhere?'
Question: 'But in this way everything would be eliminated. There cannot be just nothing.'
Answer: 'Who teaches that there is nothing? What is this nothing? (But you implied that) *you wanted to seek for something ... If you do not seek, that is enough.* Who told you to eliminate anything? Observe the Void which lies before your eyes. How can you set about eliminating it?' (*Huang-Po Doctrine of Universal Mind*, p. 41).

We have said elsewhere that Vacuity is not nothingness but plenitude which is revealed through the absence of attachment to [168] values and distinct qualities.

(4) *We are the Real*

We are Reality but we do not see it. Our own mind is the Real, but a fault in our mental functioning due to identification with past memories, prevents us from seeing ourselves as we are.

169   These ideas briefly summarize one of the bases of Zen thought which is common also to Krishnamurti.

It is written in the doctrine of Hsi Yun (*Huang-Po Doctrine of Universal Mind*).

170   'All the Buddhas and all sentient beings are nothing but universal mind, beside which nothing exists. This mind, which has always existed, is unborn and indestructible' (p. 16).

'Since we are nothing but universal mind, strictly speaking there is no such thing as "becoming" a Buddha; we have but to realize intuitively what we already are' (p. 18).

'But whether Realization is accomplished . . . its result is a state in which to be, and not something which can be performed or realized' (p. 20).

Krishnamurti used somewhat similar terms to those above when he spoke in London in 1953.

171   'Then the mind is in itself the unknown . . . the "new", the "uncontaminated". Consequently it is the Real, the incorruptible . . .' (Krishnamurti, Talks, London, 1953).

'When the mind is free from the past, from memory, from knowledge, it is the unknown. For such a mind there is no death . . .' (*idem*).

'This stillness is not an idea, it is a fact. It is the unfathomable. Then the mind is the real' (*idem*).

(5) *The Sense of freedom*

Zen thought and Krishnamurtian teaching are the two highest expressions of *free spiritual thought*.

Both encourage us to free ourselves from sacred texts, rituals, principals and traditional methods of realization. They require us to free ourselves from all outer or inner authority, including that of memories accumulated by our own past.

Very often we see Krishnamurti encouraging his audience to doubt the content of that which he has just expressed. When it happens that he expresses a thought too clearly and strikingly, and which might be systematized, he immediately asks his listeners not to repeat it mechanically, nor erect it into a system. 'All that was merely words, if you did not feel them', he often used to say.

We often notice reactions of this kind amongst the Zen masters. [171] In answer to a question of his disciple, Hsi Yun concludes saying:

'As soon as you start to think of what I tell you about mind being Buddha, attachment takes place and you rapidly tumble' (*Huang-Po Doctrine of Universal Mind*, p. 44).

We do not in any way claim to exhaust the very rich possibilities which arise from a comparison of Zen and Krishnamurti. We sought only to present here the most striking aspects. As it is [172] obvious that these comparative studies belong to the purely intellectual domain which is condemned with equal vigour by the two teachings, we shall now desist from our attempts in this direction.

CHAPTER XXVI

Divergencies between Buddhism, Zen and Krishnamurti

Certain divergencies exist nevertheless between Buddhism in general, Zen in particular and Krishnamurtian thought.

Firstly is the fact that Buddhism in general and Zen in particular are presented as 'doctrines'. This applies to Buddhism more than to Zen. Secondly, Buddhism and Zen have a religious organization, monasteries in which monks devote themselves to the attainment of 'Correct Vision'.

Krishnamurti, on the other hand tends towards a kind of integral secularization. In his eyes all organization of the truth conditions the mind.

To whoever has studied Krishnamurti deeply it would seem that the idea of a 'Krishnamurtian' monastery is the very negation of the teaching of the Hindu thinker. Some may object, however, that on various occasions Krishnamurti himself has suggested the setting up of 'communities' founded by men who had effectively realized the transformation of all false values.

At the same time we must point out that these communities ought to be free of any religious character as we generally understand it.

A difference seems to exist between Buddhism in general, Zen and Krishnamurtian thought. It lies in the domain of affectivity and sensibility.

One of the essential bases of the thought of Krishnamurti resides in the realization of a superior sensibility by which the spontaneous, rapid rhythm of Life can be seized in the instantaneity of its springing forth.

This sensibility is given us, not through a refusal of affectivity or of the various forms of love but, on the contrary, by a progressive increase of our emotional energies.

It would appear that the different forms of Buddhism and Zen dispose of the affective problem by subtly rationalizing it whereas Krishnamurti, on the contrary, tries to make us plunge into it, and transcend it, by means of a veritable volatilization of the limits of the 'I-process' effected by love itself.

Commentary on a 'Koan'

Text:

'At the beginning, the mountains are mountains.
In the middle, the mountains are no longer mountains.
At the end, the mountains are once again mountains.'

Commentaries

The interpretation of this text gives a panoramic vision of the stages leading to Satori according to Zen thought. At the same time we must insist on the fact that these phases apply to the period preceeding Satori and not to the experience itself. The latter is devoid of any sense of progression or degree: it is instantaneous.

During the period preceeding all research we do not throw doubt on anything, nor do we devote thought to the great problems of existence.

When we see mountains we merely say: 'These mountains are mountains.' Their exterior contours which are apparent to our eyes are their only reality. Rocks are but rocks, and earth is only earth.

When we awake and begin to seek we discover that nothing is permanent, that everything moves and is transformed. Instead of the rocks and the earth and the mountains we discern the action of a prodigiously active energy which moves with the swiftness of lightning. We tend progressively to notice the impermanence of things and beings. We are on the path to the discovery of the profound nature of the universe and of ourselves. Their superficial appearance tends to take on a secondary and derivative role in face of the common essence.

When we look at the mountains, during this phase, they are no longer mountains. They seem like a mirage which is devoid of all

real consistence. In reaction to our complete ignorence at the beginning we tend to orient ourselves in the directly opposite direction.

The sense of reality which we attributed to matter is transferred
to the pure essence in an equally unilateral attitude. In a word,
matter has become for us the 'veil', 'maya'.

The mountains are regarded as pure illusion.

It may happen, however, that we perceive that no scission
exists between the material world and that of pure essence. These
distinctions arise from a lack of penetration on the part of our [174]
mind. Everything is Reality. Not a speck of dust is outside this
Totality-that-is-One which the Zen masters call 'Cosmic Mind'.

From that moment, when our eyes alight upon the mountains,
we say as in the beginning: the mountains are mountains. We
have returned to matter, but we have a new vision of it. Our
vision is no longer confined exclusively to its material or to its
spiritual aspect.

It is no longer illusion, or 'maya'. The creator of illusions has
been finally unmasked: it is none other than our own mind.

Our attitude of mind has undergone a complete metamorphosis.
When we now say: 'The mountains are mountains', these same [175]
words express a panoramic vision which comprehends both the
relative 'surface' appearance and absolute Reality. It is a question
here of an integration that can neither be described nor thought.

At last we play the 'Game of the World', while free from it.
We attribute a correct value to separate beings and things. We are
free from attachment and from identification with superficial
appearances.

We are free.

Brief Survey of the Tibetan Schools of Philosophy, of the 'Oral Transmission', of the (so-called) 'Secret Doctrines'

by Mme A. David-Neel

Many absurd stories have been told concerning Schools in Tibet which diffuse a so-called 'secret' teaching. Similar stories are still retailed throughout the various Western countries. It may be of some use, therefore, to give those who are interested an exact picture of what really are these Schools in Tibet which are depositaries of Doctrines and Methods of traditional intellectual and spiritual training.

To begin with, when I say 'School', I use this term in the sense of a 'body of doctrines' expounded by successive Masters. It is not at all a question of 'classes' given by professors and followed regularly by students as it might be in an institution of university type.

In fact there exist in Tibet successions of 'Doctors of the Law' who claim to possess philosophical doctrines, and methods of development of the spiritual and intellectual faculties which, since remotest antiquity, have been handed down from master to disciple within the sect to which they belong.

All these sects claim to profess Buddhism; but it is only the profane, ignorant of religious history, who believe that there is only one kind of Buddhism. It is far from being so. The complete freedom of thought, allowed to the disciples of Buddha, has resulted in the more intellectual among them developing, through the centuries, many theories which are presented as interpretations or elaborations of the basic principals proclaimed by the Buddha.

We therefore find ourselves, face to face with divers forms of Buddhism represented by the different Tibetan Schools of the 'Oral Tradition'.

Nevertheless, if we wish to have a correct idea of the nature of these schools, we should know that the Masters generally took care not to propound theories to those whom they admitted as disciples.

These should not expect a sudden revelation of particular truths. What they will receive from the Master will be indications which will help them to cultivate a certain kind of energy by *themselves* within themselves.

'What kind of energy?' The Master would answer this question by saying that only one kind of energy existed, but that it can be used in dozens of different ways for dozens of purposes.

In this case the disciple must:

(1) develop this energy within himself;

(2) use this energy to increase the faculties of research in order to arrive at *knowledge*;

(3) use it in order to *act* in accordance with the knowledge acquired. Briefly, the aim envisaged is to effect a complete transformation of whoever undertakes this training; to make a different being of an ordinary man. An ambitious programme . . . a ridiculous programme, because impossible, or so many people will think.

But it is not to 'many people' that the teaching of the Tibetan schools of the oral tradition is addressed.

But, remember: I said *knowledge*.

Knowledge of what? . . . Knowledge of reality hidden beneath appearances. Not to be deceived by appearances as are most men. Not to accept things as they appear at first sight or as most men see them, without reflection.

Finally, *to see*, with the penetrating vision which sears through to the depth of things, and which the Tibetans call *lags thong*, that is to say: 'see more'.

I think indeed that these words 'see more' summarize the whole programme of the Schools. *To see more* in the physical domain as in the mental. And when one knows: to *act* with all the means which this knowledge procures.

Tibetans see a dangerous side to the power resulting from a profound knowledge of things in the physical field, as in the domain of the mind, and in knowledge of the mechanism which phenomena obey.

This power, they say, can express itself in different ways according to the character of whoever has it. It can serve both good and evil. It can also turn against him who has partially developed it and is not entirely its master. Dreadful tales have been told of this power. Obviously exaggeration must be taken into account, but I still have good reasons to believe in the truth of certain stories of novice-sorcerers who have met their death or lost their reason during the rites they practised. I have seen something of this at close quarters.

If I mention this, it is incidentally, because you may have heard tell of it.

The eminent Masters of the Schools of the traditional transmission are philosophers. They only see in these abnormal effects the result of a derangement of the mental functions producing derangement of the physical functions. Both *being the work of the individual himself* who is its victim.

Learning is always good, they say, on condition that one truly learns, learns *thoroughly*. Also they believe that not all men are capable of learning in this manner. Do we also not think that not all men are able to be great mathematicians and understand Einstein's theories, or other similar theories? They think moreover that most men have no desire to know, have no curiosity as to the *how* of things and their nature, and think, above all, that those who have the will and the perseverance necessary to undertake long research are few in number.

For these reasons they live in retirement, admitting few pupils, and it is that which has earned their teaching the name of 'secret doctrine'.

Above all we should not forget that the Masters of whom we speak profess Buddhism. The theories they have adopted, however mixed with Tantrism they may be, have a solid foundation of Buddhism, and you will remember the formal injunction of Buddha to his disciples is: 'Rid yourselves of erroneous ideas, acquire *correct vision*.'

Buddhist salvation is highly intellectual. It consists in seeing *that which is* instead of contemplating the phantasmagoria which we build ourselves. When they recommend the cultivation of perspicacity, intense vision, the Doctors of the traditional doctrines of the oral transmission are there in perfect agreement with the fundamental doctrine of Buddhism.

The Masters of the Schools of Oral Tradition dwell on the instantaneous and essentially transitory nature of all phenomena. They also teach that bodies which appear solid to us are really composed of particles in motion. Their solid and durable appearance is due to the prodigious rapidity with which these particles move.

This theory is found written in Sanscrit, Tibetan and Chinese books.

Then the Master of the secret School will say to his disciples: 'You think that it is so, but it is probably on the faith of what is written in books. It is not real knowledge. Have you *grasped or felt*, have you *seen* this basic impermanence, this lack of self-nature of things which are only agregates of divers elements. . . . ?'

No doubt you have not grasped these facts directly. But it is only by so doing that you will have real knowledge of them. Otherwise you will only have *faith*, and faith is the opposite of knowledge.

If he were here, one of these Doctors might say to us: You Occidentals think that light takes time to travel. You must therefore conclude that the phenomena, the events that you are seeing *now*, have already taken place and already belong to the past when you perceive them. Are you well aware of that?

Have you understood that the fact of your witnessing, as in the present, events which have occurred in a past that stretches back to infinitely distant points of the universe, should induce you completely to change your notions concerning what you call time: past, present and future.

To his disciples the Master merely asks:

Does time exist? Is there a past, a present, a future?

This question may appear absurd to us. Well, it is apparently ridiculous questions like this one that the Masters of the secret Schools encourage their disciples to ask themselves. Why? Because they want to lead them to make a clean sweep of their conceptions, and prepare themselves for a complete reversal of all their old ideas.

Time . . .? Is it true that a kind of panorama unrolls before the immobile spectator who cuts it into sections which he calls 'yesterday', 'today', 'last year', 'twenty years ago', etc.

One Master of the Chinese sect Ch'an saw things inversely. He has expressed his conception in one of these figurative declarations which the members of this sect call *kwain* in Chinese and *koan* in Japanese, which more or less means a 'problem'.

'Oh Wondrous', exclaimed the Master, 'I am on this bridge, and lo, it is not the river that is flowing, but the bridge which is moving up stream!'

A Tibetan expressed the same idea when he said: 'The landscape is motionless, it is the rider who passes by.'

There are more ways than one of understanding these declarations.

To employ a metaphor, let us consider ourselves as moving past a series of events, of phenomena lined up along our route. The position we give them is due to our own velocity. We leave certain 'landscapes' behind us, that is certain aspects of the world, certain events, certain phenomena, and because they are behind us, we call them 'past'. In saying 'past' we imagine a certain division of time, and draw a line of demarcation between the place in which we are and that on which we were yesterday; and that which is on the other side of the line we consider as dead and a nullity.

But is it so? That which we consider as finished and dead, is it really so? Does it not still exist like the mountain or the river which the rider on his journey has left behind him?

Is the past not living in the present and the future? Is it not contained in the present? Does anything other than a perpetual present exist? . . . One must ask oneself that.

However one must be careful not to believe that there are stable elements or any entities which remain unchanged subject to these changing phenomena.

Such a conception is absolutely contrary to the fundamental

principals of Buddhism and to the secret doctrines of the traditional transmission.

Impermanence is the general law. The cause perishes when the
effect is revealed, or rather, it is the destruction of the cause, its
transformation which *is* the effect.

Nothing which exists has its own nature, everything is an
'assemblage' everything is impermanent; in Tibetan this is expressed by:

'Kang zag dag med pa — Tcheu dag med pa.'*

It is the repetition of the declaration, in lapidary style, of the
first Buddhists: 'Sabbe sankhara anicca — Sabbe dhamma anatta.'

Nevertheless nothing is annihilated. The whole content of that
which we call the 'past' remains active.

Material phenomena, events of all kinds, ideas, thoughts and
even the smallest movements of the body and the mind of all
beings, all these remain as potential forces 'stored' in a manner
of speaking, to use an image, in a 'reservoir'.

The Tibetans call this 'reservoir', *Kun ji*, that is the 'basis of
everything', or, often, *Kun ji nampar ches pa*,† consciousness, or
the fundamental basic idea.

Sanscrit writers use the term *Alaya vijnana*; 'Warehouse of
consciousness'.

This 'reservoir' is not situated anywhere; it is everywhere, and is
the universe itself. Speaking approximately, it is the *subconscious* of
the universe.

This reservoir is inexhaustible although its content flows perpetually because while it flows away in the forms of activity that
make up the world, at the same time all the beings and things of the
universe continually add to it the energy which their activity
generates.

Unless I am mistaken the second law of thermodynamics, which
occupies such an important place in modern physics, is opposed to
the idea of re-using the whole of the energy given out by the
body. But the universe to which this law is applied is a universe

* Tibetan spelling: kang zag bdag med pa — tchosbdag med pa.
† Tibetan spelling: Kun g ji and Kun g ji rnam par chés pa.

which is supposed to be material. In Tibet we are on another plane. The universe, as the Tibetan Masters see it, only exists by the mind and in the mind. It is a creation of the mind and is made with the substance of the mind.

A similar idea has occurred to some physicists. In Eddington I read that 'the stuff of the world is mind'.

The ancient Hindu philosophers have given the name of *vâsanâ* (memory) to this storing of active energy; as for the Tibetans they call it *pagchag* which means propensity.

Energy is the *memory* of the universe; the propensities of the universe tend to reproduce activities which have already been manifested. They *all* tend thereto, but not all with equal force. Consequently these dissimilar and even, sometimes, frankly antagonistic forces meet and struggle, cancel each other out or strengthen each other, so much so that the activity-producing energy coming from the 'reservoir', never gives rise to activities exactly identical with those which fed it.

Nothing is absolutely predetermined. Though everything arises from causes, there is no rigid determinism allowing exact fore-knowledge of what will be.

Never, it has been said also, is an effect the outcome of a single cause. It is always due to the combination of many causes which are ranged in divers positions in time and space: some near and others distant.

Tibetans attach great importance to this distinction of the essential cause *gyu* and secondary causes *kien*,* the latter being in an indeterminate, but always considerable, number.

One of the training exercises proposed to the disciple consists in unravelling the complicated skein of secondary causes, entangled round the principal cause, and discovering the roles they have played in the events and phenomena which occur round us and above all, those occurring *within* us.

One must set one's mind to discovering the causes which have built up the individual we are today.

To know these causes is to know one's previous lives.

The Masters of the secret teaching say: In Buddhist texts the

---

*Written respectively rgyu and rgyan.

question of recalling one's previous existence is often raised. The majority of Buddhists who do not understand the doctrine dealing with the inexistence of an *ego* have adopted the ancient Hindu idea of the reincarnation of a spirit which is always the same, and which transmigrates (the *jiva* of the Hindus).

It is not thus that the initiates of the secret doctrines understand *re-birth*. To them that which is *re-born*, or *rather*, that which has persisted, consists of *forces*; and these converge to produce a physical phenomenon, an individual, the mental disposition of this individual, etc.

The dissociation of these clusters of force occurs every moment, and partially or totally different associations are formed. By being aware of this one can understand the words of the Buddha: 'That which is called a man, is perpetual transformation.'

Like all bodies, phenomena and the entire universe, what we call our *me* is a vortex into which forces hurl themselves, attracted and captured by it while, at the same time, this vortex ejects other forces which join other vortices.

The Masters of the secret sects try to train their disciples not only to understand that Universal Life is made up of movement — a physicist will understand that — but to attain an acuteness of perception which will allow them to *see* all that surrounds them, and to see themselves also under this aspect of the continual play of energy.

Having seen this, and having contemplated the spectacle of the universal life, they will see that the idea of birth and death, in the ordinary sense of the words, is pure illusion devoid of foundation.

As the great philosopher Nâgârjuna said: 'There is neither coming into existence, nor going out of existence.'

And we can compare this declaration with that of the Buddha:

'An ignorant man says that *everything is*. Another ignorant man says that *nothing is*. But for him who understands through wisdom there is neither Being, nor Non-Being.'

To sum up, I shall say that the teaching of the Tibetan Masters of the philosophical Schools called the 'Secret Doctrines' or 'Oral Tradition' consists in inspiring their disciples with the desire to penetrate that which exists behind the appearances which their senses offer them, behind the generally accepted theories, and behind the 'me' in which habit causes them to believe.

They invite them to contemplate other spectacles than those which they are in the habit of contemplating; and, above all, they invite them to see themselves as different from the person they have always known.

Part Two

Introduction to the Conclusions

ZEN being essentially practical it therefore appears opportune to conclude our studies by a general summary of the 176 methods of their application in daily life. This appears to us all the more necessary in that we wish to destroy the legend of a supposed incompatibility of Zen with the active life of the Occident. We insist particularly on this possibility of assimilation while admitting the need for a *totally different* rhythm of life. It is not only a question of 'living better'. In comparison with the average life of today Zen can be considered as a *complete revolution* of all our spiritual values which should inevitably be expressed by a new social order free of egoism.

Not only is life without egoism and personal identification not an impossibility, but it is the condition *sine qua non* of all social harmony both individual and collective. Obedience to the profound nature of things should give rise to as perfect an order on the human scale as that which stirs us when we regard the silent beauty of the vegetable kingdom. In order to be perfect this order should be the work of Life, and *no longer that of ideas.*

This rich, intense life, non-violent and silent, should be lived within the frame-work of the outside world. An abyss seems to separate us from the rhythms of this supremely natural existence, and yet nothing is more simple.

Our difficulties arise from our education, our physical and mental heredity which all bear the stamp of false values.

The fundamental transformation which is most urgent, is both physical and spiritual. We intend to dwell on certain practical aspects of this while making certain reservations. In fact we would not wish the examples, suggestions and details presented in the following lines to be adopted by the reader in a spirit of imitation. All conformism constitutes an obstacle to the supreme awakening. All conformism is the expression of a fear and of an unintelligent search for the Real.

Our approach can only be negative. The positive character of methods and so called 'practical' formulae is entirely illusory, for these only lead to comfortable states of self-hypnosis, which bear within them the invisible seeds of violence and egoism, of which the individual and collective dramas of the present-day world are the culmination.

Nevertheless we are obliged to develop certain theoretical aspects of this question, rendered indispensable by the somewhat thankless nature of Zen on the one hand and our Western education on the other.

The transformations demanded by Zen can be summarized as follows:

(1) Transformation of physical life and its relations with the psycho-physical unity.

(2) Transformation of human relations:

    (a) Importance of the fact of relationship in the Universe;

    (b) Importance of the mental attitude in the approach to these relationships.

(3) True 'letting go' effected by 'Love-Intelligence'.

CHAPTER I

Transformation of Physical Life and its Relations with the Psycho-Physical Unity

THE Zen masters, Hatha Yoga and Judo teach us that the human races of today have lost all trace of an instinctive wisdom of the body. The physical body which is disdained by many Occidental mystics, spiritually minded persons and intellectuals, *is Cosmic Mind* in the same way as are the highest mental attainments.

We can still rediscover an instinctive wisdom of the body drawing its essence from obscure biological memories going back to the beginnings of the world. The possibilities of physical life from this angle are immense.

That is the reason which leads many Zen sympathizers to practise Judo. We will not assume the responsibility here of asserting that the practise of Judo leads to the experience of Satori. Nevertheless it gives a certain suppleness to the physical body, a flexibility, a muscular and nervous relaxation which can be of great use. Judo also brings about a pacification and non-violence of thought. We know, indeed, that this pacification and non-violence apply to the peripheral, the most 'physical' layers of the mind, and do not affect the 'I-process' in its ultimate refuge. Nevertheless the results obtained can be of considerable help.

Chinese tradition gives us some interesting details concerning the origin of Judo long before the form given it by the Master Kano in the last century.

Its principles of non-resistance and non-violence were born one day in the mind of an observer who noticed that the branches of a fir-tree snapped under the weight of the snow, whilst the simple reeds, weaker but more supple, emerged victorious from the trial. This suppleness and this non-resistance figure among the bases of Judo.

We are often broken by circumstances, for we resist the law of Life.

We are no longer adequate. We no longer have the relaxation, neither the physical suppleness nor the mental agility with which to reply adequately to circumstances. Our disordered mental activity and too fertile imagination cut us off from the outside world.

The practise of Judo forces us to an attention which is completely physical and non-mental. In Judo, he who thinks is immediately thrown. Victory is assured to the combatant who is both physically and mentally non-resistant. We suppose wrongly that only thought-out and calculated moves are sound.

The practise of Judo helps us to revalue the vegetative life which our hyper-intellectualized generations too often despise. We should rid ourselves of our excessive intellectuality.

As we have seen above, mental activity conceals a fundamental character of violence whose importance escapes us. Violence and fear are the distinctive signs of thought in its deepest levels. We are often unaware of this. In the first period of training the attentive judoka can surprise in himself signs of this mental violence and fear. He will notice that they are radically opposed to the reflexes arising from the instinctive wisdom of the body. The gestures suggested by violence and fear express tense, agitated and often aggressive attitudes. The great art of Judo consists precisely in using to the maximum the force of the adversary against himself. If we try to resist him we are immediately thrown off balance, and our fall is inevitable. If we free ourselves from all mental suggestions of resistance and, on the contrary, adopt an extremely supple attitude, the defeat of our adversary is certain.

The practise of Judo is of great benefit to the impenitent 'hypercerebral'. The intensity of the exercise, and the completely physical attention required, bring a happy compensation. Equilibrium is assured because the judoka is *obliged* to exercise a vigilant and non-mental observation. He is *obliged* to rediscover the dormant corporeal reflexes of an instinctive wisdom which is directly linked with the profound nature of all things and his own being. This equilibrium is sound as no mental or spiritual discipline is involved.

Generally speaking, physical discipline is necessary. But we should also add that this physical discipline should be free of all mental identification and all craving for 'becoming'.

Its aim is essentially physical. Here once again, a piece of paradoxical advice is in place. Although necessary and indispensable, physical transformation must not be accompanied even by a secret anticipation of Satori.

The exercise of close attention, mental flexibility and the higher forms of sensibility need a body which is itself supple, sensitive and free of all toxins.

A brain irrigated by unhealthy blood can scarcely have clear ideas.

Therefore a strict alimentary hygiene is necessary, avoiding as far as possible alcohol, meat, processed or chemically treated foods, too richly prepared dishes and complicated mixtures.

Again we must insist that the putting into practise of this advice would be quite useless if a fanatical or intolerant outlook is adopted, as can be observed among certain naturists and vegetarians.

The safe-guarding of the equilibrium of the nervous system is very important in a civilization where anti-natural rhythms tend constantly to destroy it. The nervous system is the instrument of expression of the psyche. At this point we find it necessary to recommend balance in the sexual life as much as in alimentary hygiene.

Digestion is a question of nerves. By eating hastily and not chewing sufficiently we are exposing ourselves to considerable nervous expenditure. Zen masters advise us to be completely present to what we are doing. Let us take our time and, if we are in a hurry, then let us eat less.

One of the strangest paradoxes of technical civilizations lies in this fact: the more technique triumphs over the barriers of time, the less time man has at his disposal. He no longer has time to eat, breathe deeply, to live. Modern man loses his life by trying too hard to gain a living. Therefore he is incapable of dying in a healthy manner. Our present life is but a succession of incomplete actions. The agitation and impatience of modern man deprive him of the natural riches inherent in complete actions. These are only possible in the relaxation of body and mind. Impatience and avidity are the worst enemies of the nervous system.

The abuse of sexual relations involves a considerable expenditure of nervous energy and diminishes the higher forms of sensibility. Most sexual excesses are the result of purely imaginary mental suggestion rather than of simple physiological need. The Zen masters beg us to be very attentive to our manner of reacting in this manner.

We will not end this ensemble of physiological advice without mentioning the importance of sleep.

The progressive increase in the number of insomniacs is one of the evils of technical civilization. Sleep is the great restorer of nervous energy. The Zen masters advise us to conform to the rhythms of Nature. This means that whenever possible we should go to bed and rise early. Those persons deprived of physical exercise and fresh air, by reason of office-work, would do well to walk for half an hour, or an hour, before going to bed.

These practical indications should be applied with judgment by each person according to his constitution and temperament.

As we have already mentioned, the evening meal is omitted in most Buddhist monasteries. The receptivity of the deep layers of the unconscious during sleep requires a higher form of sensitivity on our part. The mobilization of nervous energy needed for digestion paralyses receptivity in the deepest parts of our being. The deepest layers of the unconscious and certain states akin to Satori may be revealed during particular phases of sleep.

These profoundly revealing phases only come to us in the complete absence of digestive processes and during a period when blood-pressure is slightly below normal. A copious meal taken late at night prevents the realization of these conditions.

CHAPTER II

Transformation of Human Relations

(a) *The importance of the fact of relationship in the Universe*

THE deeper significance of human relations cannot be grasped without the development of a few considerations [18] which may appear abstract or theoretical.

In spite of their theoretical and speculative aspects the following lines have an essentially practical aim.

We try to give real help to readers so as to guide them towards an effective experimental realization. But its strictly individual character makes our task extremely difficult.

In spite of its apparent complexity Zen psychology is a return to the practical. It simply encourages us to listen to the language of facts as they are.

But, to understand the language of facts in the sense meant by the Zen masters, we should be in *true relationship* with these facts. But we are not. Between the facts and ourselves there is the world of *ideas*.

Though we may understand most of these notions intellectually, we remain often incapable of putting them into practice.

The understanding of the language of facts should take place in the course of our daily life. It depends on approaching all circumstances in a frame of mind which is totally different to our usual one.

An insufficient development of this rather new subject may give rise to many misunderstandings.

It is, therefore, of the greatest importance to study from life the significance and nature of our *relations* from all points of view.

Most people who devote themselves to research in the inner life have a tendency to meditate in solitude. Many are content with a vision that is comprehensive and purely intellectual of these problems.

They confine themselves purely intellectually to seeking the perfectionment of certain truths to which they have adhered after a brief reading. Such an attitude of research is utterly inadequate.

Knowledge of ourselves – without which no Satori is possible – requires a lucidity of every moment, not only in our moments of solitude but *above all when we are in contact with others.*

The importance of human relations as factors of spiritual self-revelation and as a method of approach to Satori, has only too rarely been placed in evidence in contemporary Zen literature. Nevertheless we will recall this important thought of a Zen master, 'Every perception is an occasion for Satori'. His admirable development of this point of view is one of the principal bases of Krishnamurti's teaching.

The process of relationship is the process of life.

On its comprehension depend the creative or destructive qualities of our behaviour. Such are the reasons for which we have deemed it indispensable to make a few definitions on the exact significance of relations, not only regarding men but also in the universe.

True meditation is not inner passivity realized by external inaction. It is sometimes useful for us to pass through periods of rest and solitude. Let us bear in mind, however, that the complete contents of consciousness, and the unconscious cannot be fully revealed in the course of solitary meditations practised in a state of external inaction.

This kind of meditation often betrays an unconscious fear, a reflex of self-defence engendering a process of isolation.

Before reaching this domain lying beyond all experience we should reveal ourselves to ourselves in the fire of experience.

Correct meditation – an essential basis of Buddhism – is a lucidity of every instant in the course of which are revealed our emotional and mental reactions, our cravings, susceptibilities, attachments, our sensuality and violence *in our relations with others.*

The introspection realized during long periods of meditative isolation by many mystics or sincere seekers leads to states of auto-[179] hypnosis.

As an example we will cite the experience of a Hindu hermit.

After many years of solitude and meditation in forests and caves, this saintly man realized divers experiences of profound communion. His perseverance allowed him access to very high levels of consciousness where the essence of things and the unity of Brahman were revealed to him.

Some years passed and the hermit was noticed. A group of disciples quickly formed round him, each showing him profound veneration. The esteem with which he was surrounded and the intensity of his spiritual and ecstatic perceptions resulted in convincing the saintly man of the authenticity of his inner realization.

He believed himself to be freed, completely emancipated from all personal attachment and all possibility of egoistical reaction.

One day, however, he had to go to quite a big town.

Completely unknown in this highly populated region, he was nothing more than an ordinary man, completely anonymous, and lost in the great crowd. Little used to such agitation, he accidentally pushed against another pedestrian who promptly and soundly upbraided him. Greatly vexed, the hermit found himself a prey to anger mingled with indignation.

This human contact, this unexpected *relationship*, was more revealing to him than many years of solitary meditation. In the flash of an instant a whole sector of his 'I-process', which was deeply hidden in the ultimate layers of his consciousness, was revealed to him.

This is the sense in which we should consider human relations as factors of self-revelation. This complete act of becoming conscious is an indispensable condition of self-revelation without which our integration into Cosmic Mind is impossible.

The 'I-process' should be completely emptied of its content of false values, cravings and secret resistances. This cannot be realized in solitary meditation in the course of imaginary situations or relations. The relationship which is lived is the revealing mirror of the contents of consciousness and the unconscious.

The history of a universe is one of billions of *relationships* that are ever new. Everything is interrelated physically, biologically and psychologically.

Each breath of ours has a *relationship* with regard to the surrounding atmosphere. The air which enters our lungs is renewed with each breath. The cells of living things are in a continual state of *relationship*. The basis of biological life is perpetual exchange during which substances are transformed and renewed intensively owing to the flexibility and fluidity of the constituents of the cells.

The natural or manufactured objects with which we come in contact in daily life, do not escape the fundamental fact of relationship despite their appearances of fixity.

When bread was merely ears of corn, waving in the golden fields under the July sun, it was only a complex of '*relationships*', of 'interferences' between light-energy, the conditioning factors of its absorption and the mineral riches of the earth.

Everything is only interferences, residues of relations and forms of 'interference', but our attention possesses a quality of inertia which obliges it to dwell more on the residual than on the living aspect.

This bread which appears set, separate, 'residual' and victim of a sort of exclusion, resulting from the apparent isolation which its definite contours suggest to our eyes, is no less 'relationship' now than when its structure as living corn seemed to incorporate it more directly into the exchange: 'sun-light-earth-atmosphere.'

Its atoms react on the whole of the Universe right up to its ultimate confines.

The behaviour of atoms in the heart of all living or inanimate matter illustrates in a striking fashion the fundamental fact of relations.

If we had the faculty of being able to observe an atom of hydrogen, we would notice the dizzy circuits of a negative electron revolving round positive nucleus at the rate of six thousand billion times per second. But the electron only represents the two thousandth part of the mass of the nucleus. In the over-all behaviour of such an atomic system an enormous disproportion exists, between the fundamental fact of *relationships* and their intensity, on the one hand, and the derisory quantity of energy of an electron, on the other.

Moreover, we can no longer speak of an isolated atomic corpuscle.

The principals of 'exclusion' of Pauli and Fermi teach us that there exists a potential presence of each corpuscle which extends to the whole universe. Most modern physicists consider that the *Universe is only a reality in its totality*. The Zen masters have been [180] teaching nothing else for centuries.

The fundamental fact of relationship in physics has been revealed in all its implications as a result of the sensational discoveries of the antiproton in 1955.

Before that date, a certain mystery hovered over the exact structure of the constituent elements of atomic nuclei and the nature of their reciprocal relations. In fact everyone knows that particles charged with identical electricity repel each other. But there exist many atomic nuclei of heavy bodies such as lead, platinum, uranium, etc., which contain a considerable number of protons. No one was able to explain by what means the 146 protons existing in a nucleus of Uranium, for example, had the power to resist the intense repulsion arising from the identity of their electric charge, of their proximity and of their mass.

The merit goes to the Japanese physicist Yukawa for having expressed in 1936 the hypothesis of the existence of another force whose role consisted in developing an energy of linkage which is stronger than the force of repulsion of protons. This force was designated by the term 'meson' (from the Greek: middle, intermediate).

In 1947 the physicists Powel, Occlialini and Lattes discovered, in fact, a 'meson' of mass 276 approximately, presenting an affinity for the divers corpuscles of the nucleus. It was given the name 'pion'.

Recent progress in the study of accelerators of particles have permitted the discovery of positive, negative and neutral 'pions'.

This parenthesis, which seems outside our subject, allows us at last to support one of our fundamental conclusions, the separation between physics and psychology being non-existent.

No imagination is capable of conceiving the dazzling spectacle of the inter-changes — therefore *relationships* — which take place in the heart of the atomic nuclei.

The 'pions' exert their force of linkage by means of a play of exchanges both original and strange, whose philosophic consequences are immense. Thanks to their intervention the protons react amongst themselves. Neutrons react on protons and *viceversa* whilst they also react amongst themselves.

We are witnessing here the most extraordinary phenomena in existence.

It is really like a masquerade in which infernal roundabouts turn incessantly and in the course of which the *participants exchange their individuality in turn* billions and billions of times per second.

Protons lose a positive 'pion' and again become neutrons.

Neutrons join up with a positive 'pion' and become protons while identical corpuscles proceed to make intensive exchanges of neutral 'pions'. We are the bedazzled witnesses of the spectacular overthrowing of the ancient notions of individuality.

The essential notion arising from these interesting observations can be summarized as follows:

(1) *On the ultimate microcosmic scale of the Universe the fundamental fact of relations is infinitely more important than the particular nature or individuality of the connected elements;*

(2) *relations are the universal language of Cosmic Mind in the manifested world;*

(3) *perfect adequacy to circumstances is the universal expression of the intelligence of Cosmic Mind in the manifested world;*

(4) *Satori is the expression of this perfect adequacy on the human scale;*

(5) *The effective realization of Satori depends on our mental attitude in approaching these relations.*

(b) *Importance of the mental attitude in the approach to relations.*

Before embarking upon the short study of the mental attitude in human relations we will make a fairly short survey of the general evolution of the process of relationships. These may be divided into three main phases.

(1) *First phase:* In the vegetable kingdom and in certain parts of the animal kingdom relations are essentially physical. The mental

element is lacking. Plants do not resist the law of life. Their relations are perfect. Their obedience to the deeper nature of things is expressed by indisputable harmony and beauty. The presence of Cosmic Mind within them is sufficient in itself and is fully revealed on their level.

(2) *Second phase:* In the human kingdom (hyper-intellectualized) physical relations (vegetative life) are relegated to the secondary [181] plane. Mentation is intensive. *The mental function thinks that it is an entity and, as such, it corrupts the whole process of relations.* Man resists the law of life. He disobeys the deeper nature of things. The flaw in his mental function is reflected in vegetative life itself.

(3) *Third phase:* In the reign of the integrated human, the domain of relations extends only to the physical world as in the vegetable kingdom (vegetative life without mentation on the part of the living subject). *There no longer are mental relations issuing from the background of a static entity. Only thoughts without personal motive are born, and these respond adequately to circumstances.* After having passed through the phase of false relations and exhausted all the possibilities it contained, man turns towards true relations. But from that moment we are in the heart of a paradox. The true relation of Satori is Non-Mental. Speaking from the point of view of the mind, Satori is the state of no-relation.

The state of no-relation does not result from a stupid isolation. On the contrary it is the inevitable consequence of the abolition of all duality and the supreme unity of Cosmic Mind. In this resides the highest form of Intelligence. If the latter is expressed essentially by relations in the manifested universe, on the one hand, it is on the other, 'no-relation' in the non-manifested universe. *Relation and no-relation are the apparently opposite but in fact complementary facets of the same reality.*

The presence of Cosmic Mind in the heart of the man who obeys fully the nature of things is sufficient unto itself.* It does not need to be thought or objectivized in the approach to any circumstances whatever as it is the profound reality thereof, and the essence and the substance. In the man who has realized Satori

---

* A Zen master would say that Cosmic Mind is sufficient unto itself whatever the circumstances, and is in no way affected by our non-realization of Satori.

relations are limited to the physical domain. The mind only functions occasionally when social circumstances require it for communication. *This relation is no longer that of an entity, but that of an anonymous function.*

Apart from this exception, the consciousness of the integrated man exists night and day in the silence and transparence of the No-Mind.

Krishnamurti, the similarities of whose thought with that of Zen have been pointed out by us, uses the same kind of language when speaking of the no-relation of the true state of love (*First and Last Freedom*, p. 179).

'... Relationship has very little significance when we are merely seeking mutual gratification but becomes extraordinarily significant when it is a means of self-revelation and self-knowledge.

After all, *there is no relationship* in love, is there? It is only when you love something and expect a return of your love that there is a relationship. When you love, that is when you give yourself over to something entirely, wholly, then *there is no relationship*.

If you do love, if there is such a love, then it is a marvellous thing. In such love there is no friction, there is not the one and the other, there is complete unity. It is a state of integration a complete being. ...'*

However, before realizing the state of perfect integration or of 'no-relation' we ought to transform completely the nature of our present relationships such as they are.

Many philosophers have insisted on the importance of human relations. Marx considers social relationships as the highest reality.

Let us say at once that the transposition of the fundamental fact of relationships on the human scale, as we see it, differs somewhat from the purely social concept.

Our method of approach to relationships with objects, thoughts or persons determines the nature of the solution towards which we are tending.

An ensemble of factors is involved in all perception which conditions by virtue of its nature and deprives us of the experience of Satori.

* Our underlining.

Amongst these factors of our conditioning we may point out:

(1) total misunderstanding of ourselves and of our instrument: thought;

(2) our unconscious motives of attachment, our fears;

(3) our processes of choice and research;

(4) our inability to be in relationship with the Present;

(5) our mental processes of verbalization;

(6) our memory-habits and the exclusive perceptions which they engender;

(7) our tendency to compare;

(8) our fundamental tendency towards 'becoming';

(9) our refusal to see ourselves as we are.

'Every perception is an occasion for Satori' on condition that:

(1) we know the nature and function of our instrument: thought;

(2) our relationships are entirely in the Present;

(3) we are free from all motives and consequently emancipated from the process of choice;

(4) we are in a state of non-exclusive perception;

(5) we are receptive both to love and real intelligence;

(6) we are mentally and emotionally in a state of passive lucidity and consequently of not-searching and non-expectation;

(7) we are adequate.

A rapid glance over these few points reveal to us immediately their mutual interdependence in the 'I-process'.

We propose to study briefly some of these points while making clear that these headings are not restrictive and should not be treated systematically.

The elements contained in each of the above-mentioned points are so interrelated that we are obliged to limit their elaboration. To do the opposite would involve us in useless and tiresome repetition which would overload a somewhat laborious text.

MISUNDERSTANDING OF OURSELVES AND OUR
INSTRUMENT WHICH IS THOUGHT

Like Krishnamurti, Zen teaches us that we are like young apprentices who have absolutely no knowledge of their tools. Whatever the craft for which we are destined, our first task, an elementary one, consists in looking carefully at our tools.

In fact how could we carry out the simplest of tasks without examining the form of these pliers, this screwdriver, this hammer or that chisel. A preliminary study of their handling and their uses is necessary before all else.

If we take a screwdriver whose point we have omitted to examine, we may have no grip on the screw we wish to drive into a certain panel or a certain piece of furniture. We may well spoil the screw, the piece of furniture and our tool. This is our position from the point of view of the mind. We are doing hard work. *We are destroying both ourselves and others.*

Our approach to daily happenings in all circumstances is, on the psychological plane, like that of the clumsy apprentice who has not taken the trouble to look at his tools.

It is thus inevitable that we commit errors whatever we may do: we will be inadequate. In other words we will not have correct relationships.

If we had the faculty of observing our thoughts passively without the intervention of our judgment, they would themselves reveal the reasons of the fundamental flaw in their functioning.

Elsewhere we have explained the causes of this faulty functioning.

Amongst them are identification, attachment, desire for continuity, and the fear of no longer feeling ourselves to be entities.

The essential function of thought consists in communicating and expressing. It is only the instrument of Intelligence. It is not the intelligence. We shall return to this subject during the final examination of the state of Satori.

OUR PROFOUND MOTIVES FOR ATTACHMENT
AND OUR FEARS

Attachment is always the auto-defensive reflex of an unconscious fear. Attachment to others is in reality attachment to ourselves. The problem does not consist of disciplining ourselves with a view to detaching ourselves artificially. Any attitude of dependence is an obstacle to the realization of Satori.

We are obliged here to define a nuance which is as subtle as it is fundamental; *we* are in the habit of wanting to detach *ourselves from* such a person, *from* such a thought or *from* such an object. The man who has realized Satori is not detached *from* someone or *from* something. He *merely realizes a state of detachment*.

By what means? Let us remember once again that the nature of the means determines the nature of the end.

The transformation suggested to us by Zen *no longer has the avidities of the 'I-process' as a motive. It emerges directly, at the heart of what remains of the 'I-process', from an independent centre which is free from all conditioning.*

This transformation is the direct expression of the Cosmic Mind or the Zen Unconscious. It is free from all motive.

This action is that of Life itself, expressing itself through what remains of an individual who is 'psychologically dead' to himself.

In it exists the only source of new light amongst the shadows of our innumerable conflicts and woes, which will remain without solution as long as we draw inspiration from the motives of the 'I-process' in order to solve them.

OUR PROCESSES OF CHOICE AND OUR RESEARCH

Non-Mental lucidity is without choice. Generally we are very proud of being able to choose. Consciousness of self, freedom of choice, and responsibility are, according to us, the distinctive signs of the human species. They distinguish us from animality. But these distinctive signs are far from being those of wisdom, equilibrium and felicity.

We wrongly believe that we choose freely. In fact we are much more 'chosen' than we ourselves choose. We are unconsciously [184] 'chosen' through our habit of choosing, and this last is entirely conditioned by our memory-automatisms.

As we have already mentioned elsewhere, it is unwittingly that our gaze alights rather on this or that article lying amongst a thousand divers objects in the shop-window of a large store.

We think that we have chosen the article that interests us. In fact it is the article which has chosen us. The sight of identical objects or persons rouses mental or emotional reactions which come into the category of habit. Privileged paths of thought exist between the optic nerve and our cerebral engrams which lead us to react automatically in the same fashion in similar circumstances. The speed of these automatisms is such that it often happens that our eye perceives phenomena, recorded directly by the unconscious while remaining totally unperceived by our normal waking consciousness.

Whether we are chosen, or whether we ourselves choose is of relatively little importance.

The essential element to which we wish to draw attention is the following: every time that there is a conscious or unconscious act of choice there is an intervention of the 'I-process' through the sum of accumulated memories which form its substance.

Therefore there is corruption of the Present by the past.

Through the process of 'choice' we enclose ourselves within ourselves.

Choice is in fact a process of isolation resulting from a rapid and subtle act of auto-defence on the part of the conscious and unconscious 'I-process'.

The process of choice does not only exert its restrictive action when we are in relationship with physical persons or objects, it acts above all on those psychical objects which we call 'thoughts'.

We can be detached from material things while still remaining slaves to particular ideas or symbols. These should be unmasked as simple accomplices of the avidities of the 'I-process'.

Satori can only be realized in the freedom and mental transparence of the state that is without choice.

Satori is the state without choice. It is the complete act above all others.

There is no longer room for a subject identifying himself with the ideal object of *his choice*, while still claiming to remain separate from it.

There is no longer a 'son experiencing his unity with the Father'.

There is no longer an 'I-process', however purified it might be, which is united with the world.

Satori will be realized the instant we have understood the uselessness and the danger of all these dualistic notions. We should, in a manner of speaking, have forgotten everything, not by virtue of an act of personal will, but by this wonderful volatilization of the past which the living presence of the Cosmic Mind can work in us. But, in order to reach that, we must free the mind from all, absolutely all that we have read about the state of Satori itself, Cosmic Mind or the Zen Unconscious. This is very important.

The Zen Unconscious is infinitely more important, more dazzling in itself than all that we could think or say about it.

The choice of certain spiritual or mental values is not only useless, but constitutes the greatest hindrance.

It is supremely useless to choose anything whatsoever for that which we are transcends all possible or impossible choices.

Our relations with the world, with all things, with all beings should be more passive. We still have cravings though we have understood intellectually the paralysing action of our avidities. The spell by which the process of choice binds us is the characteristic expression of this fundamental and subtle craving. Nothing is more radically opposed to inner passivity than the act of choice.

Inner passivity is one of the keys of Chinese mysticism. Its influence on Zen thought is considerable.

We find it summarized in the Chinese expression 'Wei Wu Wei'. The term Wei corresponds to the words 'to act'. Wu is negative. Wei Wu Wei means therefore 'to do without acting'.

Wu-Wei concerns passivity, non-intervention of the memory-automatisms of the 'I-process'.

Wei concerns positive creative action which our personal passiveness allows to be expressed.

Creative passivity is in fact the climax of positive action.

The necessity for an inner passivity and a perfect readiness is accepted by many Christians.

The difficulty lies in the fact that we really hold on to ourselves while pretending to attain readiness.

We would like to glimpse the possibility of experiencing a few partial Satoris without thereby losing definitely the limits of our personal consciousness. There can be no half-measures in this domain. All compromise is impossible.

Let us repeat this deliberately: we lack nothing. Therefore we have nothing to choose. The part of the Real within us is sufficient in itself. It is the greatest wealth. [185]

In a certain sense the universe is more important than our recognition of the universe. Moreover the latter is conditioned by choice on the part of our habitual values.

The Zen Unconscious or Cosmic Mind is in itself more authentic than our averred experiences of it.

Our most competent meditations and speculations on Nirvâna, Satori and the divers states of Samadhi have nothing in common with the plenitude of the Zen Unconscious. They only affect us negatively by making us victims of our own mental projections. [186]

An eminent savant in atomic physics said that 'the tensorial calculus knows more physics than the physicists'. The ultimate reality of atomic relations, which the tensorial calculus tries to express on the scale of transcendental mathematics, itself knows much better than physicists and their tensorial theories, the truth of its process.

Therefore it is necessary for us to stop clouding our vision of the Real with our own creations and mental interpretations. Let us have the intelligence to allow the Intelligence of Cosmic Mind to function in ourselves as well as in the heart of beings and things. Let us allow Reality to be Its own law in us.

We find the essential bases of this creative passivity in the Tao.

Tao is eternally inactive and yet *it leaves nothing unaccomplished.*

To define the exceptional efficiency of this passive state without choice, the Tao adds:

'If kings and princes could but hold fast to this principle, all things would work out their own reformation. If having reformed they still desired to act, I would have them restrained by the simplicity of the Nameless Tao. The simplicity of the Nameless Tao brings about an absence of desire. The absence of desire gives tranquillity. And *thus the Empire will rectify itself*. . . .

Practise inaction and *there is nothing which cannot be done.*

The Empire has ever been won by letting things take their course.

He who must always be doing is unfit to obtain the Empire. . . .' (*Sayings of Lao Tseu*) pp. 30 and 31.

The inner significance of the word 'Empire' has not often been understood. It is obviously the Empire of the Real. The great error committed by most Occidentals consists in believing that a technique of action which is devoid of all personal interferences leads to inaction. On the contrary, we are witnessing the beginning of all true action.

A thought from Rinzai Zen says:

'*Have not the least thought in your mind regarding the search for Buddhahood.*' Research and choice are the same in this field.

For most of us it is here that one of our greatest difficulties lies.

The mere fact of reading a work on Zen implies in all probability an important modification in the values which we attribute to the world.

Perhaps we are free from attachment to material questions, perhaps we are free from the dogmatism and systematization of the mind imposed by religions, and perhaps we have reached the point of no longer having any desires. Or rather we have still but one desire, that of seeing, seeing quite simply, always more clearly and ever more deeply.

Perhaps we have understood that vision of the Real demands a transcendence of all our preferences, our repulsions and all gross or subtle forms of egoism.

Yet in spite of all this we seem to remain victims of an invincible inertia. Something within us seems to hold back.

We have read, studied and intellectually understood all that deals with the impermanence of beings and things, Satori and the Zen Unconscious. Yet it seems that in spite of all this — and perhaps because of all this — a final resistance has yet to be overcome.

Let us not think that it is far off. On the contrary it is very near.

It is so close that it can no longer be seen by us. It lies in the very centre of our faculty of perception.

We remain impenitently cerebral.

When we are in the open air the sight of a beautiful tree, or a sunset, no longer is for us a pure perception. We have lost all spontaneity, all disinterestedness. Often it happens that we want to 'extract' from this spectacle even its invisible quintessence.

Our first elans of admiration are too often accompanied or followed by a subtle thought: 'Everything is Cosmic Mind, all is the Body of the Buddha, all is the Zen Unconscious.'

The great majority of serious and ardent seekers go through the difficult phase preceding the third part of the well-known Koan 'the mountains are mountains'.

In the beginning in a condition of total ignorance we accept the fact that the mountains are mountains.

During the second phase we awaken to inner research. We doubt the absolute authenticity of external appearances. At the sight of great rocky masses we react in a different manner. We can think of the reality of their atomic structure which differs entirely from their surface aspects. Some of us will visualize intense electronic vortices whirling round atomic nuclei. Others will imagine an ocean of light symbolizing pure energy. The exterior aspect of the mountains, apparently static and immobile, will appear of secondary importance beside the fluid and dynamic energy in their depths. *To us* the mountains are no longer mountains.

This hyperintellectualization of our perceptions is the dominating problem for most of us.

The song of a bird, the sound of a distant bell, the sighing of the wind in the trees can evoke for us as many messages of profound unity that at the same time is real. But only too often this unity is perceived through a screen that is constituted for us by the word, the symbol of what we are seeking. Everything is

Cosmic Mind, think some people. Everything is One, say others to themselves. And others again rejoice at the possible approach of an authentic Satori.

At the moment when, in fact, the drop is going to separate and rejoin the ocean a resistance intervenes. A force, an old habit is there which tries to pronounce the diabolical words.

It is useless to become alarmed. It is useless to become impatient. It is sufficient merely to realize a state of silent observation which allows us to unmask within us the illusory character of the mental automatisms which enslave us.

Let us not deny ourselves the contemplation of the beauty of the setting sun, but let us remain passively lucid during the welling-up of eventual mental suggestions seeking the Cosmic Mind of which we have read that the sun is an expression.

Let us be more simple!

With regard to this it is extremely useful to have periods of total intellectual and spiritual repose. Leaving books aside, let us proceed to a revaluation of a vegetative life.

Let us devote ourselves to simple and concrete occupations, which require no deep thought, but giving them our whole attention.

Let us dig in our gardens and not be 'elsewhere'; let us take long walks in the open air; plant trees when the season allows.

Let us bathe in the rivers and lakes if we have the possibility of so doing. Contact with water is an element contributing to balance and rest.

Modern life intoxicates us not only by its thousand artifices which cut us off from nature, but also by the absence of exercise which it tends to impose on us.

Let us indulge in games, play tennis or train in Judo if our heart is sound.

No Satori is possible without an equilibrium between the brain, heart and hands. A compensation among these three factors should exist.

If we are hyper-intellectualized let us take up modelling, sculpture, drawing or any other manual task within our reach.

In any case let us be more simple: simple and true in our

gestures, in our words, and simple and true in our minds above all. Let us desist from assuming a mask in our relations with others. Let us be ourselves. Let us expose our fears and our cowardices. Let us learn to laugh at ourselves. By taking our-[187] selves too seriously we could reach the height of ridicule. Too many people, interested in the problems of the inner life, lack humour and cannot laugh. Never to laugh is the distinctive sign of people living in fear. No Satori is possible without relaxation of body, emotion and thought.

Let us permit our minds to lie fallow and take care of our physical and nervous equilibrium. Physiological activity is directly linked with the deeper nature of our being. By listening to that in a certain manner it is possible to establish, within us, a harmonious non-mental resonance revealing a more adequate kind of relationship.

At all costs we should avoid making a habit of mentally over-working. We must stop 'intellectualizing our actions'. We take a malicious pleasure in complicating our lives by attaching our-selves to the useless.

The instinct of preservation of the 'I-process' is capable of every perversity and of every artifice. That we should suffer from our tensions, contradictions and overwork is of no consequence to it. This is where lies the great paradox. The instinct of preservation of the 'I-process' is, in relation to the real, a condition of per-manent unbalance. It rules as master at the heart of the disequili-brium and disarray of the 'I-process'. It is dependent on them.

Whatever we may all suffer, we appear to be obstinately bent on remaining on this path, which is absolutely without issue. We have taken the stupid decision of remaining prisoners of the 'I-process' in spite of the train of suffering and servitude which it entails.

We will not conclude these considerations on the process of choice without repeating that: to choose is unconsciously a wish to perpetuate oneself.

To choose is to avoid a salutary confrontation with what we really are. The instinct of preservation of the 'I-process' absolutely refuses to allow us the exercise of concentrated attention in the momentaneity of the instant. By constantly choosing we become the accomplices of its mental tactics. We are the victims of a clever diversionary manœuvre.

By choosing we do not look at ourselves and see ourselves as we really are actually; our attention avoids the actual present and turns away to an imaginary future.

The process of choice lies at the source of all our incomplete actions.

Barely has a thought been born when another appears suddenly preventing the first one from all possibility of completion. *Our mental structure owes its complexity to a constant superimposition of uncompleted thoughts. The sum of these is expressed by the cravings of the 'I-process', and is the origin of all its violence.*

If we stopped choosing, our nascent thoughts would be able to develop fully and exhaust themselves. This is the essential condition of the effective realization of Satori.

The moment we permit a thought to run its course naturally without being hindered by the inopportune appearance of another, *we inevitably come to a moment of silence.*

This interstitial void between two thoughts is essentially non-mental. Its discovery requires the volatilization of the resistances of the 'I-process' developed by the instinct of preservation. The dissolution of these resistances cannot be carried out by the mind. It is the work of pure attention, voided of all ideation emanating from an unconditioned centre which we not only carry within us but which is our real being.

ADEQUACY

What is to be adequate?

To be adequate is to respond *fully* to all the conditions of a given circumstance. *Adequacy is the universal expression of the intelligence of Life.*

Inadequacy is the distinguishing mark of unintelligence.

If we wish to respond *fully* to all the conditions of a given circumstance we cannot tolerate the intervention of our attachments and preferences, of choice, repulsion and weakness.

The examples of adequacy are not lacking in Nature.

In their degree most animals are more adequate than us.

The realization of perfect adequacy in human relations implies the exercise of an impersonal consciousness forming the highest octave of the instinctive wisdom expressed by some animals. We will not use the word 'intuition' as it carries contradictory meanings.

Perfect adequacy implies the exercise not of a consciousness of self but that of *the pure* and impersonal consciousness.

Such a consciousness is ever open. It is not limited to the definite contours which our physical organism outlines in relation to its environment. It disregards the constituent memory-associations of our 'I-process'.

This consciousness is that of the Zen Unconscious. Its behaviour on the ultimate scale of materiality of the Universe is rich in import. *The deepest zones of the atomic world, which recent discoveries in physics force us to consider as much spiritual as material, offer us, within their limits, divers examples of the most perfect adequacy. Nothing in Nature* — with the exception of the integrated man — *is as adequate as an atomic corpuscle* (on condition that we envisage intranuclear corpuscles such as neutrons, protons, pions, and not the already individualized ensemble of a particular atomic system, clearly defined, such as the hydrogen atom).

If we examine attentively the factors of this adequacy we observe the following elements:

(1) It arises from the extraordinarily fluid and non-localized nature of the corpuscles, that is their *agility, flexibility, and exceptional freedom of movement.*

(2) Perfect adequacy comes also and above all from *lack of particularization and specialization.* Corpuscles have neither form, surface nor colour. They are devoid of nearly all the attributes, qualities and particular aspects with which we are familiar.

(3) Atomic adequacy also arises from the *effective absence of individuality amongst the intra-nuclear constituents.* For example, if we examine a Uranium atom composed of a nucleus, round which revolve 92 planetary electrons, we will say that its equilibrium is due to the predominance of 146 neutrons and 92 protons in the heart of the nucleus. Since 1955 we know that we can no longer speak of 146 neutrons and 92 protons as individualized. *They are non-existent as individuals since they disappear and appear, die and revive, thousands of millions of times per second.* We now know that this extraordinary play of exchanges saves the atomic nuclei from exploding.

In order to be adequate to the exceptional circumstances which arise in the heart of atomic nuclei protons and neutrons continually renounce their individuality. The adequacy and intensity of relationship are effected at the cost of all continuity in the connected elements.

If we examine the elements responsible for our inadequacy we notice that not only are they a result of our physical specialization, but above all, of our psychological specialization. The latter, which used to be a help, is now an obstacle.

Psychological specialization implies a withdrawal of the individual within himself. It is a factor of isolation and, as such, becomes an impediment to the establishment of adequate relations.

These comparisons are not inopportune. Eminent physicists have dwelt on the disquieting similarities existing between the [188] behaviour of atoms on the physical plane and that of man on the psychical.

If atomic life is based on the dualistic opposition between two elements of the same energetic essence, present human consciousness owes its apparent solidity to an identical process.

Let us consider an atom of hydrogen. If we were able really to see the structure of its nucleus and that of its planetary electron we would be very much surprised by the identity of their appearance. There are only two differences between them. The first and most important lies in the opposition of their electrical charges. The nucleus is positive while the electron is negative.

The second dissimilarity lies in the difference of mass.

We know that the equilibrium of a hydrogen atom is the result of vertiginous revolutions of the electron round the nucleus.

It is only by virtue of this rapidity of rotation that the negative electron manages to create a centrifugal force which neutralizes the centripetal force of attraction of the positive nucleus.

The psychological life of man is the object of a series of similar tensions between two elements, apparently opposed, but of the same essence.

On the one hand, a nucleus formed by the supposed entity of a 'thinker' and, on the other, a cloud of thoughts perpetually in movement, and which, by their very agitation maintain the illusion of a thinker.

In so far as the latter attempts to work on his thoughts he sets in motion a series of tensions which assure both his continuity and his servitude.

The study of the work of Krishnamurti from this point of view is perfectly in accord with the teachings of Zen and of modern physics.

The play of psychological tensions in man, and that of electrical tensions in the heart of atoms, is governed by the double aspect of *creativeness* and *habit*.

The behaviour of the atom is governed by the sign of *creativeness* if we observe the continual renewal and the upsurging of its energetic essence.

The behaviour of the spiritual essence of human nature is governed by the sign of *creativeness* by a similar continual renewal and up-surging.

On the other hand, the property of hydrogen, in chemistry, is the result of *habit* in the behaviour of an identical energy, differently polarized, in the form of a negative electron revolving, always at the same velocity, round a positive nucleus.

In the same way, the property of this or that particular consciousness-of-self is the outcome of the *habitual* play of tensions existing between two differently polarized aspects of Cosmic Mind: the first one formed by the *habits* of our memory-automatisms, the second formed by the pseudo-entity of the thinker resulting from the accumulated residue of these *habits*.

On the cessation of the rhythm of habit, Satori is revealed.

It is realized suddenly when the tensions existing between the supposed entity of the thinker and his thoughts shall cease.

On the human scale, Satori is equivalent to a short-circuit occurring on the atomic scale by the negative electron being precipitated on to the positive nucleus as a result of the cessation of the complex play of opposing tensions.

And, again, let us say that this experience is for us a plenitude, and not an annihilation.

Previously we defined adequacy as the faculty of responding *fully* to all the conditions of a given circumstance.

This requires on our part the possibility of observing and seeing beings and things as they are.

In fact how can we respond fully to all the conditions of a given circumstance if we cannot see its essential elements clearly.

A careful study of our process of observation shows us that only very rarely do we see beings and things *as they are really at the moment we perceive them.*

Such an assertion often astonishes us and should therefore be explained.

We are so absent-minded that sometimes we do not notice the exact details of a certain landscape or person, though optically they are perceptible. This occurs mainly when the circumstances are habitual or familiar.

Let us suppose for an instant that the silhouette of a person we know well appears unexpectedly in our visual field. It is most probable that we will not perceive the person as he is *actually.*

All that we will perceive of him is the image that we have made of him once and for all. Therefore we have not *any relationship* with this person in his present reality. *Our relation is established with the past image only, which has crystallized for ever within us.* We remain enclosed within ourselves, cloistered behind the thick walls of our habits.

We are conditioned to such an extent that sometimes we do not notice the unexpected changes or new transformations undergone by things or beings we come across every day.

This is true not only for physical changes but applies, above all, to modifications of a psychological nature.

The privileged grooves of thought, engendered by the repeated sight of identical persons or objects, lead us to react in an automatic and habitual manner during our relations with these persons or objects.

The person who has offended us will always release in us the same negative reflexes of rancour and hostility. We will not see the smile or kindly look which he may give us on the morrow of an unexpected inner transformation. Our mind will only retain a petrified and painful vision of this person. This vision will be the same a week hence, or a month, a year, twenty years. A worthy person will always be worthy, while a dishonest person will always be base.

We lose sight of the fact that the persons, beings and things which we see *are never the same*. *They are changing constantly, both physically and psychologically*. We ourselves never escape from this changing from the perpetual renewal.

Adequacy, therefore, consists in being new in each new instant.

In it is realized the living synthesis of the two aspects of Cosmic Mind:

(1) The aspect of perfect relations with environment in the manifested Universe. In it is revealed the extraordinary degree of creativeness and unicity in each instant.

(2) The aspect of non-relation 'to the depths of the non-manifested Universe' by integration with Cosmic Mind, that is non-relation through absence of all duality and by effective realization of Unity in apparent multiplicity.

NON-RESEARCH FOR THE REAL

However paradoxical this may sound, Satori does not reveal itself to those who desire it. Herein lies the greatest difficulty for most of us. In proportion to our sincerity we all traverse a phase during which its effective realization is our dearest, most constant, and [189] most secret wish.

Cosmic Mind or *the Zen Unconscious* (the words matter little) *is a reality which is not found by those who seek it.*

The old saying 'Seek and you shall find' is not necessarily true. Everything depends on the manner in which we seek.

The central Reality of Zen is only revealed to those who no longer seek it as we generally seek things.

There is positive and negative research.

During so-called positive research we proceed by successive comparisons and by referring to facts from the past or with what [190] is known.

We never leave the domain which we like to call 'positive' or 'realistic'. In the eyes of the integrated man, however, we are wandering in the land of dreams. All research undertaken in dream can only result in elements of dreams.

The utilization of so-called positive methods of research is adequate in the field of material and technical activities in the course of everyday life.

Let us recall the wise counsel of Plato: 'For each task use the right tools.'

The nature of Reality in Zen requires other working tools, other attitudes.

By using tools such as our pre-established values, intellectual certainties, our memories and our past conclusions we are heading for certain failure.

In fact the problem of implements for our research is secondary. That which Zen commands is purely and simply the cessation of all research.

We can only seek with success something which is to be sought. We can only seek effectively and find an object which is distinct from ourselves. We cannot seek or find that from which we are not distinct.

We need not seek that which is so much our own being that any attempts at mental objectivation of its presence is not only useless but profoundly ridiculous.

The Zen masters never cease insisting on the negative character of our attitude in research. They cite willingly the famous words of Obaku:*

'To use the Buddha to seek the Buddha, and using mind to grasp mind is an impossibility to the end of eternity.'

We will quote the answer given to the same problem by Master Hyakyo:

'It is as if we were to seek the ox on which we are seated.'

Denouncing the absurdities of the search for the Real, the poems of Zenrin-kushu contain the following:

'Like a sword that wounds but cannot wound itself,'

'Like an eye that sees but cannot see itself.'

We will not end this paragraph without citing this ancient text of Rinzai:

'We cannot solve past karma except in relation to circumstances. When it is time to dress let us put on our clothes. When we should take a walk, let us walk! *Do not have a single thought in your mind in view of searching for Buddhahood.*

How can this come about? Of old they said: *If you deliberately seek the Buddha, your Buddha is simply Samsara* (illusion).

Disciples of the Tao, there is no room for effort in Buddhism!

Remain as you are, without anything special. When you are tired, rest . . . The ignorant may laugh at you, but the Sage will understand. . . .

Of old they said: "If perchance you meet a man of Tao on the road, the first thing to do consists in not approaching this man with your conception of the Tao . . . For this reason is it taught that in a person practising the Tao (or, more exactly, a conception of the Tao), the Tao cannot operate (or be manifested)." '

THE NECESSITY OF THE PRESENT

[191] We are never in relationship in the Present. Our inner life unfurls in the field of a past which is no longer, or in that of a future which is not yet.

Our mental life therefore is lived in a double inexistence: firstly,

* Obaku is the Japanese name for Master Hsi-Yun (or Huang-Po).

inexistence of that which is no longer and only subsists in a state of ashes and residues of memory and, secondly, inexistence of that which is not yet. In this kingdom of shadows the light of the present is systematically excluded and hidden from our mind by a reflex of self-defence emanating from 'Tanha' (the instinct for self-preservation and craving for duration).

As we are obviously unable to be completely happy in the adoration of traces of a past which is dead, we try to mortgage the future by imaginative activities which are but a triple lie.

Firstly a lie, because the contents projected by our imagination into the future are entirely borrowed from the past.

Secondly a lie, because the *essential* content of the future is strictly unforeseeable.

Lastly a lie, because every time we arbitrarily place ourselves in the past or in the future we deny the fundamental reality of our being: the Eternal Present.

We always arrive late at the meeting of life.

We are so weighed down by the burden of our innumerable memories that we no longer have the agility and suppleness with which to welcome the Present. We are heavy in body, heavy in mind, heavy in heart and heavy in our perceptions. We can only perceive the heavy aspects of existence. The creative reality of life in the Present, its perfume, its freshness and lightness continually escape us.

We are residual in our often intoxicated bodies, we are residual in our hearts and our minds cluttered with incompleted actions, unassuaged desires and unfinished thoughts. Our perception itself is residual. We only seize residues, the extinguished debris of the Eternally present Lightning.

To arrive in time it is sufficient to become aware of the force of inertia which paralyses us. *If indeed we are seriously interested, we perceive that this act of becoming conscious, though seeming very arduous, is in fact very simple. A true and whole-hearted interest irresistibly triumphs over all obstacles.* This lucid emancipation from the past allows us to gather the supreme and ever renewed confidences of every instant.

Life becomes a perpetual song. In the heart of each thing and each finite being the infinite lies revealed. The unicity of each instant harbours possibilities of creativeness and renewal which escape all mental representation. No monotony, no fixity, no repetition whatsoever weigh down the atmosphere of a true realization.

Besides, Satori is not a 'thing' which we seize once and for all. *We* seize nothing because at that moment we are *psychologically inexistent*. More exactly it is reality which seizes us.

Elsewhere we have dwelt on the negative role of our tendency to make comparison. The process of comparison systematically hinders all direct perception of the present.

[192] When we are in an *actual* state of a certain nature we cannot compare it *simultaneously* with a state of being which is its opposite while keeping our consciousness concentrated entirely in the present instant. In fact we never compare with the opposite state itself, but with a *memory* of such state. By so-doing this we escape immediately in a simple projection of the past. We never adhere to the Present.

Reminders of the past intervene ceaselessly in our comparisons in the form of words, symbols, various mental clichés and the aroma of memories which are the essential fuel of the 'I-process'. As Alan Watts, the eminent Zen writer expresses it:

'But in reality we cannot compare joy with sorrow. Comparison is possible only by the very rapid alternation of two states of mind . . . Sorrow can only be compared with the *memory* of joy, which is not at all the same thing as joy itself.

Like words, memories never really succeed in "catching" reality . . . Memory never captures the essence, the present intensity, the concrete reality of an experience. What we know by memory, we know only at secondhand. Memories are dead because fixed. . .' (*The Wisdom of Insecurity*, p. 83).

A close examination of the processes of comparison, choice, and of the verbal expression of our states, reveals to us the absolute power of the instinct of preservation of the 'I-process'. No Satori is possible before thoroughly becoming conscious of this desperate reflex of self-defence on the part of our thirst for continuity.

Each human being possesses in the depth of consciousness a zone of influence which perpetually obeys personal motives of self-protection. This zone of influence is at once subtle, wily and all-powerful. *It knows perfectly that every experience lived fully in the present is a danger to it.*

Whatever may be his degree of superficial ignorance, each human being possesses this *unconscious apprehension* within him, and it is this which inclines us to refuse *unconsciously* to see things *as they are*, and suggests that we imagine what *they have been* or *what they could be* in so-called more favourable circumstances.

It is most important that we surprise in ourselves the operational process of this tendency. A complete and deep-seated act of becoming conscious of this can liberate us. By this we mean to say that a purely intellectual act of becoming conscious is of little use for the complete act includes both the heart and the mind. In the degree in which we approach a phase preceding Satori we tend to think with the heart and love with the mind.

Besides, this opposition should disappear finally in order to reveal to us the vividness of perception of the present.

Krishnamurti clearly denounces the conflicts and suffering imposed on us by our refusal to look at ourselves *actually* as we are.

'Your conflict can only exist between what you *are* and what you *wish to be*, between the *actual* and the *ideal*, between that which *is* and the *myth of what should be*.

The myth, the ideal are unreal. They are evasions projected by our own minds. *They have no present existence.* The present state is what you are. What you are is much more important than what you would like to be. You may understand that *which is*, but you cannot understand that which should be.

The comprehension of an illusion is impossible. All that is comprehensible is the manner in which this illusion was engendered. In order to understand that which *is*, we should be free from all distraction.

Condemnation or approval of that which is are distractions. *Comparison is a distraction: it is a resistance against the present state.*

That *which is* can only be revealed in a lucidity which is both alert and passive.' (J. Krishnamurti, *Commentaries on living*, p. 127.)

CHAPTER III

The true 'Letting-Go' effected by 'Love-Intelligence'

DR. HUBERT BENOIT, in his most interesting work (*Lâcher prise*), shows us how our thoughts, emotions, and actions are the expression of a 'desire to experience'.

The desire to feel ourselves as distinct beings is closely linked with the habit of association of which we have repeatedly spoken in this work.

The author suggests opposing 'divergent tendency' to the 'convergent tendency', which constitute the habit of association as defined by Dr. Benoit.

Our disagreement with this point of view calls for an explanation which will allow us to define the effective experience of Satori.

We only think with words. Human language is the final stage of an organization of sounds that is many thousand years old. Words are articulated sounds joined together by mental habits of association. The act of evoking a particular word automatically leads us to the evocation of another which is generally associated with it in everyday speech.

Dr. Hubert Benoit defines this tendency of association in language, and consequently in thought, by the term 'convergent language'.

He suggests the realization of a 'counter method' and the utilization of a 'divergent' language-technique in opposition to the 'convergence' habitual to the 'I-process'.

It is obvious that, in spite of all precautions and warnings, the 'counter-method' in question runs the risk of becoming merely a snare for the mind.

The value of disassociative 'counter-method' depends essentially on the motives which have inspired it.

Observing the conflicts and suffering resulting from our convergent and associative tendencies we decide to adopt a contrary method.

A Zen master or a Krishnamurti would ask us immediately 'Who' wants to be rid of the convergent and associative process? Why? What are the *motives* behind this *choice*, this change of attitude?

There are two possibilities.

(1) The first has as motive a fear of suffering. It comes from the 'I-process'. In our desire to be rid of suffering we crave methods, receipts. We designate these methods and receipts by labels that are apparently truthful and flattering to the mind. The fact of designating them by the terms of disassociative or 'divergent 'counter-methods', does not solve anything.

The practice of a method, or the application of a technique, inevitably entails a degeneration of thought by a process of imitation and personal becoming.

The Zen Masters and Krishnamurti draw our attention to these dangers. The Indian thinker points out to us that most of our spiritual transformations only represent a 'modified continuity' of the 'I-process'.

(2) There is a second possibility: that of *transformation without motive*. It would be partially the expression of an obscure urge of the Real within us.

'You cannot choose Reality,' Krishnamurti tells us, 'Reality must choose you.' The presence of Reality in us is sufficient both for itself and for us Satori is nothing but a state of availability which allows the Real to be its own law in us and by us. This law ignores all our methods.

Krishnamurti and the Zen masters suggest a 'non-method'.

This cannot come about by act of choice on the part of the 'I-process'.

How do the processes of choice and convergence cease?

Liberation is carried out by 'Love-Intelligence' and not by the 'I-process'. The solution is very simple but a general intellectual perversity hinders us from perceiving it.

We are so degenerate that we must ask ourselves again this incredible question:

What is 'Love-Intelligence'? It is the essence and substance of everything, of all beings, of the ignorant and of the enlightened.

Our mistake generally lies in thinking that it is inaccessible. It is certainly so, however, as long as we use the methods with which we are familiar. *To allow 'Love-Intelligence' to work in us is in itself the most simple task on earth. It is so simple, so near, that all methods are not only useless but form an obstacle to this state of availability.*

Love-Intelligence is the supremely natural state of being of Cosmic Mind. Each of us can experience the intelligence-aspect by means of a state of lucidity without idea during certain moments of silent observation. We all have the faculty of experiencing partially the 'love' aspect in the first surge of generosity, spontaneity and in the disinterested nature of all pure affection.

Let us repeat that there is in this absolutely nothing distant or inaccessible.

It is sufficient to allow these aspects of Love and Intelligence to operate in us, while ceasing to disassociate them artificially. The task is really very simple because, in 'Love-Intelligence', love and intelligence have never been separated. These distinctions are only arbitrary divisions on the part of the mind.

Satori is perfect availability to the infinite possibilities of 'Love-Intelligence', and it is this which confers on the 'I-process' — or, at least, on what is left of it — a disassociative and divergent attitude.

At the same time we must say that the exercise of a divergent attitude cannot recreate 'Love-Intelligence' or realize a state of availability to the Real.

As for the practice of a divergent language, as proposed by some, we do not see its utility, and we fear that it may become a snare in the same way as the practice of 'Puja' in India, and that of ritual in general.

Disassociative or divergent attitudes are consequences of Satori.

The integrated men of whom we know have never desisted from using the convergent language, with which we are familiar both before and after Satori.

The great mistake consists in taking a real or presumed consequence, whatever its nature, as a means of the realization of Satori.

Earlier we insisted on the strictly *irreversible* character of the processes of the Real.

The putting into practice of a consequence of the state of Satori, does not necessarily bring about this state.

Therefore it is not desirable for us to practice a 'divergent counter-method', for this may lead us to sink unconsciously into an opposing attitude of 'anti-convergence'.

The solution proposed by Krishnamurti is quite different and seems to us more correct. A Bodhi-Dharma, a Tsen-Tsang or a Hui-Neng could not but adhere to this entirely.

The Indian thinker suggests that *we discover the fundamental motives of convergent or associative behaviour in action in the very heart of convergence and associative habits.*

It is at the moment when it expresses itself actively, during our relations, that we should unmask our fundamental thirst for continuity, and not oppose to it, theoretically or superficially, a process of discontinuity.

When this thirst for continuity has been correctly unmasked the 'old man' within us dies by himself; and in this very death there is a rebirth. The old, being dead, that which is eternally new appears by itself.

But it would be vain to force ourselves to be new, artificially. At the heart of such a highly sophisticated novelty we shall never find the freshness nor the spontaneity of Life.

In other words, *we* will never be able to realize an authentic attitude of divergence or renewal. Our task consists in letting 'Love-Intelligence' work on our convergent centres in order to dissolve the knots of resistance.

The Effective realization of Satori is perhaps more the result of Love than of Intelligence alone.

However we must say that the usual expression 'Intelligence alone' has no meaning. True Intelligence is also Love.

Love is essentially divergent, dissociative. True Love is incorruptible. The supposed corruption of love and its associative or convergent tendencies are the work of thought.

The associative habits of the 'I-process' try to degrade the first purity of Love by possessiveness and repetition of certain mental or sensual automatisms.

It is regrettable to affirm, as does Dr. Hubert Benoit (*Lâcher prise*, p. 277) that the second half of realizing, that which is superadded to our life and crowns our development, *is devoid of love*.

Indeed the state of Satori is neither mental, nor emotional, and [193] veritable love is not an emotion only. Dr. Benoit admits this in other works.

However *if we resolutely resist Love, whatever its nature, as a result of an* a priori *entailing its systematic devalorization we are unable to be truly divergent.*

In the game of life, let us use the cards we have in hand.

These cards are our faculties of thought, love and action. No one is expected to do the impossible.

The faculty of loving exists, either latent or developed, in the heart of all beings. Our technical and hyper-intellectualized civilizations are corrupted by interest and calculation. They have left no room for education of feeling. For many generations parents and teachers have despised affective manifestations and ignored the riches which their development could bring. Events show us that the suppression of the cruelties and injustices in the world are not the result of intellectual and technical evolution.

Only the birth of a new and profoundly natural sensibility, inspired by veritable Love, can bring about the urgent transformations which are required by the heart-breaking conflicts of humanity.

We have come to the point of asking ourselves how we should love.

From ordinary love, corrupted and limited by identification, to real Love, a very simple, natural path nevertheless is open to us.

It suffices to keep intact the first flame of Love by freeing it from its points of attachment.

This liberation cannot be the work of the 'I-process'. It is Love itself that burns the bonds of associative and convergent habits. This Love is a state of being which is recreated from instant to instant. It is no longer distinct from Intelligence.

From the experimental point of view, it is, then, the *radiating intensity of veritable Love that suspends associative or convergent activities of the 'I-process' and brings mental serenity.*

Veritable Love acts through simple presence.

The 'Love-Intelligence' of Satori gives us this simple yet wonderful faculty of observing everything, both inside and out while remaining entirely free from choice and identification. This gives an astonishing sense of inner freedom. We can play the game of the world to the full while remaining free from the innumerable forms which serve as its expression.

Emancipation from the associative habits of memory is *imposed* on us by the radiation of Love. Each person can test it for himself.

In the degree in which we realize in ourselves an adherence to each present moment the very vividness of the instant lived delivers us from all clutches of the past. If we allow the omnipotence of Love to work in us we die to ourselves and become nothing but Love. The presence of this Love in each new instant is then our presence. Besides, there is, so to speak, no longer opposition between the two presences. Such a distinction never really existed.

In this state that which remains of ourselves is non-exclusive, non-accumulative, non-convergent. We are not freed from convergence by virtue of an act of choice. *We are so because it is impossible for us to be otherwise.*

The prestige of 'Love-Intelligence' projects a kind of prohibition on the agitations of the mind and on convergent aspects of the 'I-process'.

It is by this means only that spiritual realization is freed from the unceasing conditioning of thought.

An awakening to the state of 'Love-Intelligence' confers on us the strange power of penetrating to the heart of beings and things, through deep reaches of consciousness as unfathomable as the Universe itself. We are born into a new life in which are revealed faculties inexpressible in everyday speech. It would be better to speak of the power of omnipresence and 'omnipenetrability'.

However, the ideas treating of the 'gift of ubiquity', of which certain philosophers have spoken, are not absolutely adequate.

Our concepts of time and space undergo a total metamorphosis. We really live in a new dimension. Reality reveals to us strange resonances by letting us see what we are therein while in the heart of all that is around us. But, we repeat, there is no longer opposition between ourselves and that which is around us. The mask of separativity has disappeared for ever. The universe of outer appearances is progressively stripped of its opacity. In this new transparency the 'surface-world' seems to deepen irresistibly. Nothing any longer hinders our vision.

The limited becomes unlimited. The finite becomes infinite. Time reveals to us the part of eternity that we are in it. Everything becomes unfathomable to such an extent that depth and surface are integrated in a new homogeneity, completely unknown hitherto.

Beings and things have never been otherwise; only our vision has changed. An intense life is henceforward expressed in us by the ecstatic pulsations which mark the rhythm of an eternal re-creation.

But in this domain each word, each image is both a snare and a betrayal.

Words and images are concessions made to our dualistic language which is responsible for the mirages of the 'I-process'.

We must also point out that the experience of Satori *itself* is totally alien to all the above descriptions. These are suggested to the mind *after, and not during the experience*.

At this point a Zen master would call us to order by pointing out that — Satori, in any case, is not an 'experience' as we generally use the term.

The part of Love in 'Love-Intelligence' possesses the simple yet marvellous power of guiding us towards perceptions whose power is greater than that of the words and symbols which claim to contain them. This power is one of the principal keys of Satori.

Every human being possesses in a latent state this divine magic of veritable Love whose liberating and divergent qualities *act by themselves without the intervention of methods or disciplines on the part of the 'I-process'.* In certain cases such forces can work despite our egoistic resistance, and reveal to us the divine surprise.

In the mind of those who awake according to this *natural religion, the ocean of old dreams forms waves of words which break on the shores of the Eternal Present.* The content of each of them fades before the dazzling light of the instant.

In the moments preceding Satori 'thought-words' still occur. Already their development is slower. They are born, flower, fade and die. They no longer have as a motive the craving of a pseudo-entity which feeds on them to nourish the dream of a continuity that is dead.

As Suarès expresses it: it may be that 'on the ruins of the crumbling entity, another wishes to establish itself'.

But in the light of 'Love-Intelligence' each old wave breaks on the rock of perpetual renewal.

We have repeatedly insisted on the fact that in the state of Satori or liberation there is no longer an entity.

This important affirmation can actually be explained.

Every moment a thought is born, free, supple, adequate to the circumstances. Barely has this thought appeared, in answer to the requirements of adequacy of that moment, when it is entirely dissolved.

This thought is wholly free from identification with a thinker.

The perpetual play of their reciprocal tensions is ended. It may be that another thought succeeds it in answer to the solicitations of the instant. But it is entirely extinguished as soon as its role is completed.

In the integrated man thoughts only arise for purposes of communications.

It should also be said that the act of communicating or expressing is freed from the desire to project the self.

The man of Satori is no longer anything regarded as an 'I-process'. This true humility, irresistible and unaffected, is the sign of wisdom and real greatness. It allows man the realization of a new dignity, which is no longer that of an 'I-process', but that of the plenitude of Life itself.

All human beings possess in the depth of their consciousness, in the latent state, the freshness and perfume of this eternal springtime. All can discover within themselves, and by themselves, the blessing of this human and divine joy.

On the Birth of Thoughts

THE process of the birth of thoughts is rather obscure. Its study is most rewarding.

We have defined mental activity as an expression of the instinct of preservation of the 'I-process'. This definition is only partly correct. It requires adjustment.

The integrated man can exercise his mental activity while remaining completely untouched by an instinct of preservation.

In fact mental activity is *also* the expression of a universal tendency, or habit of expansion, inherent in the process of exteriorization and development of life, in the manifested world.

This tendency naturally inclines us to objectify ourselves, project ourselves.

Without this we would not be in existence.

The mental process can be compared to a giant tree grown from a minute seed.

This development, which demands years for the formation of the trunk and branches of the tree, is affected in a few moments on the plane of thought.

'Thought-roots' are born at every instant.

They can be compared to mental seeds whose first stage of formation appears in a psychical centre situated in the lower part of the spine.

Barely have they begun to germinate and develop, during the superficial act of becoming conscious by the brain, than they are expelled, smothered by the too rapid appearance of a ceaseless procession of other 'thought-roots'.

These thousands of unkept promises, unassuaged desires, incomplete or unsuccessful actions create innumerable knots of psychic forces and memory-complexes, the sum of which gives an appearance of reality to the 'I-process'.

Krishnamurti and the Zen masters suggest the realization of a different mental process.

We should concede greater attention to the mental process. We should allow the latent plant in each psychic seed to develop to its full growth.

When the tree, of which each of these seeds is the promise, has developed completely it will yield us highly revealing messages. We will have before us an open book which will give us the keys to living knowledge of ourselves.

We will see that the trunk, branches and leaves of this tree bear our imprint. The seal with our effigy is found imprinted everywhere on it so systematically, so obviously and so ridiculously that we become brutally aware of the absurd comedy we were playing to ourselves. From this moment we are no longer 'made fools of'.

Other thoughts will be able to arise in anonymous response to circumstances, but we shall no longer project ourselves in them.

Satori and the Research Techniques of Physicists

THE preceeding considerations inspired by our research into the complementarity of physics and psychology are endorsed every day by eminent scholars and thinkers. While on this subject we might point out that most contemporary physicists are *obliged* to adopt in physics a technique of research which offers surprising similarities with that of the negative approach of Satori.

In a remarkable work, *Les Conquêtes de la Pensée Scientifique*, G. Cahen, the French physicist concludes:

'The depersonalization of scientific judgment is considered an essential condition of its validity. In all calculations the physicist should fight against the precariousness of a statement which might be too individual, and against the systematization or accidental errors that an operator introduces by reason of the imperfection of his own constitution. *He should as far as possible eliminate the personal equation. Faced with the fact, he wants to be invisible, passive, impersonal, non-existent'* (pp. 277, 278).*

Is this not typically Zen language!

Concerning the necessary emancipation from our habits the author declares:

'To start on this path the seeker often must have had to make not only hypotheses, *but also to give up his well-anchored habits of thought*, euclidian geometry, three-dimensional reasoning, constancy of the mass, possibility of distinct representation of phenomena, individuality of corpuscles etc. Each of these apparently intuitive and irreducible notions has had to be abandoned, and each abandonment coincided with the progress of science.

This catharsis, this *successive abandonment of our familiar modes* of apprehension of the universe, seems an inexorable law in the development of modern theories in physics' (p. 281).

* The underlining is our own.

We have made repeated allusions to the fundamental law proclaimed by the eminent Swiss physicist Eugène Guye: '*The scale of observation creates the phenomena.*'

This law governs the whole process of our relations. [195]

It applies not only to physical research, but has important implications in the domain of the inner life.

The remarkable lines by G. Cahen, which we shall quote here, cannot fail to interest to the highest degree, not only readers familiar with Buddhist literature, but also those who are interested in the very up-to-date problems of the complementarity of physics and psychology.

The French physicist expresses himself as follows:

'The denudation of phenomena, when faced with the immediate content of our perceptions, presents two characteristics which we will demonstrate. On the one hand, this process reveals an *identity of essence between the intellect and the universe.* On the other hand, this content is progressively emptying itself of its apparent substance: matter itself tends to be but an empty form, a field of action of the structural properties of our mind, that is to say of something immaterial.

We will express thus, and in the most extreme manner, the ultimate tendency of science: *the reduction of reality to the void.* This void is not not-being, nullity. It is on the contrary, the most complete being possible since it potentially contains the universe.' (G. Cahen, *Les Conquêtes de la Pensée Scientifique*, p. 10, 1956).

From Personal Consciousness to the State of Satori

IN the course of this work I have sought to demonstrate the negative and destructive part played by our mental habits.

To such an extent are we identified with the words and symbols with which we are familiar that they reappear at every other moment. This takes place, whether we wish it or not, in all the circumstances of our daily life.

Unknown to ourselves the automatic character of our habits of memory enclose us within ourselves. Our mental habits possess a dangerous force of inertia. This force of habit must needs be revealed in us. It is absolutely necessary for us to perceive the plan according to which it operates.

The unique character of each moment of the present, its creative upsurge and its novelty continually escape us.

There is a key of fundamental importance which allows us to open the inner door which gives access to the plenitude of the Present, the heavy door which we have ourselves constructed. We can even say that it is ourselves. Its existence is due to our habitual inattention, to our constant negligence.

Correct attention is the only key which allows us not only to open this inner door but also to demolish it. It is not sufficient merely to state the necessity of correct attention; it is also necessary to explain the manner in which it should be exercised.

Those who are sincerely interested in the discovery of the Truth should be attentive. We do not realize to what extent we often remain superficial, to what extent we are careless in spite of our reading and our intellectual understanding. We do not sufficiently ponder on all the implications of the fact of 'being attentive'.

To be attentive is evidently to remove ourselves from the influence of distractions; that is a simple truth that everybody admits but that nobody puts into practice.

The most fundamental distractions are not without; they are within us; they result from the potent magic of words and symbols inseparably connected with all our thoughts.

It is absolutely necessary that our attention shall be applied *every moment*, but in order that it may be fruitful and revealing that attention should not be 'cumulative'. It should not merely be the result of reading about its necessity. We should be attentive because we have realized its importance with intensity and in a profoundly personal manner. True attention should resemble the irresistible urge of a natural function which seeks to express itself in us and through us.

We should avoid being attentive with an idea of obtaining a reward thereby, either directly or indirectly. We lack nothing. We must pounce on the secret avidity of the 'I-process' projecting itself into the future to that end.

Any expectation of a result leads to nothing. The more subtle the expectation the more damaging it is: it will lead us inevitably to a state of auto-hypnosis. The moment we wish for a result our unconscious instantly projects that result in us by virtue of a principle of compensation well known to modern psychology.

Let us never lose sight of the fact that Cosmic Mind is not a 'result'.

Therefore it is indispensable to see, to see with ever greater intensity; but, by a strange paradox, intensive or penetrating vision does not result from an act of will on the part of the 'I-process'. It is realized by perfect passivity of the mind. Perfect vision is 'non-expectation'; and for that reason it cannot be induced by any method. Perfect vision resides entirely in the intensity of the passing moment. Any secret expectation instantly paralyses that intensity. Every hope causes a rent in consciousness, separating that part of it which holds on to the present from another part that is directed towards the future. In this way 'distractions', in the pure sense of the word, are continually being created.

We should concentrate on what we are doing, our eyes wide open, without expectation, supremely attentive to the continual evasions of the imaginative mind, to its endless 'dis-tractions'.

But it is not a question of avoiding the activities of the imagination by deliberately driving them away: it is necessary to unmask the force of inertia of the 'I-process' (the 'old man') which is the cause of their appearance.

One does not rid oneself of imagination in order to acquire anything whatever; imaginative agitation disappears if we allow the force of non-cumulative attention to express itself in us.

If we have fully understood and deeply felt, both in heart and mind, to what an extent the inertia of our mental habits reveals the basic craving for survival of the 'I-process' (*Tanha*), imaginative agitation disappears of its own accord. We have understood why it prevents us from being lucid and adequate.

There is a method for the development of attention that is not cumulative; anyone can put it into practice.

We can readily observe that the fact of being more and more attentive develops in us a sort of automatic faculty of attention to the present. By really living, in the course of our daily life, in this state of observation, wherever we may be and whatever we may be doing, we will notice in ourselves the awakening of an ever clearer lucidity the intensity of which is astonishing.

This attention, which is not cumulative and is devoid of choice, operates from moment to moment. It is imbued with an increasing penetration and power of concentration on the present which no longer result from an act of personal will. At that moment we are very near to Satori, but we will not effectively realize it until the moment arrives when we shall have forgotten everything that we have read or imagined about it – including the word 'Satori' itself.

The master-key of which I spoke at the beginning of this note can now be described as follows: in the course of the effective practice of correct observation in daily life *there comes a moment when the power of attention to the present moment is more potent than the words or the symbols that pretend to contain it*. We always mistakenly believed that words and symbols were indispensable aids to our faculty of awakening. On the contrary, Satori – the state of supreme awakening, and which is perfectly natural – manifests itself as an invasion of ordinary consciousness by means of a degree of lucidity which literally annihilates words from 'within'. Henceforth symbols and words will have only a secondary and derivatory function: their use will be limited to that of instruments of conversation and communication.

Let us not lose sight of the fact that at the very moment of the experience there are no longer either words or symbols, subject or object, subject of an experience or experience itself.

Besides, the supreme attention of Satori is no longer merely attention: it is also Love. We are no longer attentive to some particular thing – although we do not lose the faculty of observing the particular when circumstances require it. The process of optical isolation is then realized in asbolute liberty, free of all identification, of all attachment to the particular object.

There is an immense difference between the familiar fact of being conscious *of* something and that of simply being conscious, in the plenitude of a lucidity without choice, freed from the duality of subject and object.

The man freed from the illusion of consciousness-of-self is the simplest and most practical man there could be. He is no longer anything but a body that has been rid of its content of personal psychological identification, which gives him the highest degree of adequacy and awakedness. Such a body rediscovers the plenitude of an instinctive wisdom whose immense possibilities are entirely unsuspected by our present-day sub-human races.

Although this superior form of the instinctive wisdom of the body is based on biological memories going back into the dawn of history, these memorial automatisms no longer give rise to misplaced echos on the psychological plane. This enables us to understand how the external life of a man who has realized Satori can be possible, for in such a man are realized the highest possibilities of creation.

Parable of the Flame and the Smoke

SATORI defies all description, all imagery, and yet certain expressions might prove useful as aids to practical realization, especially if they are approached through the heart and not by the mind (*Koan No. 1*).

Having made the usual reservations with regard to the weakness of all symbolical representation, we will say that Satori, from certain points of view, is similar to an eternally pure flame without smoke.

The Flame remains pure and without smoke for as long as there appears no dualistic consciousness of experience and person undergoing the experience.

It is within this dualistic consciousness that the only real Hell exists; the one which we create ourselves in all its details in the mirages of identification and attachment.

The eternally pure Flame remains unaffected by the mirages.

The Flame is an inconceivable reality shining in its own light.

The brightness of the Flame is unthinkable; it can be lived only in the non-dualistic integration of the Pure Act. The Flame is itself reality beyond light. The vision of the Flame as light is an objectification, consequently a degradation, affecting only ourselves.

The Flame is 'Prajna' or Wisdom. The Flame has no name; it has never borne one, nor will it ever do so (*Koan No. 2*).

Although in itself the Flame has neither source nor centre, we will say that 'for us' its source and its centre are 'Prajna' or Wisdom.

Although in itself the Flame has no 'halo', we will say that 'for us' the halo of the Flame is the Ananda or spiritual felicity.

The smoke of the Flame appears 'for us' the moment when we objectify the Ananda or felicity. The smoke grows denser and becomes suffocating from the moment when we delight in the enjoyment of the Ananda or felicity by identifying ourselves with its savour, 'rasa'. Boundless felicity is unconscious of itself. Objectification causes it to lose its unfathomable character. Although the Flame in itself has no privileged point in Time and Space – (it is not a thing, but Pure Action) – its manifestation *within us may* be localized.

The Flame is not 'perceived' as we generally perceive things. The Sage, conscious of his wisdom, is not a sage. The enlightened person conscious of his enlightenment, is not an enlightened person. An awakened person conscious of his awakedness, is not truly awakened.

However, in the body of an awakened person who is free of all dualistic perception and all consciousness of self, the Flame of Prajna or Wisdom is manifested in the proximity of two psychophysiological centres; one situated at the base of the spine, the other near the navel.

This localization which appears absurd only concerns the psycho-physiological stimulation arising from the manifestation of Prajna or Wisdom within us. The Flame is in itself omnipresent and has no privileged dwelling-place.

The Flame is ever new and creative. It leaves no traces. It is complete in itself in every instant. It is the Great Work. Its rhythm is that of creation, pure and eternally present, maintaining the worlds of the infinitely small and of the infinitely great.

The Flame is not the flux of 'something'. It is beyond mobility and immobility.

The felicity of the Flame (Ananda) is perceived by the heart. It may spread throughout the whole of the physical organism. The felicity of the Flame can leave traces. These traces form the 'rasas' or savours.

The smoke of the Flame appears at the moment of the perception of the savour. It grows dense on attachment and identification with the savour. This attachment emanates from the mind. That which remains of the 'I-process' tries to seize the savour in order to affirm itself, to play a role, to give itself importance.

Our hyper-intellectualized races are suffocated by the fumes of mental activity. The agitation of thought and the savours (rasas) are merely sensations seized upon by the illusion of the 'I-process' in its avidity for existence (Tanha).

The Flame is pure creation and not creation of 'something'. The smoke tends to become immobilized in the rhythms of the habit of identification. The smoke is a creation of our mind in the same manner as is the concept of 'thing'.

When mental and sensorial habits are all-powerful, the seat of consciousness seems to become established in the brain. Such is the position of the present 'norm' in its state of generalized inattention and neglect.

The displacement of consciousness in the brain is the last phase in the degradation of our perceptive faculties. The latter are deformed by the desire for objectification. The desire for objectification or projection of self is one of the most subtle forms of attachment and identification.

The Zen Unconscious – this infinite consciousness which is unconscious of itself in its unfathomability – comes alive when objectified consciousness no longer has its seat in the brain and is transformed into non-objectified consciousness (*Koan No. 3*).

Non-objectified consciousness, that is, the state of non-mental awakedness, has *for us* its zone of manifestation between the navel and the centre of the base of the spine. For this reason certain schools of Zen advise the direction of consciousness or the perception of consciousness towards the abdomen. This is the procedure of the Rinzaï school.

Nevertheless, the practice of this method may engender an objectification of another kind or lead to self-hypnosis.

It is important to insist that nothing should be expected of such a shifting of consciousness. Satori is not a thing which is to be expected. The practice of a mere 'trick' of the mind cannot engender an authentic experience, that is, the awakening of integration in which the duality of experience and person who experiences vanishes forever.

This would be equivalent to an attempt at reformation of the Flame with the aid of the smoke. The Flame of 'Prajna' is not a result. It is sufficient in Itself. It is completely new.

From the Flame to smoke, the process of transformation

(which exists only in our mind and in no way affects the Flame), is irreversible.

Therefore we should distrust the exercising of presumed consequences of Satori with a view to obtaining Satori. From Satori to its consequences there exists 'for us' the same irreversible process as that for the Flame and the smoke.

Nevertheless, concrete things must be put in their place, and that is only because we have misplaced them. Such is the case of the tendency that consciousness has within us in order to feel itself in the brain.

The acuteness of complete consciousness inherent in the awakening of Satori does not have its centre of psycho-physiological stimulation in the brain.

On the contrary, it appears that the intensity of the awakening is expressed on the psycho-physiological plane through the intermediary of a centre situated in the abdomen for the birth of Satori, and in the heart for the perception of the inevitable transformations brought about by Satori.

Mental automatisms resulting from attachment to cerebral engrams are seated in the brain. Their hold on consciousness is all the greater in that this only arises because of our mental activities.

Were we to allow the non-mental consciousness emanating from the abdominal centres to work without interference of cerebral consciousness, the total power of attention and the acuteness of lucidity resulting from such displacement would have an immediate effect: words, references, symbols which presumed to 'contain' consciousness would 'burst' literally and dissolve. The acuteness of non-mental attention is greater than the words attempting to describe them.

The Flame of Prajna or Wisdom is lucidity without ideation.

But in order that 'Prajna' or Wisdom may live effectively, 'Dhyana' should be realized. 'Dhyana' is the basis of Zen. 'Dhyana' is the symbol of availability, inner transparence, non-expectation. For Hui-Neng 'Dhyana' was synonymous with detachment.

Detachment cannot be the result of a reaction of the 'I-process' fighting in order to detach itself, disciplining itself in order to become indifferent or insensible.

Detachment cannot result from an act of will. It arises from an act of attention. The will emanates from the fundamental violence of the workings of the 'I-process'. True attention, although exercised by the 'I-process' (or what remains of it), emanates from the Zen Unconscious. In the very fact of correct detachment freed of all personal motive, there is 'pure action'. All pure action is the Flame of Prajna or Wisdom.

In the fact of allowing the Flame Itself to operate without any expectation, without any hope, lies one of the keys to Satori (*Koan No. 4*).

The weakness of all speech lies in the fact that words and images filling the mind are essentially dualistic. Each affirmation has its counterpart. Each thesis its antithesis. That which has been expressed here is absurd if we consider the relative world, but becomes true in the world of the Unique Reality. In order to encourage the mind to transcend the dualistic processes which imprison it, Zen uses 'Koans'. The impasse in which 'Koans' place us cannot be solved by the mind. Before the simultaneity of two contradictory affirmations – opposite but complementary facets of a more vast Reality – logic is forced to suspend its usual process. For this reason we have interspersed the preceding article with 'Koans'. Some are the negation of the phrase preceding them. This negation, from the transcendental point of view is true also. The confrontment of these negations is indispensable for the understanding of the text in a 'higher octave'. However, it is advisable to deepen the original version of the article before proceeding to meditation on these 'Koans' which form its counterpart. Koan No. 1: True heart is Intelligence, true Intelligence is Love. Koan No. 2: There is neither past nor future such as we conceive them. Koan No. 3: Objectified consciousness having its seat in the brain, has no reality in itself. Koan No. 4: In Reality there is nothing that can be compared to a flame or anything at all. Comparison is a dualistic process.

Marginal Notes

[1] 'If someone after having read this, tries to obtain the informal perception of which we are speaking, let him beware; there are a thousand ways of believing that one has it, whereas one has it not; in any case the mistake is the same and consists in one complication or another which comprises forms; one is not *simple-minded enough. In-formal and immediate perception of existence is the simplest kind of perception there can be*' (Dr. H. Benoit, *Supreme Doctrine*, p. 55).

[2] 'Anyone who attempts to write about Zen has to encounter *unusual difficulties; he can never explain*, he can only indicate; he can only go on setting problems and giving hints which at best can bring the reader tantalizingly nearer the truth, but the moment he attempts any fixed definition the thing slips away, and the definition is seen to be no more than a philosophical conception . . .' (Allan Watts, *The Spirit of Zen*, p. 12).

[3] Zen incites us to interrupt the routines of our mind.

[4] In the name of the Unity of all that exists in this manifested Universe, *be free* and detached from all separate things for you are its immortal essence (Ramlal Dayal-shanti Ghôse).

[5] The evil brought upon the white people by their exclusively intellectual culture and their cupidity . . . should be offset by a mutual comprehension of East and West (Professor Masson-Oursel).

[6] 'That which has been successfully defined has been successfully killed' (Christmas Humphreys, *Zen Buddhism*, p. 102).

[7] Faith without works is a dead faith (Saint Paul).

[8] Daily life is the proof that reveals the value of a philosophy (J. J. Van der Leeuw, *The Conquest of Illusion*).

[9] 'Satori is the sudden flashing into consciousness of a new truth hitherto undreamed of . . .' (C. Humphreys, *Zen Buddhism*, p. 154).

[10] In the man who has freed himself from his me (his past), the guiding principle at every moment is himself who transforms himself, who is constantly born of himself (C. Suarès, *Comédie Psychologique*, p. 289).

[11] 'Our productive imagination fed on the energy engendered by *habit* superimposes . . . an illusory edifice, a mirage, on its past. The cessation of the mirage is called Nirvâna' (Vajracchedikâ Sûtra).

[12] The world is undergoing a gigantic revolution. The call for a new Middle-Age today, is only a call to this revolution of the mind, a complete renewal of consciousness (N. Berdiaeff, *Un Nouveau Moyen-Age*, pp. 91 and 105).

[13] 'If you affirm divine transcendence, you are conditioning your

conception of God, and if you affirm his immanence, you are setting limits to Him; but if simultaneously you affirm both one and the other point of view, you will be exempt from error and be a model of knowledge' (Verbe de Noë, *Muhyi-d-Din. Esotérisme musulman*).

[14] 'Man, by contemplating his deeper nature, can find the whole Universe' (Professor Téchoueyrès).

[15] That which remains hovering over East and West is the Spirit, final master of the world (René Grousset, *France-Asie*, p. 777, 1953).

[16] 'Taking all in all, Zen is emphatically a matter of personal experience; if anything can be called radically empirical, it is Zen. *No amount of reading, no amount of teaching, and no amount of contemplation will ever make one a Zen master. Life itself must be grasped in the midst of its flow, to stop it for examination and analysis is to kill it, leaving its cold corpse to be embraced*' (D. T. Suzuki, *Essays in Zen Buddhism*, vol. I, p. 360).

[17] 'When the Buddha was asked his lineage he answered: "I am not a brahmin, I am not the son of a prince, I am not a bourgeois, and finally I am not anyone!" (Suttanipato).

[18] The annihilation of ALL suffering is only possible by the annihilation of our entire personality . . . (G. Grimm, *La Religion du Bouddha*, p. 127).

[19] The Buddha: 'Hearken, O ye monks, the STATE WITHOUT DEATH has been found; I present and expound the doctrine; in following these precepts you will very quickly understand, while still in this life, the final aim of the holy life (that is, exactly, immortality), you will realize it and you will remain in it' (G. Grimm, *La Religion du Bouddha*, p. 80).

[20] The Buddha: 'A perfected man EXISTS after death' or 'A perfected man does not exist after death': either, my friend, is a way of conceiving on a bodily basis (from which, precisely, a Perfected man has freed himself).

For him who has returned home there is no scale of measurement; that which, while he was alive, served to describe him, no longer exists FOR HIM.

A perfected man, FREED from corporeality, is immense and cannot be measured; he is UNFATHOMABLE like the vast ocean (G. Grimm, *La Religion du Bouddha*, p. 105).

[21] '. . . The doctrine of the Buddha diverges from Christianity on a point of capital importance. In fact, the Buddha does not found his doctrine on supernatural revelations, or mystical experiences which always end by coming into conflict with reality, and which for this reason require amendments. Quite the opposite; he proves that his doctrine is the result of direct, penetrating and normal knowledge, of the most profound and lucid thought, which makes truth "independent

of time", that is, valid for all men and at all times; a truth that does not lend itself to amendments. That is why he does not ask for faith, on the contrary, he asks that nothing should be accepted, even from him, on simple belief, but only what one has oneself recognized as being true...' (G. Grimm, *La Religion du Bouddha*, p. 62).

[22] 'Metaphysicists are conjurors, they conjure themselves away' (C. Suarès, *La Comédie Psychologique*, p. 92).

[23] The claims of the intellect are vitiated from the beginning. For how can one resolve the me by means of one of its own faculties? One might as well ask the rules of a game of chess to explain for what reason men play chess (C. Suarès, *La Comédie Psychologique*, p. 92).

[24] NIRVANA is the 'annihilation of MAYA' — a 'blowing-out of AVIDYA, or Ignorance' — and a state of Universal Inner Consciousness, rather than an extinction of consciousness... (Ramacharaka, *The Inner Teachings of the Philosophies and Religions of India*, p. 179).

[25] 'All knowledge is an aquisition and accumulation, whereas Zen proposes to deprive one of all one's possessions.

Learning, on the contrary, makes one rich and arrogant... When the spirit is all purged of its filth accumulated from time immemorial, it stands naked, with no raiments, with no trappings. It is now empty, free, genuine, assuming its native authority' (Suzuki, *Essays in Zen Buddhism*, vol. I, p. 349).

[26] The schools of Zen Buddhism lead their adepts along severer paths ... The disciple must plunge into the waters of Life. All attempts at evasion towards dialectic are immediately chastized. The Zen master knows only too well that the intellect, reduced to its own resources, can never go beyond the limitations of its sphere (Dr. R. Godel, *L'Expérience Libératrice*, p. 111).

[27] Nothing that is knowable is our profound essence, our own Me. Naturally this does not exclude the qualities which we recognize, namely BODY, MIND and WILL, from being some of our qualities, but they are NON-ESSENTIAL characteristics, mere accidents, or as the Buddha says, merely 'attributes' which we have simply appropriated (Grimm, *La religion du Bouddha*, p. 97).

[28] 'All is flow, a ceaseless flow of life in and out of the forms which, for a time, express part of it...' (C. Humphreys, *Zen Buddhism*, p. 105).

[29] 'The endless round of births is not caused by any God only the elements produced by causes and materials which constitute beings go their way. One round of action, one round of fruit, birth arising from action, and thus the world goes round (According to the Visudhi Magga).

[30] Master Eckhart: 'In so far as man knows himself, he comes to know God.

Where I am there is God, and that is pure truth.
Man in truth is God, and God in truth is man.
I perceive in this vision that I and God are one.

The soul (after its deliverance) loses its name in the unity of the divine essence, and that is why then it is no longer called soul, its name is "incommensurable essence".'

[31] '. . . The mind IS the Buddha, nor is there any other Buddha or any other mind. It is bright and spotless as the void, having no form or appearance whatsoever.

. . . but the Buddha who has always existed is not a Buddha of stages. Only awake to universal mind and realize that there is nothing whatsoever to be attained' (Hsi-Yun, *The Huang-Po Doctrine of Universal Mind*, p. 45).

[32] 'Practise the art of the "complete gift of yourself".' (Fo-sho-hing-tsan-king).

[33] '. . . Man should free himself from the material wrapping of religion' (Rabindra Nath Tagore).

[34] We can show today that what all religions, what all metaphysics, and what all philosophies were trying to seek while calling it all possible names; God, the Absolute, Truth, are nothing other than the human element (C. Suarès, *La Comédie Psychologique*, p. 68).

[35] 'Shine by yourself with your own light' (Dhammapada).

[36] Do not make for yourselves idols of any kind (Siamese Buddhist maxim).

[37] Absolute authority only exists in the lower forms of Buddhism.

[38] There is indeed freedom. When we enter the world of the Real we do experience freedom; not the illusion of freedom which was to do as we liked, to have our own way, to choose without compulsion, but a true Freedom in which we are free because then nothing is outside us to limit or compel (J. J. Van der Leeuw, *The Conquest of Illusion*, p. 173).

[39] In the quest for truth, however, we must be utterly free from prejudice and ruthlessly sincere, never accepting a fact, cherished though it may be and hallowed by universal recognition, without first challenging its reality, even though such a challenge might appear superfluous. Only thus can we prevent error from entering into our very question (Idem, p. 17).

[40] The me which has accomplished the colossal task of disassociating itself from everything, alone is able to probe doubt in its entirety, and reach the irreducible (C. Suarès, *La Comédie Psychologique*, p. 80).

[41] We no longer need the seclusion of the Church to find God and to serve Him, we see Divinity in the faces of our fellowmen and hear its music in the voices of nature. Our daily life has become the cathedral

in which we revere the Eternal. While the common activities of our human existence have become the ceremonies in which we worship the Reality which in them is manifest (J. J. Van der Leeuw, *The Conquest of Illusion*, p. 233).

42 Inscriptions on the rock of Asoka: No superstitious rites, but kindness towards slaves and servants, deference to venerable persons, independence united with respect for living creatures, these virtues and others like them, they are, in truth, the rites which should be accomplished.

43 It is only in the course of daily living that man can reach the liberty which will allow him to know Reality. In this realization, man does not become something that he was not before, he does not enter a world to which he did not hitherto belong, *but he realizes himself as he always was.* Spiritually the life of man is a slave of forms in religion, and the church, the form and the ritual faith and credulity. The ardent desire for a revelation through intermediaries is an attempt to obtain from the outside what man cannot discover in himself. It is a bondage through fear, fear of remaining alone, without the comfort and support of priests or faith, fear of offending the deity that man has created in his own image (J. J. Van der Leeuw, *The Conquest of Illusion*).

44 'You claim', you will say to me, 'that ritual is an obstacle to human development. However is it not possible that with the help of ritual and disciplines one can experience strange and splendid emotions? The ritualist feels carried away, and at certain moments believes that he is in contact with the divinity itself. Such acute joys, are they without value in your sight?

Indeed no, I even accord them a terrible value. While most people draw from this the proof that the way on which they are found must be the right one, I consider them as the worst danger threatening spiritual research. They are the treacherous sirens which lead men astray, turning them away from their difficult path to make them a prey to innumerable servitudes.

From the heart of the religions themselves, the great mystics have not hesitated to sound the alarm. In the "Ascent to Mount Carmel", a St. John of the Cross places the "path of the lost spirit", or "path of material enjoyment", parallel to the "path of the imperfect spirit", or "path of search after spiritual joys"'. (R. Fouéré).

45 There, where one imagines that one is pursuing truth, the unity of one's being, one is only chasing sensations into which one sinks lamentably. One wants to be drunk with spirituality — adulterated as it is — as others are drunk on wine

Indeed, to reach liberation is to enter into an ecstasy. It is even entering into the sole real ecstasy, that which, according to the etymology of the word, is a going-out from oneself, an escape from the condition of the me. But to experience moments of intensity, of plenitude because one is free, is one thing, but it is quite another to undergo intense sensations in the very interior of the condition of the me, without leaving that condition.

Though interior intensity is a trait of spiritual realization, it is not its distinctive trait, its criterion.

Then how shall one distinguish between the sentiment felt by an integrated man, from that felt by the ordinary man? (R. Fouéré).

[46] Whilst pure emotion is detached, that which we commonly call emotion is a state that creates a dependence of the subject with regard to the objects that arouse this state in him. No sooner have we felt this, its pretext, whether it is a being, a thing or a practice, becomes the object of our anxious pursuits or the prey of our frantic embrace. It becomes a tyrant, we become obsessed by it, intoxicated. In contrast, the plenitude of the liberated being, the plenitude of pure emotion does not depend on a particular content. Being able to subsist in all circumstances or before any object, it is not seeking any special object, nor particular circumstances. It is this detachment that matters. To feel violent joys and cloying satisfactions are in themselves valueless.

In the same way, ritual or disciplines which procure them for us are without value. Nothing can justify the use of these rituals in the domain of pure spirituality (R. Fouéré, *Disciplines, Ritualismes et Spiritualités*, pp. 28 to 30).

[47] . . . mystical vocations appearing among people who do not belong to a church, or who even are in disagreement with all churches have far less chance of being noticed and especially of being pointed out. They even have less chance of notoriety in so far as they are purer. For the purest mysticism does not appear to itself or to others as extraordinary. It is not conducive to any unusual or showy manifestation, confining itself to accomplishing profoundly and in plenitude, what others accomplish thoughtlessly and with an overwhelming feeling of inner misery.

Such a mysticism approaches directly and simply the problems and circumstances of life. It does not burden itself with superfluous celestial entities. Outwardly: barely is it revealed by the harmony of a face, a kind of spiritual touch marking the features which the busy people of every-day life have not the time to notice. That is all, that is, nothing for the lover of sensations and spectacles. Men having reached this wisdom can disappear 'without leaving a trace in the memories of the passers-by', so deeply their inner riches were hidden under humble appearances (R. Fouéré, *Disciplines, Ritualismes et Spiritualité*, p. 68).

[48] By 'false emanations of Eternity, of light and of the Real' we mean

the states which arise from a fundamental flaw in the functioning of the mind.

[49] To those who feel the mortal boredom of secular routines, to those whose passional hopes have been disappointed by the brutality or the inconstance of others, ritual offers the initial seduction of a break with the order of things from which one no longer expects anything, of a renewal, of a different experience.

Many, the author of the *Imitation of Christ* tells us, have been deceived by this idea of change.

The temptation is all the greater as ritual practise surrounds itself with rich decor, art and real poetry. The ragged poor finds that the church, decorated and illuminated, filled with perfume and music, is attractive to stay in; a fact around which one can weave dreams indefinitely; a moment of harmony which often has no domestic equivalent. So one comes, and one comes again, spell-bound by the celestial mirage. One engages oneself on this promising path, and, even if later the original exaltation has worn off, one stays there through habit, and one becomes a supporter of ritualism in the world (R. Fouéré, *Disciplines, Ritualismes et Spiritualité*, p. 72).

[50] Another attraction of ritualism, is that it promises a realization which, obtained by purely mechanical processes, owes almost nothing to intellectual effort. Such a conception could not but flatter laziness of mind (R. Fouéré, *Disciplines, Ritualismes et Spiritualité*, p. 73).

[51] I repeat the same crucial question, the terrible question which is constantly omitted and which one could call tragic in its simplicity: are the disciplines which assure the perpetuity of social, political or religious organizations capable of bringing about its individual synthesis, of procuring this durable unity of the me? . . .

The answer is indubitably in the negative . . . Far from being sources of unity and truth in intimate order, these disciplines are the causes of individual disintegration and dissimulation.

To impose a discipline on oneself, is that not to institute a duality within oneself, to split one's me into two fragments, of which one half imposes and the other suffers the discipline in question? . . . Far from uniting and harmonizing the me, all deliberate discipline tears it and warps it. . . .

The duality implied in the initial constraint is not really dispelled, even if, at times, it ceases to be perceived. It is like those wadis which one thinks are definitely absorbed by the sands, but which always reappear. . . .

From these considerations it is clear that to wish to find a solution by means of disciplines to the fundamental problems of life, is to engage oneself foolishly on an endless undertaking, in an attempt that will never end . . . because it postulates the absurdity that servile imitation and repetition can oppose themselves victoriously to the incessant universal creation . . . that it is possible to fit spirit to the Procrustean bed of habit. Foolish attempt about which we do not see that if it succeeds it would mean the arrest of creative becoming, the irremediable mechanization of the universe and its reduction to a definitely unchangeable function. All this is invisibly implied in the theories which try to make of disciplines a liberating instrument (R. Fouéré, *Disciplines, Ritualismes et Spiritualité*, pp. 14-16).

[52] 'Zen followers do not approve of Christians, even Christian mystics being too conscious of God, who is their creator and supporter of all life and all being' (Suzuki, *Essays in Zen Buddhism*, vol. I, p. 344).

[53] As we already know, our real Me is inaccessible to knowledge, because all our learning activity is directed to THE OUTSIDE, that is, on to the elements of our personality: body, sensations, perceptions, activities of the mind (G. Grimm, *La Religion du Bouddha*, p. 110).

[54] '. . . This (universal) mind is the Buddha and the Buddha is all living beings. It is not the less for being manifested in ordinary beings, nor is it greater for being manifested in the Buddha' (Hsi-Yun, *The Huang-Po Doctrine of Universal Mind*, p. 16).

[55] 'There are no things differing from each other Hence (to understand this) is called attaining complete, perfect Enlightenment' (Hsi-Yun, *The Huang-Po Doctrine of Universal Mind*, p. 44).

[56] By suggesting to us the complementarity of the notions of element and system, by showing us the individual losing his personality in so far as he merges in an organism which comprehends him, and finding it again in so far as he isolates himself, does not physics offer us suggestions of certain originality and richness of content from which general philosophy and sociology could draw profit? (L. de Broglie, *Avenir de la Science*, p. 34).

[57] Dhammapada: 'He who no longer needs to believe, but who KNOWS the uncreated, this man in truth is the greatest of men' (Grimm, p. 129).

[58] 'That which man acquires by contemplation he should spend in love' (Eckhart).

[59] 'Instead of understanding the spirit of Truth, people have taught that religion lies in the name of the Teacher . . .' (I. Khan, *In an Eastern Rosegarden*, p. 16).

[60] '. . . No one purifies another' (Dhammapada, v. 165).

[61] 'you yourself must make the effort; Buddhas do but point the way' (Dhammapada).

[62] 'To accept authority, especially in matters that concern right thinking, is utterly foolish. To accept authority is binding, hindering and

the worship of authority is self-worship. It is a form of laziness, thoughtlessness, leading to ignorance and sorrow' (Krishnamurti, *Ojai*, 1944, p. 60.)

⁶³ 'Just as one knows not the path of the sparks which, sprung from under the smith's hammer, die one by one, so is it impossible to discover the path of the perfectly Awakened who, having crossed the river of sensory desires which held them, have reached unshakeable beatitude' (Digh. Nik. XVI; Udana 8, 10. G. Grimm, *La Religion du Bouddha*, p. 147).

⁶⁴ . . . To believe that we lack something is a senseless ILLUSION; in fact we lack nothing. And it is only by reason of this prodigious ILLUSION that unceasingly increases in us the will, the impulsion, the thirst to acquire something, to acquire as much as possible, and beyond all else, a body and a mind (Grimm, *La Religion du Bouddha*, p. 58).

⁶⁵ Kant: 'The Self does not know itself.'

⁶⁶ The Upanishad: 'It is towards the outside that that which exists in itself digs its hollows, and that is why one looks towards the outside and not into the Self within.'

⁶⁷ 'There is no path towards deliverance, and that is evident since we have never really been in servitude; there is nowhere to "go", there is nothing to "do". Man has nothing directly to do in order to experience his liberty that is total and infinitely happy. What he has to do is indirect and negative; what he has to understand . . . is the deceptive illusion of all the "paths", then "satori" will burst forth, a real vision that there is no "path" because there is nowhere to go, because from all eternity, he was at the unique and fundamental centre of everything' (Dr. H. Benoit, *Supreme Doctrine*, p. 5).

⁶⁸ There is no longer a standard for him who has entered his house; describe him as you will, it will never be applicable. There, where all things are utterly annihilated, all the pathways of speech are also abolished.

⁶⁹ Approximation does not apply where the Truth is concerned. A path which does not lead directly to it is simply the wrong path. The only true one is that which links the person who says: 'I am I' to the capacity which the individual should reacquire of vibrating to the present moment when the me will have vanished. This way is its own goal (C. Suarès, *La Comédie Psychologique*, p. 305).

⁷⁰ 'When it is said: "Nothing is born", this does not mean that things are not self-engendered. According to a deeper meaning, to be deprived of self-nature is not to be born. That all things are deprived of self-nature means that there is a continual and uninterrupted "becoming", a change every moment from one "state of existence to another".' (A. David-Neel, *Le Bouddhisme*, p. 223).

[71] For we all possess the same Buddha-nature. What we lack is to be conscious of it, and favour its entire expression in ourselves, by absolute detachment, complete liberty and poverty of mind (Steinilber-Oberlin, *The Buddhist Sects of Japan*, p. 135).

[72] The absolute is present in the present. This absolute has not the characteristic of fixity, it is dynamic, perpetually changing it renews itself unceasingly (C. Suarès, *La Comédie Psychologique*, p. 120).

[73] 'There is a state in which there exists neither earth nor water, nor fire nor air, nor the domain of unlimited consciousness, neither this world, nor the other, nor the sun and moon. That O monks, I do not call either to come or to go, to appear or to disappear; without basis, without duration, without foundation is that: it is precisely the end of suffering' (Udana VIII, I, Grimm, *La Religion du Bouddha*, pp. 152-53).

[74] 'Since all the myriad things are nothing but mind and mind, itself, intangible, what can you hope to attain? Those who study the highest wisdom do not hold that there is a single thing upon which to lay hold. There is only one reality, and that can be neither realized nor grasped. To say "I am able to realize something" or "I am able to grasp something" is merely to add yourself to the ranks of the arrogant...' (Hsi-Yun, *The Huang-Po Doctrine of Universal Mind*, p. 32).

[75] 'Not that things are difficult to understand, but the fault lies in you who have not yet a sufficiently lofty outlook' (Dante Alighiere, *Il Paradiso*).

[76] This state of complete knowledge, this absolute state is so essentially natural and so entirely devoid of sensations that it can hardly tempt those who, under a pretext of seeking the truth, are only vulgar amateurs of sensation (C. Suarès, *La Comédie Psychologique*, p. 298).

[77] The progress of knowledge leads us away from the original Truth as does the river from its head when one follows its course. Near the source the water is less abundant but purer, and from all time, enlightened men have tried to retrace their steps to the source of truth. At the height of their thought we constantly find the intuition of the fundamental unity of creation' (Professor Viscardini).

[78] Today one generally agrees, and on the physical side of science this agreement is unanimous, in thinking that the current of knowledge is leading towards a non-mechanical reality. The Universe is beginning to resemble one great thought rather than one great machine (James Jeans, *Le Mystérieux Univers*, p. 168).

[78a] 'Then what is this that illuminates me within and causes my heart to vibrate without wounding it? ...

I entered and I contemplated with the mysterious eye of my soul the *light* which never changes, higher than my intelligence.

It was something entirely different from any terrestrial illumination. *It was higher than my intelligence because it was made by it*' (Saint Augustine, Confessions VII).

[79] 'So that God may enter, things must go out' (Montherlant, *Service Inutile*, p. 18).

[80] Julian Huxley once undertook this investigation. At the end of this investigation the outer world was rid of all its pretensions to objectivity; resolving itself in mental projections, it returned to the reign of the spirit, all that had originally belonged to it.

'*The spirit*' he concluded, '*is an integral part of the universe. Something of the nature of the spirit must be implied in the essence of things*' (R. Godel, *Expérience Libératrice*, p. 288).

[81] Every wave of excitement, by stimulating a centre of the nervous system, arouses at a distance an opposite process (induction in space) and provokes at the place itself an antagonistic consecutive reaction (induction in time).

Our conduct in life, our character, our intellectual operations are governed just as are simple sensations by the mechanism of induction.

In the eyes of the awakened observer, the two poles of the pair of opposites balance each other and dissolve in the radiation of unique intuition, for him appearances are resolved in non-duality (Godel, *Expérience Libératrice*, pp. 84 to 92).

[82] Such a descent to the sources requires the use of very purified psycho-techniques. At this level only an exploratory function, similar to the field of exploration, can operate.

Penetration into these regions of the mind which are difficult to explore is only possible for a consciousness which is freed from the conditioning factors of its own individuality (Dr. R. Godel, *Expérience Libératrice*, p. 149).

[83] To the mind thus established in an extreme purification of the senses and the intellect, nothing else exists besides a pure consciousness in observation. This primordial consciousness, this original consciousness . . . is the whole reality.

A certain like-mindedness unites the modern physicist, the Occidental mystic and the Hindu Sage. And this homology tends more and more to force the attention of the philosophers of our times. The common denominator that unites them in one same family is the impersonal position of their consciousness. It is manifested beyond the framework of sensory activities on a plane of abstraction, of pure dynamisms. During the instant it operates on this high level, their thought escapes the servitudes and the routines of the sensori-motor experience (R. Godel, *Expérience Libératrice*, p. 128).

[84] It appears that one of the difficulties in understanding the relationship

between mind and matter arises from the fact that we take concepts belonging to one aspect of the Cosmos and use them to describe other aspects to which they are no longer applicable.

If we wish to understand the reciprocal action, between the physical processes in the brain and the corresponding mental phenomena, we can say on the one hand, that the immaterial living element in the neurons has physical properties, since through its associated system of living waves it can influence the position and movement of atoms and electrons and, on the other hand, mental properties inherent in the 'source' and indicative of its last origin, and through such sources we immediately become conscious of certain attributes of the Cosmos. This sort of immaterial element *offers us a passage between* physical and mental phenomena (G. Stromberg, *L'Ame de L'Univers*, p. 164).

[85] A singular analogy symmetrically joins the order which governs matter and that which presides over the psychic dynamisms.

As all electro-chemical functions of the atom exclusively depend on the nuclear field, so all our determinations proceed from the axis of our being (R. Godel, *Expérience Libératrice*, p. 20).

[86] No soul is immortal, because only the resultant of all the movements of the Universe are immortal. No object is immortal, no idea, no form, nothing which one can perceive or conceive is immortal (C. Suarès, *La Comédie Psychologique*, p. 114).

[87] 'Before doing, one must BE' (Goethe).

[88] In Descartes the sleight of hand is much finer: 'Who am I?' he asks. He only answers by a series of negations- 'I am not my body, nor my passions' etc. On the other hand he claims to think and even to be thought. But he concludes most strangely: 'I think, therefore I am.' Logically he should have said: 'I think, therefore I destroy myself' (C. Suarès, *La Comédie Psychologique*, p. 285).

[89] Subjective time, there is the me. The me is an accumulation of all the desires for permanence, linked one to another by a chain which is duration. The cause which creates individual time is not the existence of objective time, but the desire felt by associations of which the me is made, to recall itself at every moment in order to perceive itself (C. Suarès, *La Comédie Psychologique*, p. 306).

[90] Every habit is a limitation of movement, and from this point of view *there are no good habits* (C. Humphreys, *Zen Buddhism*, p. 107).

[91] There is, proceeding from the mind, in terms of spiritual life, something which is in the nature of a fall, which resists change, that proceeds by rectilineal inertia which is mechanical and *repetitive*, which offers the Unconscious something which resembles the mind destroying itself to the extent of self-negation right up to death and burial. This something is *habit*; habit, generator of divisions and discourses whose acts

little by little are schematized in gestures immobile as things, then whose gestures are spatialized by *routine juxtaposition*; *habit* finally, visibly governed by two laws or tendencies: one asymptotique, for preservation, the other more effective for degeneration and wear.

Should one not take into account at the same time the whole of the data of the problem by conceiving matter under the analogy of *habit* by discerning a group of inveterate *habits*, constellations of *habits*, sunk in oblivion, dead *habits*?

Habit spreads itself on a series of successive planes on which it becomes more and more mechanical.

Everything starts in an atmosphere of liberty by an act of invention. Then comes *habit*, a kind of body as the body itself is a cluster of *habits*. And *habit* becoming inveterate, work of liberty which escapes it and turns against it, gradually degenerates into mechanicalness in which consciousness falls asleep and is buried (Professor E. Leroy, *Exigence Idéaliste*, pp. 27 and 38).

[92] The me is not the being, but a universal resistance, whose aim is its own destruction (C. Suarès, *La Comédie Psychologique*, p. 67).

[93] By evolution we do not mean to include a group of biological facts whose immediate causal link escapes our actual experience. Etymologically 'evolution' means 'unrolling'. This meaning is clear. An idea, an organ, an animal species evolve in the history of the world when the later state is potentially implied in the earlier. Evolution, therefore, is a transformation in time, conditioned by the self-nature of the thing which is in the process of transformation (Suarès, *La Comédie Psychologique*, p. 64).

[94] These remarks lead us to identify three phases of the life of the me. The first is the period of infancy during which the me is formed.

The second is the period when the me, already constituted, develops to its full flowering.

The third is the period during which the me finally gives way before the individual who has reached his maturity (maturity being precisely nothing but the possibility which the individual has of breaking his me).

The first phase is that in which Time is being built up, the second is that during which Time is destroyed, and the third is that in which man has returned to the Present (C. Suarès, *La Comédie Psychologique*, p. 308).

[95] When the 'me' has disappeared, psychological life becomes much simpler. There is no need to fall headlong every moment into new sensations with the idea of obtaining the opposite to what it is looking for (C. Suarès, *La Comédie Psychologique*, p. 297).

[96] But scarcely born, the moment lived suffers the common fate: it takes its place in the graphic system of memories; here, it is registered,

breveted, classed, compared, cognized and recognized in mummification. Henceforward it reposes somewhere in the complex web of engrams, from where memory will know how to dig it up. Does not the apparent continuity of the me — defined by its physical and psychic attribute — depend on these traces in nerve-substance? The criss-cross of memories — with their infidelities, parasites, short-circuits — weave across the organic mass a graphic by-product of the me (R. Godel, *Expérience Libératrice*, p. 173).

[97] The entity in process of formation, entirely plastic at first, hardens more and more, as a result of associations-disassociations which tend to settle in and take shape. As soon as they have solidified, the entity is there and thenceforward it advances in time (C. Suarès, *La Comédie Psychologique*, p. 290).

[98] Is our omnipresent ego, that mysterious reference-body which succeeds in insinuating itself everywhere, absorbing and claiming for itself all the activities of consciousness, anything but a sum of relative experiences? Any analysis of origin brings into relief the nature of this *artificial* complex which is the ego (Godel, *Expérience Libératrice*, p. 74).

[99] The Me is the blind spot of consciousness just as on the retina it is precisely the point at which the optic nerves enter which is blind, as the brain is completely insensible, as the solar body itself is dark, and as the eye sees everything but itself. Our faculty of knowing is entirely directed towards the exterior . . . That is why each of us only knows himself as an individual . . . But if he could be conscious of what is over and above, he would then voluntarily give up his individuality, and he would laugh at the tenacity of his attachment for it (Schopenhauer, *Le Monde comme Volonté et Représentation*, v. III, p. 302).

[100] It takes logicians, historians and critics, only to accept from the world that which they can use to make phrases.

Because I think, for my part, that you, little man, are just beginning to learn a language and grope and practise it, and still only grasp a thin film of the world.

You called liberty that power of yours of demolishing your temple, to mix up the words of the poem . . . freedom to make a desert.

And where will you find yourself?

As for me, I call your deliverance liberty.

I know two kinds of men who tell of an empire to be founded. This one is a logician, and builds by intelligence, and I call his action utopia. And nothing will come of it, because there is nothing in him.

And the other animated by a strong impulsion which he would be unable to name . . . that one has not acted by means of intelligence, but by the spirit. That is why I tell you that the spirit leads the world, and not intelligence (Saint Exupéry, *Citadelle*).

[101] The complete action which contains its own end is its own retribution. It is not bought for the price of any reward, nor is it extorted by any constraint. It is therefore a gratuitous action. It is not sought by the attraction of a representative of the future; by the fascination of an ideal from which it could be distinct. It is not directed towards any end outside itself. It springs up by itself spontaneously (R. Fouéré, *de L'Acte Complet – Spiritualité*, p. 171, 1946).

[102] ... what does it find? Nothing. It had already emptied itself. This 'I' is no longer stuffed with ideas, with sentiment, with perceptions, with memory; the notion that it is an entity is no longer based on anything (C. Suarès, *La Comédie Psychologique*, p. 87).

[103] ... in true spirituality we do not *desire the forms* of the world-image since we are already one with Reality (J. J. Van der Leeuw, p. 233).

[104] 'Tarry not with dualism – carefully avoid pursuing it – As soon as you have right and wrong – Confusion ensues, the mind is lost' (Seng Ts'an, *Inscribed on the Believing Mind* – D. T. Suzuki, *Essays in Zen Buddhism*, p. 196, vol. I).

[105] 'The Mind is no other than the Buddha himself. Truth-seekers of this day fail to understand what this Mind is, and, raising a mind on the Mind, seek the Buddha in a world outside it, and attaching themselves to form practise discipline. This is a bad way, and not at all the one leading to enlightenment ...' (Huang-po, Hsi-Yun in *The Zen Doctrine of No-Mind*, by Suzuki, p. 129).

[106] To effect the complete act, one should not seek to reconcile differences – but what is quite another thing – lose the habit of distinguishing (R. Fouéré, *De L'Acte Complet Envisagé Dialectiquement*, in 'Spiritualité', 1946, p. 209).

[107] Because it is self-sufficient, the complete act (considered by a consciousness which is placed in the very heart of the impulsion from which it is derived) at each moment of its duration is independent of all that preceeds it and all that follows (R. Fouéré, *De L'Acte Complet* etc., p. 172).

[108] '... It is like brushing the mirror. When there is no more dust the mirror shines out, leaving nothing unilluminated' (Tsung-mi – Suzuki, *The Zen Doctrine of No-Mind*, p. 17).

[109] There are no longer then, properly speaking, either emotion or thought, or effort, but a total functioning, a simple and indeed composable inner movement, an escape of energy that flows of its own accord without stopping and uninterrupted. It becomes superfluous to seek what in this flow, from which at each moment external actions are detached, belongs to emotion or proceeds from thought (R. Fouéré, *De L'Acte Complet*, etc., p. 208).

[110] Seen from without, the plenitude appears to be a void, and the

terrified individual frantically clings to this consciousness of himself, that is to say, to his own painful contradiction. This terror on the threshold of the ultimate realization, is the drama of humanity (Fouéré, *De L'Acte Complet*, p. 170).

[111] '. . . Emptiness constantly falls within our reach; it is always with us and in us, and conditions all our knowledge, all our deeds, and is our life itself. It is only when we attempt to pick it up and hold it forth as something before our eyes that it eludes us, frustrates all our efforts and vanishes like vapour. We are ever lured towards it, but it proves a will-o'-the-wisp. . . .'

[112] 'When a mind, thoroughly understanding the emptiness of all things, faces forms, it at once realizes their emptiness. With it emptiness is there all the time, whether it faces forms or not, whether it discriminates or not' (Suzuki, *Ta-chu Hui Hai*, in *Zen Doctrine of No-Mind*, p. 49).

[113] 'In Enlightenment thinker and thinking and thought are merged in one act of seeing into the very being of Self' (Suzuki, *Essays in Zen Buddhism*, vol. I, p. 66).

[114] 'Wordiness and intellection
    the more with them the further astray we go;
    Away therefore with wordiness and intellection,
    And there is no place where we cannot pass freely . . .'
(Seng Ts'an, *Inscribed on the Believing Mind*; Suzuki, *Essays in Zen Buddhism*, vol. I, p. 194).

[115] 'Everything that has a name thereby limits itself' Suzuki, *Nantchuan*, in *Essays on Zen Buddhism*, vol. I, p. 38).

[116] 'The idea of direct method is to get hold of this fleeting life as it flees and not after it has flown. While it is fleeing, there is no time to recall memory or to build ideas' (Suzuki, *Essays in Zen Buddhism*, vol. I, p. 298).

[117] 'Where the intellect is at its end, beware of uttering a word. If you do, hones will grow on you . . .' Yao-shan in Suzuki, *The Zen Doctrine of No-Mind*, p. 113).

[118] Although it may be possible from outside or subsequently to discern in the complete act the mental, emotional and physical components, these are so intimately associated that they can no longer be, from within and in their living nature, the object of a distinct observation. A kind of alignment takes place between emotion, thought and action, an alignment which makes them run together, converge in an organic synthesis, constituting in itself a simple and new reality (R. Fouéré, *De L'Acte Complet*, etc., p. 174).

[119] To maintain that the complete act can only have as author someone in whom all inner contradictions have ceased, is to say that during the

whole duration of such an act the subject concerned loses all consciousness of himself (Fouéré, *De L'Acte Complet*, etc., p. 170).

[120] If all contradiction were to cease, if the subject coincided constantly with himself, he would cease to perceive himself since all distinct knowledge supposes an initial separation between that which knows and that which is known (Fouéré, *De L'Acte Complet*, etc., p. 170).

[121] Zen is like drinking water, for it is by one's self that one knows whether it is warm or cold (Suzuki, *Essays in Zen Buddhism*, vol. II, p. 30).

[122] 'We are apt to think that when Ignorance is driven out and the ego loses its hold on us, we have nothing to lean against and are left to the fate of a dead leaf blown hither and thither as the wind listeth. But this simply is not so; for Enlightenment is not a negative idea meaning simply the absence of Ignorance, indeed, Ignorance is the negation of Enlightenment and not the reverse. Enlightenment is affirmation in the truest sense of the word. . . .'

[123] 'In Zen there is nothing to gain, nothing to understand' (Suzuki, *Essays in Zen Buddhism*, vol. I, p. 211).

[124] 'We are already Buddhas. To talk about any sort of attainment is a desertion and logically a tautology' (Suzuki, *The Zen Doctrine of No-Mind*, p. 72).

[125] 'Zen is our "ordinary mindedness"; that is to say, there is in Zen nothing supernatural or unusual or highly speculative that transcends our every-day life . . .' (Suzuki, *Essays in Zen Buddhism*, vol. I, p. 300).

[126] 'Drinking tea, eating rice, I pass my time as it comes; Looking down at the stream, looking up at the mountains, How serene and relaxed I feel indeed!' (Suzuki, *Essays in Zen Buddhism*, vol. I, p. 317).

[127]
> The Way is perfect like unto vast space,
> With nothing wanting, nothing superfluous:
> It is indeed due to making choice
> That its suchness is lost sight of.

(Seng Ts'an, *On Believing in Mind*, in *Essays in Zen Buddhism*, vol. I, p. 196, by Suzuki.)

[128] In psychology as in physics all localization of energy round a privileged point is made at the cost of the whole, entails loss of liberty, a deeper plunge into the world of duality and relativity.

[129] The Sage does not destroy anything, he is a realizer — and the most practical possible. His influence does not disintegrate but integrates. In the fire of the liberating experience the *individuality is transmuted* into light. No evil can reach it (Dr. R. Godel).

[130] The complete act which contains its own end is its own retribution. It is therefore a gratuitous action. It is not sought by the attraction of a representation of the future; by the fascination of an idea; from which

it is distinct. It is not directed towards any end outside itself. It springs up by itself spontaneously (Fouéré, *De L'Acte Complet*, etc., p. 171).

[131] An act can only be complete if it is the product of a subject in whom all inner contradiction has ceased. In other words, the complete act supposes, realizes a total concentration of the energy of the subject, a gathering of all his powers (Fouéré, *De L'Acte Complet*, etc., p. 170).

[132] Most religions and spiritual training circles confuse the 'means' of spiritual realization with its 'consequences'. This confusion results from the fact that they have not seized the fundamentally irreversible nature of the processes of the Real. This irreversible nature is in fact far more important on the psychic and 'spiritual' planes, than on the plane of matter.

[133] The practise of Judo allows the body to recover its natural and instinctive wisdom. It is in this state of mind that Zennists practise it.

[134] Those who know by themselves do not look for anything external. If they adhere to the view that liberation comes through external aid, through the office of a good wise friend, they are entirely at fault. When confusion reigns in you and false views are entertained, no amount of teaching by others, good, wise friends of yours, will be of use for your salvation (Vimalakîrti Sûtra in Suzuki, *Essays in Zen Buddhism*, vol. I, p. 317).

[135] 'Where the intellect cannot reach, in truth I tell you not to speak of it' (Iueh-chanin Suzuki, *Zen Buddhism*, p. 120).

[136] 'O my friends have no fixed abode inside or outside, and your conduct will be perfectly free and unfettered. Take away your attachment, and your walk will know no obstruction whatever' (Platform Sûtra, Hui-Neng in Suzuki, *Essays in Zen Buddhism*, vol. I, p. 218).

[137] 'Since we are already one with the Absolute, there is nothing for us to practise, achieve or attain. *All that is necessary is to reach a sudden awareness of that oneness*' (Hsi-Yun, *The Huang-Po Doctrine of Universal Mind*, p. 10).

[138] Do not imagine, do not think, do not analyse, do not meditate, do not reflect, *abide in the Natural State* (The Six Rules of Tilopa — Tibetan Buddhism).

[139] It is a mistake to think that sitting quietly in contemplation is essential to deliverance (Hui-Neng in Suzuki, *Essays in Zen Buddhism*, vol. I, p. 304).

[140] When the abrupt doctrine is understood there is no need of disciplining oneself in things external (Hui-Neng in Suzuki, *Essays in Zen Buddhism*, vol. I, p. 315).

[141] When we abide with Dhyana we are Dhyana-bound. However excellent are the merits of these spiritual exercises, they inevitably lead us to a state of bondage. In this there is no emancipation. The whole

system of Zen discipline may thus be said to be nothing but a series of attempts to set us absolutely free fom all forms of bondage (Suzuki, *The Zen Doctrine of No-Mind*, p. 27).

[142] A God that is understood is no longer a God (Terstegen in Suzuki, *Essays in Zen Buddhism*, vol. I).

[143] 'Things divine are all the more obscure in so far as they are more intelligible and luminous in themselves' (Aristotle).

[144] All our historical civilizations have been based on the Reality of the me as a being, and as a result, have been sub-human (C. Suarès, *Comédie Psychologique*, p. 66).

[145] We will take the liberty of recalling to readers the warning of Madame David-Neel referred to in the foreword to this work.

Let us not lose sight of the fact that most orthodox Buddhists of both schools consider that the similarities between Buddhism and Christianity are more apparent than real and that very often identical forms express different values.

[146] Christianity is therefore constituted not only with the teaching of Jesus himself, but with all the dogmatical and speculative interpretations that have accumulated since the death of the founder (D. T. Suzuki, *Zen Buddhism*, vol. I, p. 44).

[147] When one finds among two peoples, different in race and ideas, the same legend, with such a special circumstance, and which does not necessarily and naturally arise from the fundamental basis of the story; when moreover this circumstance is in close conformity with the ensemble of the religious conceptions of one of the two peoples, and among the others remains isolated, apart from the usages of its symbolism, a fundamental and absolute critical principal obliges us to conclude that the legend has been transmitted from the one to the other in a form already fixed, and constitutes a foreign importation which has been superimposed without mixture, on the truly national tradition and one might say of the genius of the people which has received it without having invented it. (Brother Lenormant, *Premières Civilisations*, t. I, p. 134).

[148] In this respect Greece is in a unique situation and plays a capital part. It marks the transition between the ancient cycle of polytheistic religions and Christianity. It is the Gordian knot in which are entangled all the secret threads which run from Asia to Europe, from the Orient to the Occident (E. Schuré, *Les Grands Initiés*, p. 265).

[149] India powerfully influences the current of intellectual and spiritual life of these different peoples (China, Assyria, Persia, Greece). The missionaries sent by Asoka into these countries, played a preponderant part in the transmission of this light. Does not Pliny show them established on the shores of the Dead Sea? Is it not these missionaries of Asoka and Buddhists who later gave birth to the Therapeutes and

the Essenes of Judea and Arabia who taught Jesus? (Revel, *Les Routes Ardentes de l'Inde*, p. 34).

[150] Verily, verily, I say unto you, Except a corn of wheat fall into the ground and die, it abideth alone: but if it die, it bringeth forth much fruit (St. John, chap. XII, v. 24).

[151] Die to your experience, to your memory, die to your prejudices pleasant or unpleasant. In your death is the incorruptible. That is not a state in which there is nothing, but a creative state. It is this renewal which, if one allows it to do so, will disperse our problems and our torments, however complicated and painful they may be. *It is only in the death of the me that there is life* (*Krishnamurti Parle*, p. 125).

[152] Men who are not liberated hold in horror that which is the joy of liberated men. No one is rich in God who is not entirely *dead* to himself (Eckhart, ed. Pfeiffer, p. 600).

[153] No man putteth a piece of new cloth unto an old garment, for that which is put in to fill it up taketh from the garment, and the rent is made worse.

Neither do men put new wine into old bottles: else the bottles break, and the wine runneth out, and the bottles perish: but they put new wine into new bottles, and both are preserved (St. Matthew, chap. IX, vv. 16-17).

[154] *Darkness alone filled the All* without limit, for the Father, the Mother and the Son were again One.

The seven sons were not yet born from the *Tissue of Light*. Darkness alone was Father-Mother.

Behold, O Lanoo, the radiant child issue of the two: *shining space, issue of dark space, which emerges from the depths of the great dark waters* (Extract from the Tibetan Kandjur-Bhak-hgyur, *Tibetan Studies* — 14 — Calcutta, 1912).

[155] THAT . . . Light of all lights . . . object of Wisdom . . . is in the depths of all beings (Bhagavad Gita, XIII, 17).

[156] In the sight of him who is veritably awake, what is our waking-state and our sleep? They correspond to in the same degree with lethargic states; we are somnambulists.

. . . Before consciousness in us can realize the true nature of the state of vigil and *establishes itself in this light*, all error should have been dispelled (Godel, *Expérience Libératrice*, p. 294).

[157] In the eyes of the Sage nothing is changed as regards the contour of forms, *but the vision is of light whereas ours is dark* (Godel, *Expérience Libératrice*, p. 260).

[158] There neither the sun, nor the stars, nor this fire are shining. When he shines, all things shine after HIM. It is with the splendour of Brahman that everything is shining (Shvetashvatar Upanishad, 44).

[159] Supreme in omniscience and in goodness, without rival in His splendour, the reign of *Light* is the abode of Auharmazd (Zoroaster, *The Bunjahis of the East*, v. 3, 4; v. 2).

[160] The intention of the Catholic disciplines is altogether different from that of Zen (Suzuki, *The Zen Doctrine of No-Mind*).

[161] The fully conscious man modifies himself unceasingly, instead of identifying himself with an object — his entity — he identifies himself with the *raison d'être* of this object: Life. If at a given moment he has to choose between life and himself, he will choose life without hesitation. This constant identification with Life does not carry with it, and cannot carry with it, suffering. A God who suffers is only a poor unconscious being who has not known how to identify himself with Life (C. Suarès, *La Comédie Psychologique*, p. 115).

[162] Attach yourself to nothing besides the original pure Buddha-nature (Hsi-Yun, *The Huang-Po Doctrine of Universal Mind*, p. 30).

[163] Truth is understood by the mind, and not by sitting in meditation (Hui-Neng in Suzuki, *The Zen Doctrine of No-Mind*, p. 27).

[164] He who seeks learnedness gets daily enriched. He who seeks Tao is daily made poor (Lao-Tzu in Suzuki, *Essays in Zen Buddhism*, vol. I, p. 349).

[165] Not to be attached to form means Suchness. What is meant by Suchness? It is not to think of being and non-being; it is not to think of good and bad; it is not to think of having limits or not having limits; it is not to think of measurements (or of non-measurements) (Shen-hui's teachings in Suzuki, *The Zen Doctrine of No-Mind*, p. 88-9).

[166] One no longer encounters this sense of the future which is heavy with expectations, with fears and with all kind of hope. One no longer waits for a future in which one could at last live completely (Fouéré, *De L'Acte Complet*, etc., p. 174).

[167] When one dog barks at a shadow, ten thousand dogs turn it into a reality (Chinese saying in Suzuki, *Essays in Zen Buddhism*, vol. II, p. 234).

[168]
'Try not to seek after the true,
Only cease to cherish opinions . . .'
(Seng Ts'an in Suzuki, *Zen Buddhism*, vol. I, p. 284).

[169] A Perfected man, freed from corporeality, is immense and cannot be measured; he is unfathomable like the vast ocean (The Buddha).

[170]
'Not knowing how near the Truth is
People seek it far away — what a pity.
They are like him who, in the midst of water,
Cries in thirst so imploringly.'
(Hakuin's Song of Meditation in Suzuki, *Essays in Zen Buddhism*, vol. I, p. 334).

[171] It is useless to seek holiness in poverty and solitude, holiness is everywhere we are, since the Eternal is everywhere.

[172] Truth has nothing to do with words; it is far beyond them, it is impossible to be described, it has nothing to do with idle reasoning and philosophical speculation (Manjusri — Avatamsaka Sûtra in Suzuki, *Zen Buddhism*, vol. II, 19.

[173] The mind is the destroyer of the Real.

[174] In truth he who sees all things in this Self, and this 'Self' in all things will never again be separated from THAT' (Ishupanishad, 6).

[175] The state of the disintegrated 'I' cannot be described. The disintegrated 'I' acts. It acts in space and time. It acts because he is there where insoluble problems are no longer asked, because they have been transcended....

... to imprison oneself is not truly an action. To act, is to do away with prisons (C. Suarès, *La Comédie Psychologique*, p. 90).

[176] We suppose wrongly that the absence of egoism entails a mutilation of the intellectual or affective faculties.

The extinction of the process of personal consciousness with which we are familiar, permits us, on the contrary, to realize the higher forms of love and intelligence.

However paradoxical this may seem, we only reach the plenitude of our creative faculties and of our originality by dying to ourselves.

The unity and originality resulting from the transcendence of ourselves no longer bear the marks of our pettiness, stupidity and personal cravings. They are the expression of impersonal Life in a particular place and in particular circumstances.

[177] Sleep is a strange but most important thing. During sleep, the inner organism, having a life of its own, is renewed by itself. It is obvious that the less we intervene in the inner organism, the better it will be. The organism will be healthy and natural in its functions in the degree in which the mind avoids taking charge of it (J. Krishnamurti, *Commentaries on Living*, pp. 39-40).

[178] 'There is only one real luxury, and that is human relations' (Saint-Exupéry).

[179] The Zen masters suggest that we realize a state of pure lucidity without ideation.

[180] 'The Universe is only a reality in its totality. Phenomena are only a convention (G. Cahen, *Les Conquêtes de la Pensée Scientifique*, p. 284).

[181] God, this ultimate Reality which our ego tries to seize is only revealed when we lose sight of all temporal things, cease to trust in our intellect, and transcend the 'rational' way. In the vision of the Lord there is no duality, *no relationships*.

As long as we are occupied in looking, we are not yet ONE with what we are looking at. As long as something is still the object of our intuition, we are not yet one with the ONE. For there, where there is only the One, only the ONE can be seen (Maître Eckhart, *Sermons*, ed. Aubier, p. 241).

[182] The approach to the problem is more important than the problem itself.

The method of approach conditions the problem and its outcome. The manner in which you examine the problem is of the greatest importance, for it will be coloured by your attitude, your prejudices, your fears and hopes. A correct relationship with the problem is the result of a lucid approach without choice (J. Krishnamurti, *Commentaries on Living*, p. 99).

[183] The real work of detachment does not consist in detaching oneself from everything with the exception of one thing, even if it be the idea of detachment itself; it consists in detaching oneself from everything, in detaching oneself from the very source of our detachment. It is not a question of the letting-go of this or that; it is a question of 'letting-go' (Dr. H. Benoit, *Lâcher Prise*, p. 277).

[184] 'But what we ordinarily mean by choice is not freedom. Choices are usually decisions motivated by pleasure and pain' (Allan Watts, *The Wisdom of Insecurity*, p. 110).

[185] 'The Knower of Brahman who is firmly convinced that Brahman is unknowable, knows him perfectly. But he who thinks he knows him, certainly knows him not' (Commentary of Sankara).

[186]
'He by whom Brahman is not known, knows It;
He by whom it is known, knows It not.
It is not known by those who know It,
It is known by those who do not know It.'

(Kenapanishad, II, 3).

[187] 'A sad saint is a sorry saint.'

[188] 'The laws of matter are in fact extracted by our mind from its own substance, and applied to elements which, also, are isolated by the intellect in this totality which constitutes the universe' (Cahen, *Les Conquêtes de la Pensée Scientifique*, p. 269).

[189] 'Seek not to push thy investigation too far in case thy head falls off. Thou questionest me on the nature of a divinity about which one should not reason' (Brihadaranyaka Upanishad, 3, 6, 1).

[190] 'Our conscious thought is altogether of the nature of a dream, it is a dream; the representation it gives us of the world is illusory, for it represents a world entirely centred on ourselves, whereas the centre of the world is both everywhere and nowhere' (Benoit, *Lâcher Prise*, p. 68).

[191] 'The power of memories and expectations is such that for most

human beings the past and the future are not *as* real, but *more* real than the present' (Allan Watts, *The Wisdom of Insecurity*, p. 31).

[192] 'Life is complete in each moment — whole, undivided, and ever new. The future is everlastingly unattainable. The fulfilment of the divine purpose does not lie in the future. It is found in the present, not by an act of resignation to immovable fact, but in seeing that there is no one to resign' (Allan Watts, *The Wisdom of Insecurity*, p. 131).

[193] 'It is Love and not hate that puts an end to hatred' (The Buddha).

[194] 'Modern science, in its physico-chemical branch, has come to support Buddhism with all its might.

It has been known for a certain number of years that where our senses see substance, form and colour, there are really only occurrences in time and space, forces submitted to the incessantly variable flux which determines different states of equilibrium. . . .

The latest conceptions of the atom have shown that it finally breaks down into an energy which is transformed each fraction of a second . . .

A change in perspective is just dawning, and science, each day sapping its way further into the world of appearances, brings us nearer the truths divined and proclaimed by the Buddha' (Maurice Percheron, *Le Bouddha et le Bouddhisme*, pp. 168-9).

[195] 'When inquiry is linked with certain means of obtaining indispensable and irreplaceable information these means have a part in the very form of the inquiry. The knowledge derived from it bears in itself the systematic or maybe accidental characteristics of the informative methods applied, like laws that have necessary *a priori* structures' (Gonseth, quoted by G. Cahen, *Les Conquêtes de la Pensée Scientifique*, p. 9).

INDEX